Endgame in the Western Sahara

About the Author

TOBY SHELLEY has reported from many countries in the Middle East, North Africa and sub-Saharan Africa over the course of twenty years as a journalist. He works for the *Financial Times*. Previously he was regional energy news editor for Dow Jones Newswires. He contributes regularly to *Middle East International*. His published work includes chapters in several books published by Zed and Khamsin, and a short work on Palestinian trade unions in the West Bank. He first visited the Sahrawi refugee camps in 1988 and has followed the issue for many years.

Endgame in the Western Sahara

What Future for Africa's Last Colony?

TOBY SHELLEY

ZED BOOKS
London & New York

in association with

WAR ON WANT
London

Endgame in the Western Sahara was first published in 2004 by
Zed Books Ltd, 7 Cynthia Street, London N1 9JF, UK, and
Room 400, 175 Fifth Avenue, New York, NY 10010, USA

www.zedbooks.co.uk

in association with
War on Want, 37–39 Great Guildford Street, London, SE1 0ES
www.waronwant.org

Designed and typeset in Monotype Joanna by Illuminati, Grosmont
Cover designed by Andrew Corbett
Printed and bound in the EU by Biddles Ltd, King's Lynn

Distributed in the USA exclusively by Palgrave Macmillan, a division of
St Martin's Press, LLC, 175 Fifth Avenue, New York, NY 10010

A catalogue record for this book is available from the British Library
Library of Congress Cataloging-in-Publication Data available

ISBN 1 84277 340 2 Hb
ISBN 1 84277 341 0 Pb

Contents

Acknowledgements

Many Sahrawis opened their houses and tents to me as I collected material for this book. It is to them that the most thanks are due. Inside the territory, countless activists spent long hours explaining, discussing and arguing, despite the risks involved in associating with foreign journalists. I thank them for their trust, their friendship and some memorable nights under a Saharan sky. I salute the bravery of ordinary Sahrawis who spoke their minds to strangers. In the camps also I found assistance and lively debate.

I thank not only the officials of Polisario in the camps and in Europe for giving me their time but also diplomats and officials of Morocco, Algeria and Mauritania.

Friends and colleagues encouraged me to pursue the idea of writing this book. One in particular bears heavy responsibility – John Torday, travelling companion and raconteur with whom I first visited the camps fifteen years ago.

At Zed Books, Robert Molteno took to the idea of the book with an enthusiasm that spurred me on.

Of course, there is a special word of thanks to Fiona, Joe and Tom for their support.

I dedicate this book to Miriam in the *barraque* at Dir Yeddak, to Ahmed that he may continue to play in his desert, to Fadel Ismael, whom I wish I had known better, and to my father, whom I still miss.

Chronology

1884   Spain commences the colonisation of the Western Sahara as the European powers agree to divide the African continent between themselves at the Berlin Conference.

1898   Ma el Ainin establishes Smara and continues resistance against Spain and France.

1912   France and Spain confirm frontiers of the Western Sahara.

1913   French troops seize Smara.

1934   Spain and France embark on a joint campaign to pacify the Sahrawi tribes.

1957   Sahrawi fighters attack Spanish positions. Spain and France respond with Operation Écouvillon and thousands of Sahrawis are displaced to the Tarfaya Strip.

1965   The UN calls on Spain to begin decolonisation of the Western Sahara.

1969   Harakat Tahrir is formed to campaign for Sahrawi independence. It is crushed a year later and its leader never seen again.

1973   The Polisario Front is formed and launches its first raids against Spanish positions.

1975   A UN commission notes majority Sahrawi support for independence. The International Court of Justice rejects Moroccan and Mauritanian claims of sovereignty over the territory. Morocco responds with its 'Green March' over the border. Spain reneges on promises of a referendum of self-determination for the Sahrawis and cedes the Western Sahara to Morocco and Mauritania.

1976   Tens of thousands of Sahrawis flee to refugee camps in Algeria. They report napalm attacks and slaughter of live-stock by Moroccan forces. The formation of the Sahrawi Arab Democratic Republic is declared.

1979   Mauritania signs a peace agreement with Polisario and retreats from the Western Sahara where the territory it held is taken by Morocco. The war between Polisario and Morocco continues unabated.

1981   Morocco commences building fortified sand walls, or berms, around the territory to combat Polisario.

1988   Polisario and Morocco accept a UN and OAU proposal for a ceasefire to be followed by a referendum of self-determination for the Sahrawis, based on 1974 Spanish census data.

1989   Polisario leaders meet with Hassan II of Morocco.

1991   The UN creates Minurso to oversee the implementation of the peace plan. The ceasefire commences.

1992   The referendum is delayed for the first time of many.

1997   Morocco and Polisario sign the Houston Accords on the modalities of a referendum.

1999   The process of voter identification goes ahead. Hassan II dies. A series of protests commences in the territory controlled by Morocco.

2000   A provisional list of 86,000 voters is published. Morocco floods Minurso with 130,000 appeals, throwing the process into further crisis.

2001   James Baker presents his Framework Agreement, replacing a referendum for the Sahrawis with a vote in which Moroccan settlers would form an automatic majority after a period of autonomy. Morocco issues oil 'reconnaissance' licences to Total and Kerr-McGee. Mohamed Daddach is released from twenty-seven years in detention and met by crowds in Laayoune and Smara. At the end of the year there is rioting in Smara.

2002   Morocco's Mohamed VI declares the referendum process to be obsolete.

2003   Baker's second version of his proposals is accepted by Polisario as a basis for negotiations but is rejected by Morocco.

2004   Morocco continues to reject any referendum that would include independence as an option. The UN supervises the first, limited family visits between the refugee camps and the occupied territories.

Foreword

José Ramos Horta

The histories of the Western Sahara and East Timor ran parallel for many years. Both countries endured not only European colonial rule but abandonment and incomplete decolonisation when the imperial powers collapsed in the mid-1970s. Then, both countries faced invasion and colonisation by local powers, repression verging on genocide and denial of their national identities. In both cases, independence movements fought against enormous odds to assert a right recognised but not pressed by the UN Security Council and the UN Secretariat – the right to an act of self-determination.

Across the years the leaderships of the East Timorese and the Sahrawi independence movements maintained contact and expressed solidarity with and understanding of each other. I note a comment in this book that Sahrawi demonstrators in the Moroccan-occupied part of the Western Sahara chanted 'East Timor, Western Sahara' as they marked the release of political prisoner Mohamed Daddach, a recognition at street level of the links between our two peoples.

Where our modern histories diverge – for the moment – is in the achievement at great sacrifice of a referendum for the people of East Timor in 1999. And, of course, that led to a massive vote in favour of independence. We are now embarking on the daunting task of building our state. For the Sahrawis the opportunity to determine their own future as a people remains an objective that they continue to struggle for in the occupied territories, in the refugee camps and in the wider diaspora.

I am told it is many years since a book on the Western Sahara was published in English. I hope that this book will bring to a new audience an understanding of the struggle of the Sahrawis and the contexts, regional and international, diplomatic and military, in which that struggle lies.

In the past little has been written in any language about the situation in the Moroccan-occupied portion of the Western Sahara. This book begins to correct that omission, looking at the demographic and economic conditions in the territory as well as the development of new kinds of struggle since 1999. The author has spoken to the people who are moulding their own history despite living under occupation, the militants who are building a civil society to confront the legacy of fear. These former political prisoners, families of the Disappeared, unemployed workers, students, like their kin in the refugee camps, have a determination that we Timorese understand well, a determination to ensure that our future will be decided by us.

I have visited the refugee camps in Tindouf twice in the last few years, and over the years have met many Sahrawis, leaders and common people. At first sight when one meets women and children living in precarious though well-managed camps, one cannot but cry out for them and fall in love with this brave and humble people. The Sahrawis are moderate Muslim Arabs, open to the West but still retaining their cultural values and religious beliefs.

I have always believed that a free and independent Western Sahara would serve as a bridge of dialogue in the Arab world and between the Arab world and the West. The ancient Kingdom of Morocco would benefit from an independent Western Sahara, as I am sure the Sahrawi leaders would make every effort to normalise and enhance relations with their larger and richer neighbour. On the other hand, allowing this problem to fester will only deepen the frustration and anger of an otherwise very peaceful people.

The world is familiar with the suffering of the Palestinians living in refugee camps for over fifty years but is less familiar with the plight of another Arab people also languishing forgotten in refugee camps, denied their right to freedom and dignity. The Kingdom of Morocco is one of the many champions of the Palestinian cause and rightly so. Then, one should ask, why such different attitudes towards the Sahrawi people?

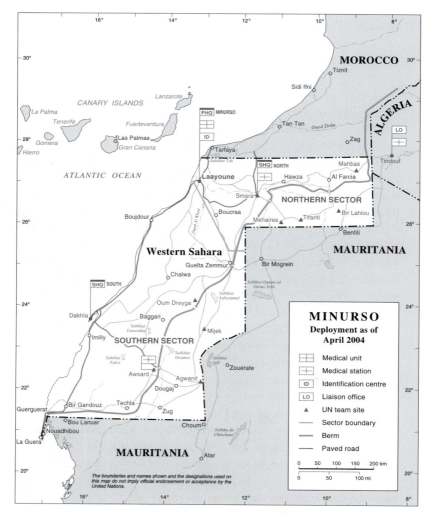

Map of the Western Sahara

Introduction

In 1975 Moroccan and Mauritanian forces moved into the Spanish Sahara under the auspices of a deal arranged with Madrid as Franco lay dying. So started a new phase of conflict over a territory the size of France with a population the size of Lyon, rich in phosphates, fisheries and, perhaps, oil. Local independence movement Polisario turned its guns from the retreating Spain and onto new adversaries. By 1976 the territory, now known to the world as the Western Sahara, was a battlefield. Much of the Sahrawi population fled to refugee camps in southern Algeria. Those who remained were to be subsumed by waves of settlers and harsh repression. Three decades later, the Western Sahara has gone through sixteen years of war and almost as many of a ceasefire predicated on a referendum that never happened. The last Africa file in the UN's decolonisation dossier remains open.

The Western Sahara issue is now at a turning point. In the territory controlled by Morocco – the vast majority of the land area – Sahrawi activists are seeking out and creating space in which to construct a Sahrawi civil society, building organisations, supporting detainees, staging protests. They are pushing at the boundaries, and the Moroccan response since mid-2002 has been to ratchet up repression albeit not to the levels seen before 1998. The question here is whether nationalist Sahrawis under Moroccan rule will be able to sustain and develop their activities sufficiently to be able to pick up the baton that their brethren in the refugee camps cannot carry at present.

In the refugee camps the 1991 ceasefire created the conditions for changes in political orientation and social organisation. Polisario nodded towards global trends declaring itself in favour of private enterprise, foreign investment in a future state, and multiparty democracy. The collectivism of camp life has diluted, with consequences good and bad. But the years of neither war nor peace have deprived the refugee population of their agency in their own future – their guns and their votes. The referendum that was to follow the ceasefire never came, leaving some 160,000 people exiled in one of the most inhospitable parts of the Sahara. This situation cannot be sustained for ever, but which of the erosive forces will prove the more powerful: normalisation of exile and abandonment of the quest to return; defeatism; or a militant anger uncontrollable by the current leadership? Polisario's leadership recognises that there must be movement if these forces are to be resisted. Morocco, for its part, benefits from the passage of time both in the territory it controls and in the camps.

The landscape of the conflict is regional: Moroccan competition with Algeria for dominance within the Maghreb. The Western Sahara is one of the expressions of that competition. That is not to say that Sahrawi nationalism is an Algerian invention for it clearly is not, but the sustainability of an independence struggle led from the camps is contingent on lack of an overall settlement of differences between Algeria and Morocco. That regional landscape is shaped by the tectonic forces of global trends and power politics. The US and France and Spain have designs on the economies of the Maghreb and vested interests in stability of the subregion on their terms. The three players compete at some levels, of course, but it is clear that the power elites in Algeria and Morocco are being nudged towards economic liberalisation that, particularly in the case of Algeria, could challenge long-held conceptions of self-interest.

In 2003 there were signs that elements in the Algerian elite were preparing to relax their position on the Western Sahara. Would these come to anything or be blown away by another spat between Rabat and Algiers as has happened in the past? Then, in the UN Security Council, Kofi Annan buried the Settlement Plan that from 1988 had

dominated attempts to find a solution. But he only did this after the
Moroccan king had pronounced the plan dead and while Polisario
was still trying to breathe life into the patient. Annan, with the support of the US, UK and France, had since 2001 promoted a scheme
advanced by James Baker, Annan's special envoy on the Western
Sahara and one-time US secretary of state. The plan, initially accepted
with enthusiasm by Morocco and rejected in horror by Algeria and
Polisario, envisaged a period of autonomy for the territory under
Moroccan provisional sovereignty, followed by a vote to decide
between integration with Morocco or independence. Crucially, the
plan threw out the hitherto sacred notion of a Sahrawi people who
would determine their fate and introduced the idea of a referendum
in which settlers would also vote. That move failed but Baker came
back in 2003 with a second iteration, unchanged in its fundamentals
but more detailed.

With the dust yet to settle in the Security Council after the invasion of Iraq, Algeria opted to welcome the proposal but hedge it
with numerous conditions. Morocco too expressed many reservations, apparently now seeing dangers not evident two years before.
Polisario's denunciation of the document was bitter but it was also
detailed, giving cause to wonder if it constituted a negotiating position rather than outright rejection. Leaders of the movement denied
this, only to shift their stance in the days before the Security Council
met at the end of July 2003. Pressure, including from Algeria, had
been intense. Now Polisario would accept the Baker document as
the basis for a solution, agreeing to some elements and saying the
most objectionable parts – principally the electoral roll – should
be discussed. The main thing was to try to move things forward,
hold back the forces of erosion, keep the Security Council involved
and deny Morocco the weapon of time. The move was described
as tactical, a means of putting the ball in the Moroccan court. But
was this clever diplomacy or the beginning of a collapse of the
movement's position and a sign that Algeria was finally suing for a
constructive peace with its western neighbour?

The outcome of the Western Sahara dispute is clearly of great
import to a few hundred thousand indigenous Sahrawis and their kin
in southern Morocco, northern Mauritania and western Algeria. But
as they have been told over the years, their fate is only of concern

to the international community inasmuch as the interests of major powers are affected. As James Baker told them, the Western Sahara is not Kuwait and troops would not be sent in to uphold the rule of international law there. There are US and European interests that may come to the fore. The quest for oil off the coast of the territory would spur more interest, and a destabilising crisis in Morocco could also force the Western Sahara up the agenda.

These considerations apart, the fate of the Western Sahara is significant to the international community for several reasons. It will constitute a judgement on the permissibility or otherwise of the wave of local imperialism that was rejected in Eritrea, Namibia and East Timor, and on the sanctity of inherited borders. As states built on inherited borders implode across West Africa and as secessionism remains a threat to numerous states across the world, anything that constitutes a sign of international legitimacy for one outcome or another has clear significance elsewhere, however much the lawyers may argue one case is different from another. The tattered credibility of the UN, perhaps never more ragged than now after the US and UK invasion of Iraq, will be further tested by any process and outcome in the Western Sahara. At the subregional level, a settlement will express a new turn in relations between the states of the Maghreb and the Maghreb's relation to bigger economic powers. Finally, but linking back to the matter of US and European interests in maintaining stability in Morocco, any outcome in the Western Sahara will have consequences for the nature of the Moroccan state. Much is made of the argument that the Moroccan monarchy is the key to stability there and that an exit from the Western Sahara would imperil the monarchy. But there is an economic and political cost–benefit analysis to be done here, and the dictum that a nation that enslaves another cannot itself be free should be factored into that analysis: consider the restrictions on press freedom excused by the sanctity of territorial integrity; consider the subsidies and expenditure enabling control of the territory while the dispossessed of Casablanca turn to suicide bombing.

The aims of this book are straightforward. It seeks to bring the nationalist Sahrawis living under Moroccan rule into focus as agents of their own history and highlight the importance of the natural resources of the territory, known and presumed. Largely due to lack of access to the occupied territories, previous work has concentrated on the Sahrawi refugee community organised by Polisario. The book locates the Western Sahara dispute within the subregional landscape and the tectonic pressures of geopolitics and economics that shape it. As little has been written in English about the dispute for two decades, this book also serves as an update on previous accounts. Then it looks at Polisario and its putative Sahrawi Arab Democratic Republic, identifying some of the strains faced and the political and social developments within the movement and its constituency. Finally, it identifies scenarios for the future, endgames for the Western Sahara.

Wherever possible the book has been based on new material gathered in visits to the subregion, formal interviews and informal discussions with Sahrawis living under Moroccan rule and in the camps, and also with Polisario, Moroccan, Algerian, Mauritanian and other diplomats and officials based in the Maghreb and in Europe. Most newspaper references are to online editions. Most of the translations are my own and so I take responsibility for errors.

I

International Context:
The Maghreb from 'Cold War'
to 'War against Terror'

In June 2002, the Moroccan security services leaked the news that they had detained members of an al-Qaeda cell. The group allegedly planned an attack on US or British military shipping in the Straits of Gibraltar, launching the assault from the Spanish possessions of Ceuta and Melilla on Morocco's Mediterranean coast. The area is a thoroughfare for vessels joining and leaving Nato's Mediterranean fleet and the US Sixth Fleet. Some 50,000 vessels transit the Straits each year. Some 10 per cent of them carry crude oil or petroleum products. Algeciras, an important Spanish container port, lies within the Straits.[1]

The alleged plot came less than two years after the USS *Cole* was badly damaged by suicide bombers in a dinghy at the Yemeni port of Aden. The suspects, all Saudi nationals, were picked up after an investigation involving US, British, French, Spanish and other intelligence agencies, it was said. Within a few days the Arabic press cited Moroccan officials saying the intelligence services were investigating the banking system in search of funding mechanisms for terrorist organisations.[2] At the same time, out came reports of a Moroccan secret agent who, it was said, had penetrated al-Qaeda and warned Washington in 2001 of a large-scale attack planned for the summer or autumn.[3]

The unpacking of this tale says much about the nature of Morocco's relationship with the US and Europe and, by extension, with its neighbours and the rest of the world. That, ultimately, provides the geopolitical backdrop to more than a quarter of a century of Moroccan rule over most of the Western Sahara.

The narrative has trusty Morocco working alongside Western intelligence services to prevent an attack by non-Moroccan, Muslim radicals on the jugular of the Mediterranean, one of the most strategically important shipping routes in the world. The foiled plot plays on US sensitivity over the USS *Cole* incident, and release of the story – the suspects having been arrested some weeks earlier – comes as the US and world media begin to gear up for the anniversary of September 11. To show this is no one-off swoop, we then have ongoing investigations into terrorist funding and a tale of long-term and heroic attempts by a Moroccan agent to infiltrate al-Qaeda and warn of its plans ahead of the 11 September attacks on New York and the Pentagon. For good measure, the actual attack would have been out of Melilla or Ceuta, demonstrating that Spain's occupation of these strategically important ports does not bring with it security for Nato.

For Europe and the US, Morocco's strategic value comes down, as it always has done, to the three determinants cited by estate agents: location, location, location. Most crucially, it plays Scylla to Gibraltar's Charybdis, guarding the route into and out of the Mediterranean. But, as Hassan II famously noted, Morocco's roots are in Africa and certainly its interventions there have been important. Then, as one of the two Maghreb countries with a sizeable population and large standing army, the kingdom's North African location matters.

Since independence, the skill of Moroccan foreign policy has been to lever the advantages of the country's location, to be useful to the West, to be considered trustworthy and deserving of support of all sorts but without losing all independence of action. In his nearly forty years on the throne, Hassan II managed this task adroitly, during the Cold War apparently kicking out US bases in Morocco but in fact removing them by agreement with Washington, and signing what at the time was a gargantuan long-term trade deal with the Soviet Union. In the Western Sahara, Morocco's success was in keeping the US and France onside and persuading the Soviet Union it had no interest in entering the game.

If sentry duty in the Mediterranean was Morocco's most basic role it was not the only one. Rabat was also counterposed to Algiers – a friendly kingdom with traditional values and a large remaining French population against a radical would-be leader of the 'Third World', Opec price hawk, a militant within the Non Aligned Movement, a founder of the Tricontinental, a state born of revolutionary war from which the *colon* masters had fled. With ongoing border disputes between the two countries, most notably the Sand War of 1963, playing up the distinction served Rabat well while assuring the West that Algeria was being watched locally. Rabat found the communist bogey useful for other purposes too. To this day, Morocco and its supporters continue to assert that the founders of Polisario were Leninist, Guevarist, Maoist cadres. In earlier years, the labels were meant to frighten; now they are used to suggest misplaced idealism, naivety, susceptibility to foreign blandishments.

In sub-Saharan Africa, Morocco has proved its usefulness too. It was there that Mobutu Sese Seko fled after his ousting, the final chapter in a history of close relations between two regimes. Twice in the late 1970s Moroccan armed forces helped suppress rebellions against Mobutu, a key US and French ally. In 1977 France and the US coordinated the deployment of 1,500 Moroccan troops in Shaba province. A year later US planes took Moroccan troops to what was then Zaire to help put down another revolt. Rabat was also complicit in US support for Unita in Angola and the MNR in Mozambique and, supposedly, in coup attempts in Benin, Chad and the Comorros.[4]

As the reworking of the accounts of Polisario ideology demonstrates, with the end of the Cold War, Morocco has had to repurpose itself. Opportunities have not been slow in arising. The Berlin Wall came down in 1989 and by 1990 the US and its allies were readying themselves for war with Iraq. Vital to the acceptability of the war was the token participation of Arab countries. Morocco was one volunteer. Then, although the crusade against Islamism went live after September 11, it should not be forgotten that since the end of the Cold War, Islamaphobia had swollen to take up rhetorical space left by the demise of the Soviet Union. Iran had not been defeated by Western-backed Iraq after a decade of war. In Palestine and Lebanon the finger was pointed at increasingly influential and well-organised Islamist groups. Throughout the Arab world and beyond, the Afghan Arabs were coming home to roost. Having defeated Soviet forces in Afghanistan at the behest of the US, thousands of Islamist Arab fighters had returned home and many were organising, much to the distress of their own governments.

In Algeria the annulling of the December 1991 election, which an Islamist party would clearly have won, threw the country into seemingly endless bloodletting. At times that would allow Algiers to make the point that it knew more than enough about the 'War on Terrorism' and that it would welcome help in suppressing certain émigré oppositionists.

Yet it was with Morocco's interests that the West's concerns about Islamic radicalism chimed. Holding the chairmanship of the Al Quds committee of the Islamic Conference Organisation, charged with safeguarding the Muslim world's interests in Jerusalem, the Moroccan monarchy has been an important diplomatic voice of 'moderation' in the Palestine conflict and in the Muslim world. Indeed, although publicly opposing the Camp David Accord between Tel Aviv and Cairo, Rabat has long been a back channel of communication between the Israeli state and some Arab governments. The high-level Israeli presence at Hassan II's funeral underlined this. There have been reports that one reward for this has been Israeli military assistance to Morocco in the Western Sahara.

At the subregional level, the chaos in Algeria has been of obvious and legitimate concern to Rabat. It has also allowed Morocco to highlight itself as a bastion of moderation. But growth of Islamism inside the kingdom has added to other, abiding expressions of the instability of the kingdom as currently constituted. The Casablanca bombings of May 2003, carried out by Islamist radicals native to the slums of the city, only underlined this.

The story is a familiar one in the Arab world. An ill-managed economy, widespread poverty, enormous inequalities of wealth, communities fractured by urbanisation and emigration, entrenched elites, lack of political freedom spawn organisations that work at the grassroots and espouse a mixture of supposedly traditional values and radical answers to the social malaise. The 2002 general election saw a legal – and therefore relatively unthreatening – Islamist party gain joint third place, and there was serious discussion about whether it would be drawn into the governing coalition. While this party was deemed acceptable as an election contender, there was real concern that the level of support it drew hinted at widespread sympathy for something more worrying. In the weeks between the release of the story of the arrest of al-Qaeda suspects and the election, over four hundred people linked with two radical Islamist groups were arrested, supposedly because of possible connections with al-Qaeda, while in Casablanca there was a high-profile court case against members of a Salafist organisation on charges that included murder.[5] The government denied the timing was related to the election but two messages were clear: first and for domestic consumption, that political boundaries remained; second and for overseas consumption, the threat faced by the regime is the same as the threat faced by its key supporters and Morocco is playing its part on behalf of all. Overseas observers read the message. A Spanish think-tank said the electoral rise of an Islamist party demonstrated that Morocco was no exception to the regional growth of political Islam and confirmed the 'irreversible instability of the country'.[6]

'On the international scene, Morocco appears to be one of the most reliable friends of the West within the Arab world', was how a Nato subcommittee summed up the country's geostrategic stance.[7]

The two most important bilateral relationships for Morocco are clearly those with the US and France, the former as superpower and the latter as the dominant former colonial power and the primary trade partner. The relationship with France is now mediated at times by the institutions of the European Union but it can be argued that the EU is a conduit for French interests rather than the other way round. Notwithstanding long-standing French scepticism about Atlanticism, Paris and Washington clearly share the objective of maintaining Morocco as a stable and pliant ally while increasingly competing at an economic level as globalisation advances and countries like Morocco privatise, deregulate and take down tariff barriers. Fruitful arms trading straddles both interests, playing a role in securing the regime in Rabat and earning profits.

US ambitions for the Maghreb

The US approach to North Africa took a new turn in 1998 with the Eizenstat Initiative of the eponymous Treasury deputy secretary. Eizenstat had two stated and intertwined aims: to boost bilateral trade between the US and Morocco, Algeria and Tunisia (Mauritania being economically irrelevant and Libya being under US sanctions); and to break down intra-regional trade barriers to maximise private-sector led development.[8] Eizenstat said: 'We felt US companies would be most interested in trade and investment if they could operate on a regional basis. By investing in one country and then exporting to the entire region, they could reach a market of some seventy or eighty million people.'[9]

Prior to the collapse of the vestigial Middle East peace process, signalled by the Al Aqsa Intifada in the occupied Palestinian territories, the US had other, explicitly political, hopes for its US–North Africa Economic Partnership. As Eizenstat told an Israeli audience:

> Your economic and political well being will be enhanced as the economies of your neighbours grow and as you are integrated into the Middle East. Other countries in the region, from Egypt and Jordan to Morocco and Tunisia to states in the Gulf are implementing structural reforms, getting their fiscal houses in order, privatising, deregulating. Here, the peace process can also be a key to the encouragement of greater trade between the rest of the Middle East and Israel.[10]

If the political strand of the project was in abeyance in the Palestine conflict, the continuation of US linkage of economic and political policy strands in the case of the Western Sahara was made explicit by Marc Grossman, under-secretary of state for political affairs during a visit to Algiers. There he said, 'Greater regional economic cooperation would facilitate the political resolution of the conflict over the Western Sahara'; settlement of the issue would, in turn, attract foreign investment to the Maghreb, he stated. The issue could only be understood by taking into account both economic and security questions, he continued, adding that US investors would be more attracted to the Maghreb if Morocco, Algeria and Tunisia settled their differences.[11]

A writer from one of Algeria's independent newspapers described Grossman's comments as an application of the tenets of US management of low-intensity conflicts, namely: minimum direct intervention (the Carter doctrine); preservation of regional equilibrium of forces (Kissinger); an exit strategy (William Perry); and exploitation of the interdependence of political and economic issues (Anthony Lake).[12]

The accompanying diplomatic démarche was the US decision in 2001 to support the Framework Agreement that would, to all intents and purposes, hand over the Western Sahara to Morocco.

In 1995, work began on a US–Morocco free-trade agreement. Such agreements exist with only two other states in the wider region, both key US allies – Israel and Jordan – indicating both the importance that Washington attaches to Morocco and its confidence that Morocco will provide the open access and deregulated environment that US companies want. The Eizenstat Initiative came from a Democratic presidency but the importance attached to relations with Morocco is bipartisan.

Indeed, it was the decision of Republican president George W. Bush to accelerate the free-trade agreement talks. He also reactivated US assistance to Morocco's experimental nuclear power programme and under his presidency an 'open skies' agreement was signed in 2001. The aim was to have the free-trade deal in place before the end of 2003, and governmental and business delegations were frequent visitors to Morocco once the fast-track process was announced.[13] As will be seen, the strengthening of US–Moroccan economic relations was accompanied by moves to reinforce military links.

The US Trade Information Center identified the non-agricultural sectors of the Moroccan economy as offering the best prospects for US companies: telecommunications, electrical power systems, environmental equipment and services, water resources equipment, tourism and oil and gas exploration.[14] The deregulatory and privatising policies of the Moroccan government draw constant praise from the US, and Morocco was recently named 'Country of the Year' by the US Trade and Development Agency.

Opportunities are also seen for US agricultural exports. And here a subtext of US economic policy in the Maghreb appears. A US Trade Information Center briefing document is candid:

> Morocco has begun implementing an association agreement with the European Union, which provides preferential tariff treatment for EU industrial exports to Morocco, putting American producers at a disadvantage.... As agriculture was largely excluded from Morocco's trade agreement with the EU, tariff elimination under a free trade agreement would give US exporters significant tariff advantages over the EU as well as other competitor suppliers.[15]

All that is for the future. To date US–Moroccan trade has been limited, just $610 million in the first half of 2002.[16] In 1996–2000, the US percentage share of Moroccan imports declined from 7.4 per cent to 5.6 per cent while France's share rose from 20.8 per cent to 24.3 per cent,[17] a trend Washington intends to check as and if globalisation increases corporate opportunities in Morocco and the wider Maghreb.

US military involvement with Morocco is long established. As will be seen, in order to nurture the strategic relationship the US has succumbed to Moroccan demands that American *matériel* be used against Polisario.

The George W. Bush administration has made no secret of its policy of reinforcing relations, including military relations, with its friends in the Arab world. Defense secretary William Cohen said:

> We are witnessing a transformation of the leadership in the region with King Abdullah of Jordan, the new Emir of Bahrain, and now we are seeing a new king in Morocco – so there is a new leadership that is starting to engage. They are much more engaged, certainly with the United States.[18]

Of Morocco in particular, Cohen said:

> During the Cold War ... they were very strong supporters of the United States and we had a very significant contribution to their military capability. Following the breakup of the Soviet Union that diminished. What we are doing now is trying to expand the nature of the relationship beyond what it has been.[19]

He went on to say that the US intended to assist Morocco in modernising its forces and restructuring its military, noting, perhaps with reference to the Western Sahara, 'because they have their own security concerns'. He also said he wanted to promote joint exercises and 'an expansion of their participation in the region, on a multilateral basis'.[20] In early January 2003, US and Moroccan troops carried out a joint exercise in the very south of Morocco, close to the Western Sahara border, a move interpreted as hostile to Polisario.[21]

During the Cold War, US military aid to Morocco amounted to $40 million a year but that fell back to only $4 million.[22] But the stated financial value of military aid is no reflection of the depth of a strategic relationship even if trends within it may be indicative.

Just as Morocco's free-trade agreement with the US picks it out from the overwhelming majority of Middle East and North African states, so does its receipt of grants under the Foreign Military Financing programme – Israel and Egypt take the lion's share, with the crumbs distributed between Jordan, Morocco and Tunisia.[23] The figures above refer only to direct government-to-government deals. Provisional figures from the Africa Demilitarisation Program of the Center for International Policy put the value of direct commercial sales (DCS) licences for US companies to sell arms to Morocco in 2000 at $51.3 million. The value of deliveries under direct commercial licences for 2002 was estimated at nearly $25.7 million.[24] The same report ranks Morocco as the second biggest beneficiary of DCS licence agreements in Africa in 2000, exceeded only by Egypt, and for foreign military sales (company to government) third after Egypt and Tunisia.

Cohen's comment that US military assistance and sales to Morocco needed to be reinforced after dropping off with the fall of the Soviet Union is borne out by the trend in US arms deliveries to Rabat. In the period 1973–77 they amounted to $79 million, rising sharply to $470 million as Morocco ploughed more and more military resources into the Western Sahara. For the next five years deliveries ran at $280 million but then for 1987–91 (the Berlin Wall coming down right in the middle of the period) they dropped to $210 million and for 1992–94 slid to $160 million,[25] after the Western Sahara ceasefire.

The US military presence in Morocco originated during the Second World War. By August 1950 the US Air Force had developed operational storage sites for nuclear weapons at the Nouasseur, Sidi Slimane and Ben Guerir bases in French-controlled Morocco. There were also marine detachments, Seabee battalions and communications stations. In 1958, Morocco was used as a staging post for US military intervention in Lebanon. Thereafter, the newly independent Morocco declined to renew the leases on the bases and US forces began to withdraw. But this show of independence was a sleight of hand, for 'SAC [Strategic Air Command] felt the Moroccan bases were much less critical with the long range of the B-52, and with the completion of the Spanish bases in 1959'.[26] And the withdrawal was less than hurried. Indeed in 1960, there were 20,000 US military personnel in Morocco, more than anywhere else in Africa.[27] The pull-out was largely completed by 1963. But it was 1977 before the last US military personnel officially left the naval facility at Kenitra (Port Lyautey) used to support the Sixth Fleet and for anti-submarine operations,[28] in the wake of a new basing agreement between Spain and the US.

The formal withdrawal of the bases did not remove Morocco from the network of US strategic stepping stones. Leaving aside other forms of US military and intelligence presence in Morocco and the build-up of arms sales supporting Rabat in the Western Sahara, the issue of bases and access was raised again in 1982. Hassan II then agreed to allow Morocco to be used as a staging post for US president Ronald Reagan's Rapid Reaction Force. A series of joint exercises involving US and Moroccan air, sea and land forces followed, and Congress voted funds to upgrade US military facilities in Morocco.[29] The use of Morocco as a listening and broadcasting post was stepped up at the same time with an agreement for the construction of a new site in northern Morocco coming in 1985 and the first contract awards being made by the US army a year later. Morocco allows US Navy port visits and right of transit for the US Air Force. There is extensive joint training. For instance, US and Moroccan fighter aircraft carry out joint exercises every two years, and twice a year Moroccan and US airforces carry out joint airlift exercises.[30] There are also regular naval visits by Nato forces.

Ever since Moroccan forces went into the Western Sahara there has been a degree of tension in Washington over the use of US weapons in the Western Sahara, in much the same way that use of British military equipment against the Palestinians and the East Timorese has caused embarrassment to a British government keen to promote arms sales to key allies but less keen on being seen to be associated with the less savoury policies of those allies. Nonetheless, the advocates of support for the Moroccan armed forces have prevailed.

Only weeks after the Green March, Hassan II sent an envoy to the US with a shopping list. He came away with assurances of a steady supply of arms, including F5E aircraft. Kamil reports that Morocco was even offered the use of US Navy aircraft on the carrier *Little Rock*.[31] Reports of the use of US-supplied weaponry in the Western Sahara, and Hassan II's blunt assertions that he would use arms he had paid for as he wished, embarrassed the new Carter administration and a ban on deliveries was announced. That this had little long-term impact is clear from the figures given above for arms deliveries – 1978–82 being the period when deliveries peaked.

Again according to Kamil, with the front door closed it was necessary to use the back door. In 1978, he says, Kissinger and Vernon Walters – for some time the CIA man with the Morocco file – supervised the delivery of weapons from Jordan, Iran, Taiwan, South Korea and South Africa. Meanwhile Hassan II sent a signal to Washington by sending military delegations to South Korea, Egypt and Bucharest. The message was clear – if the US will not sell, then others will.[32] The message was understood and the Carter administration signed off on the sale of a $200 million air defence system. Morocco then put in an order for Rockwell OV-10 and Cobra helicopters designed specifically for counterinsurgency.

By 1979 the sales were proceeding at a merry pace, with: the approval of sales of CH-47C helicopters via Italy; the sales of spares for F5s; ammunition sales; and most importantly the go-ahead for a $200 million Northrop Page intrusion detection system for spotting troop and transport movements in remote areas, clearly intended for use in the Western Sahara.[33] The next year, with the US concerned for the stability of Hassan II's rule after the toppling of the Shah of Iran, came another big package of arms sales all with clear counter-insurgency applications and justified on the grounds that a strong Morocco would be more likely to negotiate a peace.[34]

By the time the Reagan administration came to office the arms sales policy was clear. The US no longer had qualms about being seen to arm Morocco in its war in the Western Sahara. Indeed by 1981 and 1982, Washington was allowing Rabat to buy cluster bombs and use them against Polisario. In 1981 a senior Pentagon official visited Moroccan positions on the berm built by Morocco to keep out Polisario fighters and there were reports of Moroccan forces being trained by the Green Berets.[35]

Jealous France and post-colonial Spain

The reinvigoration and remodelling of US interests in the Maghreb evidenced by the Eizenstat Initiative, and in Morocco in particular with the fast-tracking of the free-trade agreement, the increase in military cooperation and the nomination of former secretary of state James Baker as UN broker for the Western Sahara conflict, is a challenge to the economic and political power of France in former colonial stamping grounds. By early 2003, there were press reports of European concerns that the US–Morocco free-trade agreement would provide a back door through which American goods would reach EU markets and of competition for influence between Washington and Paris.[36] A French trade minister went so far as to say a free-trade agreement with the US would be incompatible with deeper Moroccan economic relations with the EU.[37]

According to the minutes of a French parliamentary committee, academic Benjamin Stora

> drew attention to the reinforcement, discreet but real, of the American presence in the Maghreb, as much at the economic level, with signing of contracts between Algeria and several American companies in the hydrocarbon sector, as much as on the political level through the mediation efforts undertaken by the US in respect of Morocco on the question of the Western Sahara. He underlined that France could not leave to the US the responsibility of alone playing the role of mediator in a conflict that is at the heart of Moroccan preoccupations.[38]

In early 2003 it seemed that Jacques Chirac was responding to the reveille. At the same moment that he challenged the US and British rush to war in Iraq, dusting off de Gaulle's standard, the French president launched a counterattack in North Africa. First, Algeria's president, Abdelaziz Bouteflika, flew to Paris for talks rumoured in sections of the Algerian press to include an attempt to break the Western Sahara impasse. As France had long been the staunchest of Morocco's allies on the issue, any shift from partisan to mediator in talks with Polisario's principal supporter carried the suggestion of a rebalancing of French strategy in the Maghreb. Then, in early March, he made the first French presidential visit to Algiers since independence. There he and his counterpart signed the 'Algiers Declaration', which, taken together with his speech to the Algerian parliament, signalled a move to put French–Algerian economic relations on a par with French–Moroccan relations. On the question of the Western Sahara, he appeared to dilute earlier French enthusiasm for the reworked 'Framework Agreement' drafted by UN special envoy

James Baker, saying only that it merited serious consideration but insisting progress towards a solution could be made through dialogue between Morocco and Algeria.[39] For the people of the Western Sahara, the French démarche accompanied debate around the future reliability of Algerian support for Polisario. Would warmer relations between Algiers and Paris – even if, in part, generated by the latter to counter Washington's influence – result in more pressure to settle the Western Sahara dispute over their heads?

The 1996 association agreement between the Maghreb countries and the European Union was in part a counter to growing US influence in North Africa. But for France, says an Algerian diplomat, the agreement is also part of an intra-EU power play. According to this interpretation, Paris was concerned that the balance of French and German interests within the EU had been disturbed as central and eastern Europe came back within Berlin's sphere of influence. To restore the balance, France sought to strengthen its own economic and political pale in the Maghreb.

For now, France remains by far the primary economic and political partner of Morocco. French equity investments account for a third of all overseas investments in Morocco and 40 per cent of industrial investments. And while French investors have not shown as much interest in Moroccan privatisation stocks, some 520 French companies have Moroccan subsidiaries. Another 800 companies have been established in Morocco with French money. Almost all the best known French multinationals operate in Morocco, among them Renault, Citroen, TotalFinaElf, Aerospatiale. French companies employ 70,000 workers in the country.[40]

In trade, too, France is dominant, accounting in 2000 for 33.6 per cent of Moroccan exports and 24.3 per cent of imports. Spain, in second place, is a long way behind with 12.7 per cent of exports and 9.8 per cent of imports.[41] Trade relations are backed up by export guarantees and credits.

French loans have accounted for the majority of financial aid to Morocco, and Paris is the leading contributor within the EU MEDA programmes for Morocco and within the Paris Club of lenders. Between 1996 and 2000, France agreed to convert over FF3 billion of Moroccan debt, enabling French investors to buy into Morocco at reduced costs.[42]

Morocco is also one of a very small group of countries deemed eligible for both concessional funding from the French development agency and from the emerging countries' reserve (RPE).[43]

France runs a structural trade deficit with Morocco that derives from other aspects of the close post-colonial relationship between the two countries, namely the high numbers of French tourists who go to Morocco, transfers of money out France by Moroccan investors, and of course migrants' remittances.[44] In 1997 there were 722,000 Moroccans living in France, some three times as many as in the Netherlands, the second most important destination for Moroccan migrant workers.[45]

It was not until 1999 that there was first talk of formal military cooperation between France and Morocco.[46] French bases in Morocco were closed in 1961, two years ahead of schedule, due to tension over the war in Algeria. The talk of cooperation came as Paris moved to shore up the authority of Mohamed VI in the wake of his father's death with visits from President Jacques Chirac and Prime Minister Lionel Jospin. But cooperation had been in place for many years. Moroccan complicity with France and the US in military operations in Africa has already been mentioned.

As far as the Western Sahara was concerned, opposition to its independence came in the form of direct armed intervention against Polisario as the independence movement showered military humiliation after humiliation on the government of Mauritania, the weaker of the two beneficiaries of the Madrid Accord that partitioned the territory. In 1977 and 1978 French aircraft took off from Senegal to launch sorties against the guerrillas.[47] The French armed forces have also provided military training for the Moroccan army.[48] The direct intervention in the late 1970s harked back to earlier days. It was French troops whose flying column destroyed parts of the religious complex at Smara in 1913 as they waged war against the legendary Sahrawi leader Ma el Ainin. In 1958, five thousand French troops and seventy aircraft were deployed in coordination with Spanish forces to crush Sahrawi resistance. Indeed, a Sahrawi fighter of the first half of the twentieth century regarded the French as the primary danger until the 1930s, and referred to fifty-five battles fought against them by camel-borne raiders.[49]

France led the pack in the arming of Morocco during the hot

phase of the Western Sahara conflict with weapons deliveries worth $210 million in 1973–77, soaring to $1.1 billion in 1978–82, dropping back to $440 million for 1982–86. From 1987 to 1991 the figure was a more modest $50 million, now well behind the US, and $60 million in 1992–94 after the ceasefire, again behind the US.[50] For the first three quinquennia, France's share of deliveries to Morocco ranged from 42.5 per cent to 57.9 per cent. Coming further up to date, French ministry of defence figures for 1991–2000 put deliveries to Morocco at €248.8 million (some $250 million), the highest figure for any country in Africa and dwarfing the €54 million of deliveries to Algeria.[51]

The position of Spain, the former colonial power, has passed through several stages since it signed away the Western Sahara to Morocco and Mauritania on the rather notional condition that the views of the Sahrawis would be respected. Spanish economic interests in Saharan phosphates and fisheries were to be safeguarded and Morocco was to ease the pressure for the return of Ceuta and Melilla, enclaves on the Mediterranean coast.

The Francoist right was appalled by the loss of dignity, not least because the army had said clearly that it could resist a Moroccan invasion attempt. The geostrategic implications of the Madrid Accord were worrying. Withdrawal under duress from the Western Sahara would surely weaken Spain's hold on the northern enclaves by showing that Madrid would back down under pressure. Similarly, the deal could only complicate matters in the Canary Islands, Spanish territory just off the coast of southern Morocco and the Western Sahara. In the 1970s there was a flurry of pro-independence activity in the islands.

The first post-Franco administrations tried to placate Morocco and Algeria. Limited quantities of weapons were sold to Rabat and Nouakchott while the fiction of Spanish recognition of the Sahrawi right to self-determination was repeated. But the problems inherent in the Madrid Accord did not go away. The phosphate production that Spain wanted to keep a grip on ground to a halt due to Polisario attacks and has never reached its full potential. The Spanish trawler owners whose interests Madrid had also wanted to protect soon came under attack too. Algiers puckishly hosted and encouraged Canary Islands and Basque secessionists.

As the summer 2002 spat over the barren rock variously known as Leila and Perejil reminded Madrid, neither Rabat nor the Moroccan people have renounced the claim to the Mediterranean enclaves and their adjuncts. The issue has blown hot and cold over the years, with the Moroccan government periodically blowing on the embers in furtherance of domestic approval or diplomatic gain. In 1986, unrest in Melilla was particularly violent with Spanish paramilitary police crushing the protests of Moroccan inhabitants of the town, at least one demonstrator being killed, and the spokesman for the Moroccan community relocating to the nearby town of Nador.

It was the Spanish Socialist Party governments of Felipe Gonzalez from 1982 to 1996 that repeated the betrayal of the Sahrawis in the eyes of Polisario diplomats.[52] His party had recognised Polisario whilst in opposition but on coming to power expelled its representative. In the Polisario analysis, Gonzalez's focus was on Spanish integration into the European Union and on economic development. The former required a good working relationship with France, the country that had hosted many Spanish leftists during the Franco era, and rocking the boat in the Maghreb was not conducive to that. Morocco was willing to assist in the latter, offering investment opportunities to Spanish businessmen, maintaining Spanish access to fisheries under Rabat's control, and offering compromises over agricultural exports. Over time, Gonzalez moved closer to Morocco, actively lobbying Latin American countries not to recognise the putative Sahrawi Arab Democratic Republic.

The subsequent conservative government of Jose Maria Aznar changed the Spanish alignment to one of support for the UN referendum plan and scepticism about attempts to replace it with a transitional autonomy arrangement for the Western Sahara. Then, in 2003, it became a convert to reworked proposals and actively lobbied Polisario to accept them. Polisario had no illusions that Aznar harboured sympathy for Sahrawi independence per se, nor did its diplomats believe the collapse of the arrangement over fisheries (see Chapter 4) spurred Spain into a churlish change of stance. Rather, Aznar was viewed as a conservative pragmatist whose approach harked back to the geostrategic concerns of the Spanish right in 1975, concerns that look all the more convincing as the enclaves issue rumbles on and the search for oil complicates territorial issues in the waters around the Canaries. There is a view in Spain that Rabat has discriminated against Spanish oil company Repsol in the award of exploration licences in its territorial waters.[53]

As will be seen, the relationship between Spain and Morocco, redolent with the complications of colonialism and its aftermath, can at times be nothing less than vitriolic. At the same time, Sahrawi diplomats believe Madrid's policy of active neutrality over the Western Sahara is part of a wider Spanish attempt to reassert itself as a player in the Maghreb rather than concede the subregion to France and the US.

Yet, notwithstanding Spain's significance in the Western Sahara issue and the importance of its temporary membership of the UN Security Council in 2003–04, it is France and the US who are the principal external players. Their efforts (with the active participation of others ranging from Saudi Arabia to the UK), sometimes in tandem and sometimes not, to maintain and develop Morocco as a strategic ally and economic partner amount to a battle against two major destabilising factors: the chronic weakness of the kingdom's economy and the social tensions that produces; and the conflict over the Western Sahara. The two are intimately interlinked. The war and the maintenance of control over the majority of the territory have entailed enormous financial costs and political risks. The costs are still mounting and the risks become apparent at times such as 1999 when, on the death of Hassan II, the passing of power from a well-practised autocrat to his untried heir was quickly followed by a wave of unrest in the Western Sahara, and all at a time when the kingdom was suffering from increasingly frequent drought and oil prices were on the rise.

The split between the US, the UK and Spain on the one hand and France and Russia on the other over the 2003 invasion of Iraq by American and British forces could have an impact on the Western Sahara dispute had Aznar been re-elected in the sprint of 2004. French influence over Washington was diminished. Spain might have been able to extract repayment from the US for its support over Iraq, in which case the Western Sahara might not have been at the top of the list of matters Madrid wanted resolved, but for the first time it was on the list, said Mohamed Khaddad, a senior Polisario diplomat.[54] Until the US decides the issue must be dealt with, there will be no solution, according to Brahim Mochtar, another senior Polisario of-ficial.[55] In mid-2003, there were indications that just this might have happened. The US drafted a Security Council resolution endorsing a set of proposals drawn up by James Baker, the UN secretary-general's envoy for the Western Sahara and former US secretary of state. As will be seen in a subsequent chapter, Morocco was horrified. The draft was subsequently watered down but passed nonetheless. In a repeat of the run-up to the invasion of Iraq, Washington, London and Madrid lined up against Paris, which lobbied on Rabat's behalf. For Morocco the lesson was bitter. Long-standing ally Rabat might be, but in Washington perceived US interests come first. It now looked as if Washington had decided this irksome dispute should be ended for the sake of wider US interests in the Maghreb. Paris was sidelined in the Security Council but nonetheless scored valu-able points in the competition for influence over Rabat.

Notes

1. Lloyd's List, 3 June 2002.
2. Al Hayat, 15 June 2002.
3. The Times, 12 June 2002.
4. Stephen Zunes, 'The United States and Morocco: The Sahara War and Regional Interests', Arab Studies Quarterly, vol. 9, no. 4, 1987.
5. Al Hayat, 4 August 2002; 8 August 2002.
6. Angel Perez Gonzalez, 'La cuestion del Sahara y la estabilidad de Marruecos', Real Instituto Elcano de Estudios Internacionales y Estrategi-cos, 12 November 2002.
7. Report to Nato Secretariat by the subcommittee on Nato enlargement and the new democracies, May 1999.
8. Speech of Stuart Eizenstat at the North Africa Ministerial Meeting, Washington DC, 18 April 2000.
9. Speech of Stuart Eizenstat to the International Relations Institute, Algiers, 23 June 2000.
10. Speech of Stuart Eizenstat to the Van Leer Forum, Jerusalem, 31 October 1999.
11. Louisa Ait Hamadouche, 'Cooperation maghreine, conflit sahraoui et investissements américains', La Tribune d'Alger, 7 November 2002.
12. Louisa Ait Hamadouche, 'Les États-Unis font-ils pencher la balance dans le conflit sahraoui?', La Tribune d'Alger, 9 November 2002.
13. For example a seventeen-company trade delegation to study the potential of the free trade deal reported in Al Hayat, 23 October 2002. A week later the US named its negotiating team, according to Maghreb Arabe Presse,

1 November 2002, and a visit by US secretary of trade Don Evans was announced days after that said MAP on 6 November 2002.

14. US Department of Trade website: http://web.ita.doc.gov/ticwebsit.

15. Ibid.

16. US Census Bureau website: www.census.gov/foreign-trade/balance/c7140.html.

17. Economist Intelligence Unit, country profile on Morocco 2002, p. 66.

18. Charles W Corey, 'Morocco's King Mohamed VI Part of New Leadership in Region, Cohen says', *Washington File*, 10 February 2000, http://usinfo.state.gov/regional/af/security/g0021004.htm.

19. Ibid.

20. Transcript of Cohen's remarks on African peacekeeping, 11 February 2000, issued by US embassy in Tel Aviv.

21. *L'Expression*, Algiers, 6 January 2003.

22. American Forces Press Service, 22 February 2000.

23. *Sunday Times*, 22 October 2000.

24. http://ciponline.org/Africa/aid/dcs.htm.

25. Anthony H. Cordesman, 'Military Balance in the Middle East III: North Africa – Country Analysis', Center for Strategic and International Studies, Washington DC, December 1998.

26. Global Security website www.globalsecurity.org/wmd/facility/nouasseur.htm.

27. Leo Kamil, *Fueling the Fire: US Policy and the Western Sahara Conflict*, Red Sea Press, New Jersey, 1987, p. 6. Much of the information on US–Moroccan military relation in the 1970s and 1980s is taken from Kamil.

28. History of Port Lyautey: http://portlyautey.com.

29. Kamil, *Fueling the Fire*, pp. 76–7.

30. USAF in Europe news service, 1 February 2001 and 4 April 2001.

31. Kamil, *Fueling the Fire*, p. 15.

32. Ibid., pp. 31–2.

33. Ibid., p. 43.

34. Ibid., pp. 48–9.

35. Ibid., pp. 69–72.

36. *Al Hayat*, 18 January 2003; 5 February 2003.

37. Agence France Presse, 19 January 2003.

38. Committee on Foreign Affairs, Defence and Armed Forces, chaired by Xavier de Villepin, 26 January 2000.

39. Interview given to Algerian newspapers *El Watan* and *El Khabar*, 1 March 2003, reproduced on the website of the French presidency www.elysee.fr.

40. Report to the French National Assembly by France–Morocco Friendship Group following a delegation to Morocco, 19–24 November 1999.

41. Economist Intelligence Unit, country profile on Morocco, p. 43.

42. Ibid., p. 47.

43. Website of French embassy in Morocco, www.ambafrance-ma.org/kiosque/coopfrma.

44. Ibid.

45. Mara A. Leichtman, 'Transforming Brain Drain into Capital Gain: Morocco's Changing Relationship with Migration and Remittances', *Journal of North African Studies*, vol. 7, no. 1, 2002.

46. Jose Garcon, 'L'élan du Coeur de Jospin au Maroc', *Libération*, 6 November 1999.

47. Werner Ruf, 'The Role of World Powers: Colonialist Transformations and King Hassan's Rule', in Richard Lawless and Laila Monahan, eds, *War and Refugees*, Pinter, London, 1987, p. 90 n44; and Kamil, *Fueling the Fire*, pp. 32–3.

48. Ruf, 'The Role of World Powers', p. 81.

49. Interviews with author.

50. Cordesman, 'Military Balance', p. 13.

51. French Ministry of Defence, annual report to Parliament on arms sales, 2000.

52. Interview with the author, April 2003.

53. *Tiempo de Hoy*, 18 February 2002.

54. Interview with the author, 12 June 2003.

55. Interview with the author, 10 June 2003.

2

Cain and Abel:

The Western Sahara and the

Struggle for Regional Supremacy

Two minutes later the Land Rover climbed out of the far side of the town past a radar installation on a bluff and, beside it, a power station. Smith was left with an impression of people in uniform.

Tindouf was the main town contested by the Moroccans – stolen from them, they said, by the colonial divisions. The little town was far more than it appeared. It was the gate to the Sahara and the old caravan routes south. It was also the key to any invasion of or by Morocco: for there, like slices of a pie, Algeria, Morocco, Mauritania and the old Spanish Sahara faced one another.[1]

Algeria has been the most long-standing and important backer of Polisario. Continuation of its political and logistical support has been vital to the Sahrawi independence movement in its current form. That being the case, understanding the Algerian stance is important. So far beyond the heyday of the 'Third World' revolutions to which Algeria was a beacon, Cold War over, economic globalisation rampant, and Algiers and Washington at some level sharing in 'war against terrorism', some of the pillars of support are crumbling.

The refugee camps that are ultimately the base camps for Polisario's fighters lie within Algerian territory, so the movement's military and civilian reservoir exists only with Algerian complicity. The camps are reliant on food and other necessities supplied by the international community and these, notwithstanding traditional cross border trading with Mauritania, enter through Algerian airspace or along Algerian roads. The camps are located near Tindouf, a town that has a wider significance in the history of Algerian–Moroccan relations.

Algeria has not intervened directly in the fighting in the Western Sahara since early 1976 when there were two skirmishes between Algerian and Moroccan forces around the waterhole of Amgala. But at the diplomatic level Algeria has, to date, fought with persistence and skill, arguing that the Western Sahara is an issue of incomplete decolonisation by Spain and that as people of a non-self-governing territory the Sahrawis must decide their fate through an act of self-determination, a referendum. That has been the public position of Algeria since the closing years of the Spanish occupation although Morocco argues that in July 1975 then foreign minister of Algeria, now president, Abdelaziz Bouteflika agreed to Moroccan and Mauritanian partition of the Western Sahara in return for ratification of a border agreement between Algiers and Rabat. There have also been periodic bilateral discussions that might have produced a settlement that Polisario was unable to resist. For instance, Abdelhamid Brahimi, later prime minister of Algeria (January 1984 to November 1988), in 1980 proposed that the Western Sahara be discussed alongside other issues, including the option of routing a gas pipeline to Spain via Morocco. The talks went ahead in February 1982 between President Chadli Benjedid and Hassan II. Apparently, agreement in principle was reached and Brahimi remains convinced that the issue would have been settled had Chadli remained in power.[2] A diplomat cites three more instances over the years.

A former foreign minister with over two decades of involvement in the Western Sahara issue, Ahmed Attaf cites two points of principle in his country's position: that of the inviolability of borders inherited from colonial powers and that of the right of self-determination.[3] Attaf argues that the first principle, a basic tenet of the Organisation of African Unity (now the African Union) invoked to safeguard the fragile post-colonial states and maintain peace on the continent, has been violated only twice: by Somalia over the Ogaden and by Morocco over the Western Sahara.

A counterargument is that as a country carved up by France and Spain, had Morocco accepted colonial boundaries it would have remained in bits, 'the victim of a veritable colonial dismemberment'.[4] Former prime minister Abderahmane Youssoufi lists six treaties (including the Madrid Accord) signed to constitute the current territory controlled by Rabat[5] and the issue of the Spanish-held *presidios* of Ceuta and Melilla remains. Indeed, in the 1960s Morocco formally registered a reservation on this clause of the OAU charter. And the crucial UN resolution on decolonisation does allow for reintegration of divided territories where national unity or territorial integrity has been disrupted. That allowance clearly applied to territory that was incontestably part of Morocco but could not be applied so blithely to the Western Sahara.

On the matter of self-determination, Morocco (and Mauritania in the past) argues that a scratch meeting of the Spanish-instituted *djemaa* or assembly of Sahrawi notables exercised the right at a session convened in Laayoune by Morocco in 1976. It has also argued that the notion of a referendum that it now renounces as obsolete was first proposed by Hassan II. The notion that the Sahrawis have been consulted in any meaningful way about their future is, of course, scorned by Polisario, by Algeria and, indeed, by the international community. The comparison drawn is between the Western Sahara and East Timor. The latter was regarded by Indonesia as an integral part of its territory, was ruled for well over two decades by Jakarta, only to become independent finally through the application of UN General Assembly Resolution 1514, a referendum on self-determination.

For Morocco, Algeria's support for Polisario (which Algeria would style as support for the right of Sahrawi self-determination) is a conspiracy to contain the kingdom geographically, economically and culturally and, in so doing, to cripple the prospects of regional integration. The Western Sahara issue, for Morocco, is a bilateral issue between Rabat and Algiers. Morocco consistently portrays Polisario as a tool of Algeria, a puppet that allowed the Algerian regime to fight a proxy war against Morocco and that still allows it to maintain the threat of renewed conflict. The message pervades official statements, the comments of officials, the government press agency, the political parties and their media outlets, and the recitations of Polisario defectors.

Typical is an article published in *L'Opinion*, a newspaper of the Istiqlal party, the party of Morocco's independence struggle and the progenitor of other establishment parties in the kingdom. The article begins by noting that Algeria has always sought to portray itself as the disinterested and zealous proponent of right and international law:

> Yet, beyond the hollow slogans and the official phraseology – self-determination, the right of people to decide for themselves and other sham principles – the reality is completely different and it proceeds from geopolitical and geostrategic interests, henceforth evident to all.
>
> Algiers searches more and more openly to extend its hegemony over all of the sub-region, commencing through the dismemberment of the territorial integrity of Morocco.[6]

Fear of a puppet state to its south was expressed by Morocco to the 1975 UN Mission to the region, prior to Spanish withdrawal:

> Morocco's primary concern was the presence of an intruder, the creation of a puppet state which would separate the north and south of the Sahara. The fruitful womb of Africa consisted of that part of the continent which ran from the African bulge to Tangiers; it must not be occupied by, or at the mercy of, an intruder.[7]

While it is not stated explicitly, it is reasonable to assume the puppeteer in mind must have been Algeria.

The conflict has been portrayed as bedevilling attempts to move forward with construction of the Maghreb Arab Union, set up in 1989 as the vehicle for the economic integration of the states of the Maghreb. It was proposed in a 'naive démarche'[8] of the union's founders that Morocco and Algeria normalised relations, leaving aside the issue of the Western Sahara for the UN to sort out. The MAU never took off. Despite the complementarities of the Moroccan and Algerian economies, levels of cross-border trade have remained pitiful. Three years after the MAU was formed, Morocco took only around 3 per cent of its imports from other members of the group and sold to them just 7.5 per cent of its exports. For Algeria the percentages were 2.6 per cent and 2 per cent.[9] The borders between the two neighbours have been closed to citizens despite widespread intermarriage since 1994 – the latest closure. At the diplomatic level the organisation has been a fiasco. In June 2002, a planned summit of the MAU fell apart when Mohamed VI decided not to attend, apparently because of the impasse over the Western Sahara. Attempts to reschedule the summit fell again in January 2003 on the same stumbling block.

Yet if one interpretation is that regional integration is blocked by the Western Sahara dispute, there is the more convincing argument that the failure of the MAU and the Western Sahara dispute are, for Algeria and Morocco, expressions rather than causes of their rivalry. For the former Algerian prime minister Abdelhamid Brahimi, a passionate and long-standing advocate of economic integration, a powerful body within the Algerian military, seen by many analysts as the only real power in the land, has donned former president (1965–78) Houari Boumedienne's mantle of opposition to integration.[10] He cites reported comments by Khaled Nezzar, retired military strongman and still a powerful figure, saying he would never forgive President Chadli for trying to create a Maghreb union that would dilute the notion of Algerian primacy. Continued support for Polisario achieves the end of this clique, according to Brahimi, who sees no room for 'mini states' in the subregion. Such remarks chime with Moroccan charges that Algeria is Balkanising the Maghreb.[11] However Brahimi says he has no sympathy for Moroccan 'expansionism' but is a regionalist who believes that, rather than a nationalist approach, could provide a means of solving the conflict.

Looking at the opposing stances of Algeria and Morocco through the optic of realpolitik rather than legal and political principle, we see the two most populous states of the Maghreb locked in a contest for influence both within the sub-region and beyond. Addi describes it thus:

> Since the independence of Algeria in 1962, relations between the two 'brother countries' – who never stop proclaiming their ties fashioned by language, history and religion – have always been on the brink of rupture, with the exception of the period 1969 to 1974. This permanent belligerence manifested itself in the form of military confrontation at Tindouf in 1963 and, since 1975, put the two countries on the verge of confrontation over the subject of the Western Sahara. The contradiction between the proclamations of unitary faith and the animosity of relations finds its roots in the authoritarian mode of legitimation of power in each of the two countries.[12]

At the ideological level, an evangelical Algeria was perceived as a threat to a Moroccan monarchy with a new king who needed to prove his credentials to a nationalist movement that had been the vanguard of the independence struggle. According to Abdelhamid Brahimi, by the 1970s Boumedienne's vision was of Algeria as a 'Japan of Africa', an economic powerhouse and subregional leader, in this case built on oil, the price of which was rising as producer countries asserted themselves against the foreign oil companies. An expansionist Morocco threatened this project. So did other developments in the Maghreb, and in 1972 Boumedienne threatened to intervene to prevent a proposed union between Libya and Tunis.

The first expression of Addi's 'permanent belligerence' was the brief Sand War of 1963. This helped set the scene for the Western Saharan dispute. Tindouf, the location of the Sahrawi refugee camps, lies in the westernmost part of the great bulge of southern Algeria that comes as close as two hundred kilometres to the Atlantic seaboard. It also lies at the centre of Istiqlal's sketch map of Greater Morocco that lay at the heart of the party's ideology for decades, an ideology adopted by the monarchy in 1958.

In 1957, as France worked up its exit strategy from North Africa, the subject of Morocco's border with Algeria was raised. Paris suggested a partnership with Rabat that would allow exploitation of mineral reserves in part of what became the Algerian Sahara. Morocco's sovereign refused, saying he would discuss borders with Algeria after independence. This has been held up as an act of principle and it may have been in part, but it was also based on common sense.

The claims to the old caravan city of Tindouf and other areas along the border and deep into southern Algeria are redolent of the complications of many post-colonial territorial squabbles – nation-states attempting to formalise and solidify relationships that, prior to the arbitrary territorial divisions of the colonial era, were malleable, or to express inter-communal relations in terms of territorial sovereignty. An agreement between Morocco and then leader of the Algerian provisional government, Ferhat Abbas, had given Morocco hopes that it would gain some of the territory that fell to Algeria on independence. But Abbas was replaced by Ben Bella after independence and he made clear there would be no territorial concessions.[13]

In 1963 tensions boiled over. Istiqlal republished its map of Greater Morocco, taking in Western Sahara, present-day Mauritania, and much of Senegal, Mali and Algeria. In September, the Istiqlal-linked press said Algerian troops had moved into Moroccan oases and the town of Tarfaya. In October, the Moroccan government reported attacks on three of its eastern outposts. Algeria claimed Moroccan encroachment on its territory. A worrisome little war commenced in the south but then spread north to the border town of Figuig. It was over in weeks, with an OAU-brokered ceasefire taking effect on 1 November. Morocco claimed to have got within 12 kilometres of Tindouf.

Algeria recognised the border demarcation decision of the OAU commission almost immediately – it was little changed from the border inherited with France. However, haunted by the sketch of Greater Morocco, the Moroccan king and government were unable to accept, even assuming they wished to. It was 1989 before the government in Rabat ratified the border agreement reached in 1972 in which it renounced its claim of sovereignty over Tindouf. And, as the agreement has never been approved by the Moroccan parliament, ratification remains incomplete. As Moroccan ambassador to London, Mohammed Belmahi, has said, while the issue of Tindouf is not live, it will be 'pending' as long as the larger territorial dossier is open.[14]

In this historical context, it is little wonder that the Algerian government told the visiting UN Mission in 1975 that, 'it could not fail to take an interest in the future of a territory which adjoined its frontiers'. Its interest was 'based on obvious geo-political considerations' and it 'should not be disregarded in the search for a solution to the problem of the Spanish Sahara'.[15] Indeed, President Boumedienne, with remarkable prescience, went so far as to ask the mission, rhetorically, 'Was Spain thinking of a transfer of powers to Morocco, to Mauritania (or both simultaneously) or to the local population?'[16] The development of the situation might create a security problem in the region, he warned.

So, for Morocco, Tindouf is a ghost of territorial ambitions of the recent past and the lair of the movement that has sought to frustrate its core expansionist project. For Algeria, Polisario could help to frustrate Moroccan expansion not only to the south but also to the west, diverting its military resources and demonstrating how serious Algeria was about defending its border. At the same time, practical defence of the principle of inviolability of colonial boundaries in the Western Sahara has helped Algeria to underpin the legitimacy of its own boundaries, for, as Joffe points out, 'The one state [in Africa] that has been particularly anxious to make use of it has been Algeria, in large measure because it is extremely difficult to define a pre-colonial Algerian state with the same territorial extent as modern Algeria.'[17]

Khaled Nezzar, the former Algerian defence minister and career soldier, explicitly linked the two territorial questions: 'This question of the Sahara was not fomented by Algeria. It had been an abscess that developed badly and that suppurated because Morocco had expansionist designs over our country.'[18]

When Abderahmane Youssoufi, Moroccan prime minister from 1997 to 2002, was asked about relations between Morocco and Rabat, he said:

> Put yourself in the place of the Moroccans. If you Algerians heard, day and night, Morocco saying the Reguibat region of Algeria must be an independent state and that one led some inhabitants of that region to Agadir in order to make them a camp, a flag, what would you think?[19]

Youssoufi posed what he intended to be a nonsense in order to argue that the Sahrawi independence movement that Algeria has supported is just such a nonsense. Yet a legacy of disputed borders, the inflated territorial ambitions of Istiqlal's founders, the pressures on the Moroccan monarchy of legitimation, may well have bequeathed a fear in Algeria that border disputes could be reopened, that the nationality of the inhabitants of the town of Tindouf might again be contested, just as the nationality of the inhabitants of the surrounding camps was contested. As Hodges put it:

> If Hassan succeeded in flouting the principle [of inviolability of inherited borders] in Western Sahara, against its people's will, to solve his internal political problems, there was a real danger, whether he formally ratified the 1972 Algerian–Moroccan border convention or not, that he would be encouraged to revive the old claims to parts of Algerian territory if and when political

circumstances at home once again required new diversionary tactics abroad. Furthermore, if Hassan got his way in the Sahara, the FAR [Moroccan army] would be within striking distance of Tindouf.[20]

Periodically the Moroccan government reactivates its claim to Ceuta and Melilla, Spanish enclaves known as *presidios* on the Mediterranean coast of Morocco. As anachronistic as Gibraltar, with which they have often been compared, the two ports have been held by Iberian powers since the fifteenth century and have remained so after the decolonisation of the rest of Morocco. Apart from their military function, Ceuta and Melilla are important ports. Morocco charges that up to $5 billion a year of goods are traded through the two ports. Given that they are unproductive towns, this traffic amounts to Spanish-approved smuggling in Moroccan eyes. The continued existence of the *presidios* has deprived a region of Morocco that was underdeveloped in the colonial period of access to the best harbours on the coast and vital customs revenues. This in turn has boosted migration from the region to Europe and encouraged the cultivation and smuggling of drugs from the Rif mountains, phenomena the EU says it wishes to curtail. It has also undercut attempts to establish industries in Casablanca, further imbedding chronic unemployment and, arguably, providing a breeding ground for Islamism, a phenomenon of concern to the Moroccan and EU (and US) governments.

Relations between Morocco and Spain are difficult and will remain so for the foreseeable future. There is a list of festering issues, including: the *presidios*; access to Moroccan (and Western Saharan) fisheries; and the Western Sahara, for which Spain now advocates self-determination. A Moroccan diplomat expressed a common suspicion when he argued that Madrid seeks to control Moroccan access to European markets and frustrate it at the political and diplomatic levels.

When a dispute over a rocky outcrop just yards off the Moroccan Mediterranean coast erupted in the summer of 2002 and Algeria appeared to side with Spain, citing again the principle of accepting inherited borders, suspicions of a conspiracy ran wild. In an ambassadorial briefing, which was no doubt replicated elsewhere, the message was that the wording of official remarks out of Madrid and Algiers on the rock – known as Leila or Perejil – was so close as to prove coordination. More, there was a joint Algerian–Spanish conspiracy to isolate Morocco. At the territorial level, this consisted of Spain maintaining a stranglehold on the economic development of the north through control of Ceuta and Melilla, while Algerian interference in the Western Sahara sought to prevent Moroccan access to sub-Saharan Africa, throttling ambitions to establish Morocco as the principal overland route into Europe.

Again, the theme echoes concerns expressed to the UN Mission before the Spanish withdrawal from the Western Sahara. Ironically, given the subsequent Madrid Accord, representatives of the Front de Libération et de l'Unité, a Moroccan-sponsored, integrationist organisation, denounced what it termed the 'Spanish–Algerian plot'.[21]

Leila was allowed to fade as an issue as September 2002 general elections in Morocco approached. But the thesis that there existed 'a deliberate will to isolate Morocco, victim of a double and irascible hostility',[22] developed further with the signing of a treaty of friendship between Madrid and Algiers. This would see Algerian hydrocarbons sold to Spain with the proceeds recycled into investments in Algeria, favouring binational joint ventures, and perhaps bringing Spain in as an investor in Sonatrach, the Algerian national oil company, ran one line of reasoning.[23] Less speculative but of more economic and symbolic significance was the decision to build a second natural gas pipeline to feed Spain from Algeria. An existing pipeline avoided the expensive and demanding direct undersea route and transits through northern Morocco. Agreed during the illusory MAU honeymoon of 1989, this rare example of Algerian–Moroccan economic cooperation provided Morocco with transit fees and volumes of gas. But the new pipeline carrying gas from the Hassi Rmel field will cross the Mediterranean direct from Oran to Almeria, a move Rabat would see as 'a stab in the back', according to one observer writing in a France-based publication.[24]

At the level of international diplomacy over the Western Sahara, the new cosiness was discomforting for Rabat. The air of confidence that Moroccan officials exuded in the run-up to the April 2002 debate in the UN Security Council on an autonomy plan, deriving from its support from the US, UK and France, had dissipated. As the year drew to a close, not only had it lost two attempts to have the plan approved, largely due to the active opposition of Algeria and Spain, but now Spain was about to take its turn on the Security Council just as James Baker was due to come back with revised ideas.

A successful Moroccan integration of the Western Sahara has potentially enormous implications for the Moroccan economy and while the territory's resource base may have been a factor in the decision to claim it, economic advantage seems unlikely to play a part in Algerian policy. It lays no claim to the Western Sahara and so access to its resources would be indirect even if a Sahrawi state were a client. An export route via the Atlantic coast is on offer from Morocco in the context of a settlement of the Western Sahara issue. Indeed, there is an argument that the conflict has harmed Algeria economically by preventing joint exploitation with Morocco of iron ore deposits around Tindouf at Gara Djebilet and Abdelaziz Mecheri. These could be transported more quickly and easily through southern Morocco to the Atlantic than three times as far to the Mediterranean. A joint project was discussed in the 1960s but foundered on territorial disputes and, clearly, has not been pursued since the Western Sahara dispute developed, although Morocco says it could be revived after a settlement.

Changing interests in a changing world

If Algeria's stand over the Western Sahara is viewed as part of a wider-ranging competition for subregional supremacy, two questions arise. First, whose interests does the stand serve and, second, is it susceptible to change? Addi referred to the 'authoritarian mode of legitimation of power' in Morocco and Algeria. It is widely held that in Algeria economic and political power is vested in the military *decideurs* or simply *le pouvoir*. Of President Abdelaziz Bouteflika, the French newspaper *Libération* said: 'Certainly he has immense freedom of speech. But on condition that he respects 'the domains reserved for the sovereignty of the military': army affairs; distribution of oil earnings; management of FIS [the Islamic opposition party]; Morocco and the Western Sahara.'[25] An academic commentator remarks that 'ultimate political power remains the prerogative of the Monarchy in Morocco, the senior military leaders in Algeria and the state president … in Tunisia'[26] and that 'in Algeria it is the senior figures in the country's military who make all the key decisions in the state ... Until this current reality is changed, discussion over political parties, their role, their platforms, their meaning and their typology will remain no more than ... a mildly interesting academic study.'[27] Hugh Roberts, whose analysis of the Algerian state and its components is compelling, presents a structure in which the separation of the military from the political was abolished with the birth of the FLN. The dominance of the army, which he calls a 'shamefaced sovereign which formally denies its right to the allegiance other sovereigns unhesitatingly, indeed proudly, demand', is not for him the result of coup or conspiracy but a structural outcome of an ongoing historical absence of constitutionalism in Algerian politics.[28]

In another of the mirrored accusations that bedevil the disputes of the Maghreb, the Algerian military is said to use the closure of borders with its neighbours as a means of regulating and profiting from smuggling, while senior Moroccan officers are accused by Polisario of controlling much of the fishing and trading activity in the Western Sahara.

If the Algerian position on the Western Sahara has been a pillar in the structure of power within the country as well as a cornerstone to its closely related policy towards the subregion, then it will not shift except as part of broader changes. The very consistency of the Algerian stance since the Green March testifies to this, notwithstanding the periodic sounding out of Rabat on other options and recurrent rumours of rapprochement.

Looking at the factors in play at present, what might influence Algerian thinking? Having survived and controlled more than a decade of Islamist insurrection and secular (in both senses) unrest in the Kabyle regions, the decideurs look invulnerable to domestic pressures and may well have been able to entrench and extend their power. But Algeria's ruling stratum is not monolithic. There have been numerous fallings out and reshuffles within the political class. In 1975, the decision to oppose Moroccan (and Mauritanian) occupation of the Western Sahara was not unanimous. The then foreign minister argued Morocco should be allowed the territory in exchange for definitive recognition of Algerian sovereignty over Tindouf.[29] Whether generational change in the upper echelons of the security forces and their allies would bring a reassessment of domestic and external relations would depend in large part on the extent to which power and influence could be bequeathed to a new generation.

International financial institutions and donor countries have supported the Algerian government through the 1990s, increasing the disenchantment of ordinary citizens, argues Volpi.[30] But the Eizenstat Initiative signalled the beginning of a US engagement with the Maghreb (excluding Libya) that runs contrary to the current reality of closed borders, minimal integration and pitiful volumes of subregional trade. It offers Algeria the prospect of investment beyond the hydrocarbon sector but predicated on the creation of a wider, integrated subregional market. As the failure of the Maghreb Arab Union has shown, that cannot be achieved while the Western Sahara dossier remains open. Meanwhile, Morocco is moving ahead with a Free Trade Agreement with the US.

The time may be coming when the ideological and geostrategic logic behind supporting Polisario is pitted against potential economic gains. If the desire and perceived need to attract more and more broadly invested finance from the US and Europe is now weighing against more traditional, more domestically based revenue collection by the Algerian government and elite, that certainly militates towards a settlement of the Western Sahara question geared to the needs and demands of potential foreign investors.

Yet there are other drivers towards change. For the average Algerian, the Western Sahara issue is of little practical concern. However, the closure of the border with Morocco, not a direct consequence of the Western Sahara conflict but an expression of the wider tensions between Rabat and Algiers, is very much a concern to hundreds of thousands of Algerians and Moroccans. Not only does the closure inhibit cross-border trade (except for smugglers) but it has divided thousands of intermarried families. Tens of thousands of people are trapped on one side of the border or the other, unable to join their loved ones.

A reopening of the border would bring immense prestige and popularity to the Algerian politician able to present it as his achievement. With presidential elections due in 2004, part of the Algerian press was quick to assert that President Bouteflika's February 2003 visit to his French counterpart was to broker a deal – support from

Chirac for his re-election in exchange for a change in policy on the Western Sahara. President Bouteflika was once foreign minister, the foreign minister who argued in 1975 that Morocco should have the Western Sahara in exchange for a border agreement with Algiers. Given the preponderance of an entrenched military or former-military elite in Algerian affairs, even a long-standing and well-connected politician such as Bouteflika would be unable to effect a major change in policy over the territory without backing, so any change would suggest that at least part of *le pouvoir* was prepared to 'globalise' its economic base. That said, as noted elsewhere, over the years Algeria has been willing to 'fly kites', testing out alternative solutions. As foreign minister Abdelaziz Belkhadem said in the course of a visit to Rabat billed as the presage to a Moroccan–Algerian summit, 'Faced with complicated situations, it is wise not to believe in stereotypes and easy expedients.' In a comment suggesting the imminent launch of a kite, he continued, 'the present leaders at the highest levels of all the interested and concerned parties can overcome the blockage to make history'.[31]

Weeks later President Chirac made his historic trip to Algiers. There he asserted to parliament that the prosperity of the country depended on its integration into the global economy and France's eagerness to further the process through development aid and private investment. Not only was French private capital ready and waiting to invest in Algeria – and not only in the hydrocarbon sector – but Paris would champion the country in the international institutions.[32] But Chirac then went on to echo a theme of his US competitors, saying that subregional prosperity required Maghreb integration and that in turn demanded Moroccan–Algerian dialogue. The main blockage there was the Western Sahara dispute, of course, but progress on that could be made bilaterally, he told the Algerian press.

So, Morocco's most important political and economic partners, whilst in competition for influence in the Maghreb, were singing from the same hymn sheet. Both were telling the Algerian government that they wanted to broaden their investment there outside of the oil and gas industries but that subregional integration was necessary. While Algeria's hydrocarbon wealth and the strategic needs of Europe and the US in the wake of September 11 and the Iraq crisis meant the country could negotiate from a position of some strength, the offers on the table from Washington and Paris showed signs of provoking debate in the ruling circle.

Indeed, it was no lesser a person than Khaled Nezzar, cited by Abdhelhamid Brahimi as an epitomy of Algerian supremacism, who stirred things up. In an interview with *La Gazette du Maroc*[33] he said the issue of the Western Sahara should no longer separate the 'the two brother countries'. In an age of great regional blocs it was necessary to create 'our own Maghrebien space' and there had never been any really serious attempt to solve the Western Sahara problem. Resorting to the language that had signalled the demise of the UN Settlement Plan and its replacement by the Framework Agreement (see Chapter 9), he said that his preference 'would be to go towards the thesis of no winner, no loser'. It was necessary, he continued, 'to find the adequate formula permitting integration of the Sahrawis, to return to the country in the framework of an agreement'.

Days later an Algerian daily picked him up on the issue.[34] There he was more cautious and played the part of the simple soldier, saying, 'I've never claimed it was necessary or necessary not to create a Sahrawi state.' That was for the politicians to decide, but Algeria should not remain at arms for a hundred years to support the creation of a state, he opined, pointedly denying that the military stood in the way of a settlement.

The retired general's remarks were quickly put aside as those of someone who represented no one by the officially sponsored Algerian National Committee for the Support of the Sahrawi People, but given his continued influence his comments pointed up the pressures on the long-standing Algerian position on the Western Sahara.

In May 2003, in the wake of the invasion of Iraq and only days after the thirtieth anniversary commemoration of the founding of Polisario – attended by distinctly second-order Algerian political figures – the UN secretary-general issued one of his periodic reports on the Western Sahara. This one presented and recommended a reworked version of the autonomy plan prepared by his personal envoy, James Baker. As will be seen, the Framework Agreement of 2001 and its successor formalised the ditching of the peace process signed in 1991, granting the Western Sahara an autonomous status under Moroccan sovereignty pending a referendum. In the reworked version, voters would choose not just between independence and integration with

Morocco but also on continued autonomous status. But, absolutely crucially, the electoral roll would comprise not Sahrawis but those Sahrawis and adults resident in the territory since the end of 1999 – that is, the Moroccan settlers who outnumber the Sahrawis.

In June 1991, the Algerian response was blistering. The plan 'intends to eliminate the Sahrawi specificity, the concept of the Sahrawi entity and finally the very notion of Sahrawi people', said its memorandum to the Security Council.[35] Two years later, it greeted the revised version as 'a gamble for peace in the Maghreb – a gamble which should be taken by all concerned with determination and sincerity'.[36] The long response was very strong in the guarantees it requested, maximising the role of the UN in defining the detail and method of implementation of the plan. Indeed one immediate interpretation was that this was Algerian diplomacy at its best, assessing the mood of the Security Council and Kofi Annan's threat to propose UN withdrawal from the Western Sahara issue, and deciding to agree the plan in principle while hedging it with safeguards it calculated Morocco would not accept. For Polisario, the bleaker assessment was that this was a signal that the economic and political pressures and trends discussed above had finally convinced Algeria to transform its diplomatic stance on the Western Sahara from one founded on conviction to something much more contingent.[37]

At the very least, the Algerian response was a significant change in posture and tone. Polisario stood alone in calling the proposed plan 'unfair and fatal to the Saharan people',[38] but ultimately agreeing to proceed with it as a basis for a settlement after coming under intense pressure, including pressure from Algeria.

The supporting players

Mauritania requires some mention in a discussion of the subregional context, although it has played only a supporting role to the main actors since the end of 1979 when its troops withdrew from the Western Sahara. Ranked 139 out of 162 countries in the UN's human development index, it is one of the poorest countries in the world. Some 50 per cent of the population lives below the poverty threshold, over 20 per cent of the workforce is unemployed, and

life expectancy is around fifty-one years. The country has a population of under 3 million but a high growth rate – in the mid-1970s
the population was little over one million. The population is eth-
nically divided between the Moorish northerners, who are former
or current nomads, and the black southern farming population.
Competition for access to fertile land along the River Senegal has,
in the recent past, exacerbated historical tensions and led to (reciprocated) expulsions of black Mauritanians into Senegal. In short,
Mauritania has little weight to throw about when compared to its
northern neighbours.

As France imposed its territorial definitions on 'its' tranche of
West Africa, it gradually moulded what would become Mauritania
into a state from what had previously been a mosaic of shifting
local alliances. The area became a civil territory ruled from further
south under the French West Africa administration in 1904. In 1920
it gained the status of colony. In November 1960 it became independent – formally at any rate. Rezette remarked in the mid-1970s
that, 'even in our day many ministers and high functionaries of this
state leave their office in the evening to return to the family tent,
the only habitat really befitting noble nomads who want to remain
known as such'.[39]

Yet, despite its obvious limitations, Mauritania staked a claim to
the Western Sahara in its year of independence. Rezette argues that
it had to do so to justify its own existence for Morocco, which had
a minister for Mauritanian (and Saharan) affairs until 1963, claimed
Mauritania as its own and that 'either the Western Sahara is Moroccan
and Mauritania is Moroccan by virtue of the same reasoning, or
Mauritania has an independent existence and there is no reason why
this existence should not extend to the Spanish Sahara'.[40]

Yet the cultural ties between the inhabitants of Mauritania and
those of the Western Sahara were strong and binding, and they remain so. Sahrawis will remark that Algerians and Moroccans are of
a kind and so are Sahrawis and Mauritanians. In another acknowl-
edgement of the closeness yet distinctiveness of the two, both sides
in the Western Sahara conflict on occasion seek to discredit advocates of their adversary's cause by describing them as Mauritanians
– imposters but credible imposters. And the ties can be familial and
confusingly close. Leading Polisario figure Ahmed Baba Miske, who

has also mediated conflicts in the Sahel, represented Mauritania in the UN in the 1960s. Indeed, in its early years, Polisario proposed a federation between Mauritania and a Western Saharan state.

The linguistic, tribal, familial and cultural closeness of the people both sides of the border was expressed in Mauritania's claim to sovereignty at the International Court of Justice where it said Sahrawis and Mauritanians were both of the *bilad Chinguetti* (loosely, the country of Chinguetti, a religious centre in Mauritania that is of importance within Islam). This link, while perhaps more significant to the communities implicated, had even less tenure in the territorially based opinion of the ICJ than had Morocco's claims based on authority exercised over dignatories of some tribes in parts of the Western Sahara.

But Mauritania and Morocco had come to an understanding well before the court uttered. In October 1974, Hassan II declared that the two governments had reached agreement. According to Rezette, they had agreed the Western Sahara should be split along the lines of Franco-Spanish agreements of 1900, 1904 and 1912.[41] This is certainly the impression of the reports of Mauritanian comments given by the UN mission of 1975.

When the forces of Morocco and Mauritania moved into the Western Sahara, the latter found itself in possession of a swathe of desert and a population of just a few thousand. True, it had the port town of Dakhla and a large area of abundant fisheries, but the major population centres and the phosphate mine, conveyor and export facility fell to Morocco. From the start, the Nouakchott government was losing money in the territory.

By April 1976, Polisario was striking deep into Mauritanian territory.[42] Columns of raiders struck Chinguetti, Zouerate – the iron-ore mining town from which derived the country's only significant export earnings – and even the capital itself. By September a new Franco–Mauritanian military agreement was in place. By the following year the Mauritanian armed forces had grown from 5,000 men to 17,000 and Moroccan troops and attack aircraft were being stationed in Mauritania. Concerned about the instability the conflict was creating in Mauritania and the possible knock-on effects for French former colonies in the Sahel, President Giscard d'Estaing organised direct intervention. In Operation Lamantin, French Jaguar aircraft attacked Polisario columns twice in December 1977, inflicting heavy casualties. The pretext was that Paris sought the release of a handful of French workers seized by Sahrawi fighters.

The Mauritanian economy collapsed under the weight of the war, combined with rising oil import prices, sedentarisation and drought. A coup in Mauritania in July 1978 led Polisario to declare a truce. The new leaders in Nouakchott, egged on by Paris, raised the idea of a Sahrawi state within the borders of Tiris al Gharbia, the Mauritanian-held section of the Western Sahara. This was acceptable neither to Morocco nor to Polisario and Algeria. One year on, Polisario resumed military operations against Mauritania. Within days, Nouakchott buckled, voting at an OAU meeting for a referendum on the future of the Western Sahara and then, in early August 1979, reaching an agreement with Polisario to withdraw from the Western Sahara and renounce its claims. According to Hodges, the Mauritanian sector, the Rio de Oro or Wadi ed Dahab, would be handed over to Polisario. In the event, while the whole area was militarily contested for some time, Morocco airlifted troops into Dakhla and annexed the southern part of the Western Sahara on 14 August.

In time, Mauritania recognised the Sahrawi Arab Democratic Republic, although it allows no ambassadorial presence in Nouakchott. It signed up to the Settlement Plan and consistently urged the principal parties to make progress. But although consulted as an interested party like Algeria, Mauritania's weakness prevents it from taking an active role. No Mauritanian response to the Framework Agreement was published by the UN. Its position is restricted to saying it will support any settlement agreed by the principals and urging them to reach such a stage.

Mauritania maintains relations with the parties to the conflict – although relations with Morocco were tense after 1979 – and stands as neutral ground where divided families may meet up. 'Equilibrium' is a key word in the vocabulary of Mauritanian diplomats – equilibrium between Morocco on the one hand and Polisario and Algeria on the other. But anxiety remains. A senior diplomat said Morocco refuses to interpret Nouakchott's neutrality as less than support for Algeria and Polisario.[43] He referred to the period in the 1970s when Moroccan troops were based in northern Mauritania as akin to an occupation, and worried that Moroccan nationalists would press forward with the slogan that Mohamed V regained Morocco, Hassan II regained the Sahara and Mohamed VI will regain Mauritania.

The north of the country has long hosted thousands of Sahrawis, many of whom work at Zouerate. But, according to local reports,[44] the number of Sahrawis in the north of Mauritania multiplied after Polisario began to encourage liberalisation of the economy of the refugee population in the camps. Refugees moved from the camps to Zouerate and Nouadhibou where they set up small trading enterprises and then began buying land and real estate. The suggestion was that the extent of this phenomenon was a cause of alarm to Nouakchott, which feared the development of Sahrawi-dominated areas along the border with the Western Sahara. Mauritanian officials make no pretence of being able to police the desert frontiers.

A settlement of the Western Sahara issue would help to stabilise Mauritania's government, where coups have been generated in large part to amend Saharan policies. With oil discovered offshore and exploration licences for gold and uranium issued, durable peace to the north would encourage economic growth while free transit across the Western Sahara would open up valuable trading opportunities to one of Africa's poorest countries.

The constitution of Polisario's Sahrawi Arab Democratic Republic defines the Sahrawis as Arab and African (and Muslim). Although its principal backer, Algeria, has been a major influence in the Arab world through the inspiration of its liberation struggle, its formidable diplomacy and its oil revenues, it is on Africa that Polisario has relied for diplomatic support and recognition. To some extent this reflects an Africanist orientation of Algeria, but more importantly it is pragmatic. Morocco is better placed to garner support from regimes, frequently conservative, monarchic, or both. That said, the movement has made forays into the Arab diplomatic circus.

Algeria has been Polisario's longest-standing supporter but was not its first. Indeed, the movement's founder was briefly arrested in 1973 and the first significant support came in early 1975. It was the other Maghrebian revolutionary state, Libya, that first armed and trained Polisario fighters, as early as 1973. But that support was transitory. Libyan leader Muammar Qaddafi, spurned by Algeria in his pursuit of the ideal of Arab unity, managed to forge a short-lived agreement with Hassan II in 1984. The US was shocked but Libyan arms supplies to Polisario stopped (even if Libyan representatives continued to turn up at anniversary celebrations in the Tindouf camps). Then Hassan II pulled off a dangerous political coup, meeting in July 1985 with the Israeli prime minister, rehabilitating himself with Washington and ensuring the end of the marriage of convenience with Tripoli.

The Moroccan–Israeli talks – after which there were reports of Israeli military help to Rabat in the Western Sahara – angered Syria and for a while Damascus publicly supported Polisario, which in turn upped its anti-zionist rhetoric.[45] Tunisia courted Moroccan fury in the mid-1980s as it appeared to offer an unofficial form of recognition to Polisario, for example inviting it to attend a conference of 'progressive parties of the Mediterranean basin' in 1986.

Saudi Arabia, a close ally of the Moroccan monarchy and funder of its arms purchases, has presented itself as a mediator on occasion. In 1987, King Fahd tried to broker a deal between Rabat and Algiers at a meeting between the respective heads of state at Oujda in Morocco.[46] Years later a plane belonging to a member of the Saudi royal family would take UN envoy James Baker to Tindouf to try, again unsuccessfully, to construct a peace deal.

Morocco has, over the years, alleged that Polisario was supported by, and in turn supported, Middle Eastern political players that would raise hackles in the West and in the conservative Arab regimes. For example, it charged Iran with arming Polisario,[47] which in turn it accused of training and arming Islamicist militants. At the same time, Polisario was receiving training from Ahmed Jibril's splinter group, the Popular Front for the Liberation of Palestine – General Command, according to the Moroccan government.[48]

Notes

1. John Ralston Saul, *Baraka*, Granada, Rexdale ON, 1983, p. 268. This is perhaps the only thriller to be written in some large part around the Western Sahara conflict.
2. Interview with the author, 27 September 2002.
3. Interview with the author, 4 October 2002.
4. 'Report of the UN Visiting Mission to Spanish Sahara', UN Document A/10023/Rev 1, 1975, pp. 80–81.
5. 'Le Sahara empoisonne nos relations', interview in *Liberté-Algérie*, 25 September 2002.

6. Moussa Hormat-Allah, 'Espagne–Algérie: Une alliance contre nature', *L'Opinion*, 25 November 2002.
7. 'Report of the UN Visiting Mission to Spanish Sahara', p. 112.
8. Lahouari Addi, 'Introuvable reconciliation entre Alger et Rabat', *Le Monde Diplomatique*, December 1999.
9. Derived from Abdelhamid Brahimi, *Le Maghreb à la croisée des chemins*, Centre for Maghreb Studies/Hoggar, 1996, p. 327.
10. Interview with the author.
11. See, for example, report in the newspaper *Al Hayat*, 25 July 2002.
12. Addi, 'Introuvable reconciliation'.
13. Benjamin Stora, 'Representations of the Nation that Unite and Divide', *Journal of North African Studies*, vol. 8, no. 1, 2003, p. 23.
14. Discussion with the author, 30 January 2003.
15. 'Report of the UN Visiting Mission to Spanish Sahara', p. 35.
16. Ibid., p. 117.
17. George Joffe, 'The International Court of Justice and the Western Sahara', in Richard Lawless and Laila Monahan, eds, *War and Refugees: The Western Sahara Conflict*, Pinter, London, 1987, p. 17.
18. *La Nouvelle République*, Algiers, 12–19 March 2003.
19. 'Le Sahara empoisonne nos relations'.
20. Tony Hodges, *Western Sahara: The Roots of a Desert War*, Lawrence Hill, Westport CT, 1983, p. 194.
21. 'Report of the UN Visiting Mission to Spanish Sahara', p. 64.
22. Hassan Alaoui, 'Un mariage de raison entre petrole et politique', *Le Matin*, 7 October 2002.
23. Ibid.
24. Cherif Ouazani, 'L'Axe Alger–Madrid', *Jeune Afrique l'intelligent*, 14 October 2002.
25. Jose Garcon, 'Bouteflika, un an sans grand bilan', *Libération*, 15 April 2000.
26. Michael J Willis, 'Political Parties in the Maghrib: The Illusion of Significance?', *Journal of North African Studies*, vol. 7, no. 2, p. 2.
27. Micahel J Willis, 'Political Parties in the Maghrib: Ideology and Identification. A Suggested Typology', *Journal of North African Studies*, vol. 7, no. 3, p. 24.
28. Hugh Roberts, *The Battlefield: Algeria 1988–2002, Studies in a Broken Polity*, Verso, London and New York, 2003, pp. 200–211.
29. Stora, 'Representations of the Nation that Unite and Divide', p. 25.
30. Frederic Volpi, *Islam and Democracy*, Pluto Press, London, 2003.
31. Algerian Press Service report, cited in ARSO weekly news 2004, week 6, www.arso.org.
32. Speech to the Algerian parliament, 3 March 2003, reproduced on the website of the French presidency, www.elysee.fr.
33. 10 March 2003.
34. *La Nouvelle République*, 12 March 2003.
35. Report of the Secretary-General on the situation concerning Western Sahara, 20 June 2001, S/2001/613 annex 2.

36. Report of the Secretary-General on the situation concerning Western Sahara, 23 May 2003, S/2003/565 annex 3.
37. For further discussion of this topic, see later chapter.
38. S/2003/565 annex 3.
39. Robert Rezette, *The Western Sahara and the Frontiers of Morocco*, Nouvelles Editions Latines, Paris, 1975, p. 120.
40. Ibid., p. 144.
41. Ibid., p. 145.
42. For a detailed account of this period, see Hodges, *Western Sahara*.
43. Interview with the author, February 2003.
44. *Al Hayat*, 3 February 2003.
45. *Mideast Mirror*, 12 March 1987.
46. *Financial Times*, 5 May 1987.
47. *Al Arab*, 2 February 1987.
48. Moroccan government release, believed to be from early 1990.

3

Morocco:

Unstable and Counting the Cost

of the Green March

The kingdom bequeathed to Mohamed VI is hostage to two problems 'liable to overturn the equilibrium of Morocco: poverty and the Western Sahara'.[1] The two issues are tightly intertwined. A key determinant of the outcome of the conflict over the Western Sahara will be whether the nature of their relationship can be changed. War and occupation impose a financial burden on any economy. The social cost is all the greater and all the more stultifying for a developing country. Inevitably, much of the strategy of an independence movement will be to maintain and maximise the financial (as well as political and military) costs to its enemy. In the case of the Western Sahara, geography and climate have assisted Polisario in this aim. Even after more than a decade without fighting between Polisario and Morocco, Algeria has remained convinced that the cost of maintaining and equipping an army along the berms and in barracks in the Western Sahara would be a major factor in eventually deciding Rabat to sue for an internationally recognised settlement. Anecdotally, it is recounted that UN envoy James Baker remarked to the general in command of Moroccan forces in the Western Sahara that the Texas–Mexico border is of a similar length to that delimited by the defensive berms but that Texas could not afford to build and defend such a structure.

For the occupying government, controlling the social cost and the consequent domestic political dangers is important in the first stages but the grail is conversion of the occupation into a profitable economic integration that will alleviate rather than exacerbate domestic tensions. Chapter 4, on the natural resources of the Western Sahara, illustrates the potential wealth to be unlocked and, in the case of phosphates and fisheries, already being unlocked by Morocco. But for now the Western Sahara is a cash sink rather than a cash cow for Rabat.

Growth in the Moroccan economy slowed from an average of 3.9 per cent a year in the 1980s to 2.7 per cent in the 1990s. With population growth averaging 1.9 per cent, income growth per capita has been minimal, negative even in the second half of the 1990s.[2] According to the International Monetary Fund, real growth in GDP in 2000 was just 0.3 per cent and had been negative the year before.[3] Industry and services have become increasingly important compared to agriculture and mining. Manufacturing accounted for 18.7 per cent of GDP in 2000 against 10.8 per cent for agriculture, forestry and fishing, and 2.9 per cent for mining, according to the national bank. But agriculture continues to account for 45 per cent of employment and is an important export earner. Its decline in relative importance to GDP reflects in large part its vulnerability to droughts, which have devastated output in recent years.

The country runs a structural trade deficit in goods, with exports typically covering 70–75 per cent of imports[4] but, given the importance of its agricultural exports to the EU, as volatile as climatic conditions. So, in the first four months of 2001, cover fell to 65.5 per cent because of weak citrus and fishery exports.[5] With the EU accounting for some two-thirds of Moroccan exports of goods, there is a high degree of dependency on European economic conditions. Demand growth for Moroccan goods was weak in 2002, increasing the incentive to push ahead with a free-trade deal with the US.

The value of Moroccan merchandise exports in 2000 was some MD79 billion ($7.9 billion) but two categories of invisible exports are crucial to the country – tourism and remittances from migrants – each contributing some $2 billion a year.[6] Even more than for merchandise earnings, these two sources of income are dependent on Europe. Some 1.9 million of 2.4 million foreign visitors in 2000 were from the EU, with another 100,000 from non-EU Europe.[7] Then, some 1.6 million of 1.9 million Moroccans living overseas are in Europe.[8]

The vulnerability engendered by this dependence is clear. After the attacks on the US on 11 September 2001, the global airline and tourism trades went into a tailspin. Tourism to the Arab world was particularly badly affected. Morocco's receipts for tourism slumped by 31 per cent in the first four months of 2002, a poor start for a campaign to increase the dependence by quadrupling income from tourism by 2010, and a disaster for the 600,000 people employed in the sector. Then came the war against Iraq and the Casablanca bombings.

The regulation of migration has been a key motivation for the EU in developing its association agreement with Morocco. The priority in the social field cited in the March 2000 agreement was reducing migratory pressure and resettling illegal migrants.[9] Mara Leichtman questions the positive effects of migration on labour-exporting countries and points out that for Morocco the episode of legal migration at any rate is drawing to a close:

> Facing Morocco in the new millennium is an end to emigration as an alternative source of employment, due to decline in demand of labour in countries of employment and the resulting immigration policies.... Morocco has depended on remittances for so long, that their decline could cause a serious economic crisis for the country if necessary measure are not taken in advance.[10]

She is sceptical about the ability of the provisions of the EU–Morocco agreement to solve the problems posed by this reverse trend.

Increasing economic openness under pressure from trade partners and international financial institutions has brought the familiar phenomenon of cherry-picking by foreign investors and resultant loss of control. French foreign minister Dominique de Villepin specified transport, electricity and banking as sectors French investors are interested in and that are currently under state control.[11] In an excoriating description of Morocco's economy, long-time Maghreb watcher and resident Francis Ghiles notes: 'Many local entrepreneurs have sold their businesses to large international groups rather than modernise. This brings risks, notably that of leaving too much of the fruits to foreigners with, as a corollary, the flight of decision making overseas.'[12] He goes on to cite AXA buying Compagnie Africaine d'Assurances, Danone buying Bisco, Coca-Cola taking bottling companies in Fez and Marrakesh, and Cimport acquiring cement maker Asment. That key Moroccan companies were becoming pawns in the hands of multinationals became clear to all as French utility group Vivendi plunged into crisis two years after taking a 35 per cent stake in the privatised Maroc Telecom and the Moroccan and wider Arab press wondered for weeks in whose hands the stake would end up. Again as Ghiles points out, inward investment into Morocco has often been for the purposes of picking up privatised stock, not creating new businesses. Around half of all receipts from privatisation have come from abroad.

The consequences of a weak and dependent economy include poverty, and Morocco has plenty of that. Officially, the percentage of unemployment typically runs in the high teens to low twenties in urban areas (21.5 per cent in 2000[13]). The government says there are 180,000 new job-market entrants each year and to absorb them a minimum GDP growth rate of 6 per cent is needed.[14]

In the UN's *Human Development Report* of 2002, Morocco comes in at 112 in the aggregated human development index out of 160 countries, one place below Namibia. In a subregional context, only Mauritania scores lower in North Africa. GNP per capita used in the report is from 1999 and for Morocco is just over $3,000. The adult literacy rate is given as 48 per cent.[15]

Inevitably, poverty breeds resentments, and throughout the post-independence period the urban poor in particular have periodically erupted from their bidonvilles to riot. While the radical left had little success in organising the dispossessed, Islamists have made inroads. This has increased establishment concerns and, after the gains made by Islamists in the 2002 general election, may well have pushed the government of palace-appointed technocrat Idriss Jettou into announcing an acceleration of basic development targets such as universal access to drinking water. Further announcements came the following spring when it emerged that the perpetrators of a wave of suicide bombings in Casablanca were residents of one of the most notorious bidonvilles where a radical Islamist faction had made inroads.

The government's budget for 2003 was projected at MD139.5 billion (some $14 billion), a modest growth of 1.8 per cent over 2002 but greater than the forecast growth in receipts.[16] The budget for 2000 was MD119.5 billion.[17] Cordesman puts the Moroccan defence budget in 2000 at $1.8 billion,[18] which at an exchange rate of approximately ten dirhams to the dollar means 15 per cent of government expenditure goes on the military rather than economic development or social needs. In 1991, the spend per person in the armed forces was around $6,500[19] against a per capita income of scarcely more than $1,000.[20]

Arms imports have continued apace. Seddon is among those to have said these costs have been in addition to general defence spending.[21] Between 1985 and 1995, the bill for arms imports was some $1.9 billion,[22] although some of the tab may have been picked up by Saudi Arabia.

Assessing military expenditure on the war and subsequent ceasefire in the Western Sahara is an exercise in guesswork and approximation, not least because some military expenditure would have been incurred anyway and because some of the costs translate into savings elsewhere. Given the high levels of urban unemployment, the army is a useful sink for the jobless and the poor. A Moroccan soldier held by Polisario remarked that the army is the destination of the poor who have virtually no economic safety net – 'There are no property developers' sons in the army', he added.

Yet the timing and scale of the expansion of the armed forces was directly connected with the war in the Western Sahara and the garrisoning of the territory. There were 56,000 men in the FAR in 1974. Between 1974 and 1982 the army almost tripled in size due to the war against Polisario.[23] But the years of ceasefire have brought no reduction. By 2002 the kingdom had a total of 198,500 actively under arms, scarcely changed since 1990, the year before the ceasefire with Polisario, with a further 100,000 conscripts and 150,000 reservists.[24] The regular army accounted for some 175,000 men.

Economic costs versus political benefits

The Western Sahara has been the repository for many thousands of Moroccan soldiers. Estimates of the number garrisoning the territory have run to 170,000.[25] Even under the referendum plan, 65,000 would have remained in barracks in the territory while the vote took place. Clearly, without the Western Sahara the Moroccan government could have maintained a smaller army but suffered higher official unemployment rates. Alternatively, it could have run the dangers inherent in a large standing army within striking distance of the centres of political power. Over the years, there have been plenty of rumours that senior officer support for remaining in the Western Sahara has been bolstered by corruption such as control of the tobacco trade over the Mauritanian border and fishing vessels. As it is, the forces based in the Western Sahara, whether because of or despite the remoteness, have spawned their share of plots against the regime. As one commentator put it: 'disbanding or reducing the armed forces would only add to the unemployment problem and probably cause trouble among the 80,000 troops getting double pay in the Sahara'.[26]

In 1983, US Congress heard estimates that Morocco was spending $1.9 billion a year on prosecuting the war.[27] Seddon argued that estimates of the effective cost of the war tended to be on the high side. He cited estimates published in 1980 in the range of $2–5 million a day.[28] Direct costs of the war in 1987 were around $1 million a day, he estimated, but noted that on top of this came all the attendant costs of occupation.[29] Direct military costs may have come down with the completion of the berm-building programme, allowing Moroccan troops to sit and wait for guerrilla attacks rather than burn up fuel and vehicles in a hopeless game of chase. Cordesman refers to the war becoming 'slightly more affordable' in the decade from 1984.[30] Certainly the walls of sand limited Polisario's ability to attack economic targets. The harassment of fishing vessels was much more difficult and there were no more attacks on the Bou Craa phosphate mines, where excavation had been made impossible for six years.

As noted elsewhere, one Moroccan estimate for the infrastructural spend in the Western Sahara between the mid-1970s and 2002 was around $1 billion, with more pencilled in. Other estimates are much higher, with Thobhani citing an unreferenced $1–1.5 billion spend between 1975 and 1985 alone.[31] But the cost of ports, desalination plants, roads and airports should also be seen as capital investment necessary for the future economic exploitation of the Western Sahara. However, significant private sector investment, particularly from overseas, will not come so long as there is no resolution of the status of the territory.

Then there are the unknown costs of maintaining the settler population in the towns of the Western Sahara where the official economic activity rate for 2000 was just 43.2 per cent, the lowest for any region recorded by Morocco.[32] The many tens of thousands of northern Moroccans and ethnic Sahrawis from southern Morocco transferred to the towns of the Western Sahara subsist for the most part on government jobs and government subsidies. Settlers receive tax breaks, subsidised goods and services. Those given jobs receive special high rates, while those without work get hand-outs through the government's workfare scheme.

However important the financial accounting, the political items on the Western Sahara balance sheet will be at least as important in determining whether the Green March ends in profit or bankruptcy for the Moroccan leadership. The credibility of not only the Makhzen – the ruling elite – but the whole establishment political class and its attendant electronic and print media has been staked on the 'recovery' and integration of the 'southern provinces'.

Ironically, Hassan II may well have seen his Green March into the Western Sahara as a move to stabilise Morocco or, at least, to underpin his own power. An army coup had failed in 1971. An airforce-led attempt came close to killing the king just a year later. A leftist move to provoke an uprising collapsed a year after that. The political parties were clamouring for more influence. The 350,000-strong wave of Moroccan civilians who crossed the border as the army made its move further along the frontier provided the king with 'a personal triumph necessary to the stability of his throne, with his restless army occupied in the desert'.[33]

'The king's next move, launching the Green March into the Western Sahara, was a master stroke. It greatly strengthened his domestic position because all the parties rallied round him on the issue and observed a virtual political truce for fifteen years',[34] according to one observer. Another says the Green March 'allowed the king to assert, once again, his domestic hegemony and his domination of the nationalist discourse', adding that not only were the parties shepherded into line but tentative moves towards a human rights discourse were transformed into citizens' rights, 'with a clear emphasis on the defence of the unity and the independence of la Patrie'.[35]

Hassan believed that Polisario would fade away after Morocco and

Mauritania partitioned the Western Sahara, or at least would not be able to cause significant problems.[36] By 1979 the size of Morocco's desert army had been doubled to 80,000 men, Mauritania had retired wounded from the fray, guerrilla attacks were reaching into southern Morocco, and Hassan, attacking Algeria for its support for Polisario, said the conflict had 'reached the threshold of the intolerable'.[37]

After the seizure of the Western Sahara, the exercise inside Morocco was transformed from one of mobilisation and co-option into one of containment. This required denial of casualties, denial of Polisario attacks, and even refusal to acknowledge the existence of Moroccan prisoners of war. A postcard from Casablanca, posted in 1988, says 'you have brought our son back', a simple affirmation that Rabat had swept under the carpet the fate of men it had lost as prisoners to Polisario fighters. Lieutenant Ben Salah Abdel Majid, sous-officier Hamdani Abdelsalam and corporal Yusfi Heddu sounded resigned when they explained that they knew their government denied their existence as prisoners of war. Abdel Majid had already been held for nine years; the others were snatched from the berm in 1987. They believed POWs released by Polisario were simply re-imprisoned in Morocco to prevent them from talking about the war and the conditions faced by rank-and-file Moroccan troops. Would their journalist interrogators send photographs of them to their families to prove they were still alive?

It was to be years before Rabat openly acknowledged the existence of the POWs. Then, as governments will, it effected a 180-degree manoeuvre and began agitating domestically and internationally for the immediate release of the prisoners, denouncing their detention as a human rights abuse.

In this context, of course, for a newspaper to raise issues of 'national unity' was to invite closure – not that the state-subsidised, party- and palace-linked major dailies were likely to be tempted to offend. As for dissidents, 'the Western Sahara provided the state with another rationale for repression ... to advocate autonomy for the disputed territory was to write one's own prison sentence',[38] wrote one academic human rights commentator (although, ironically, advocating *autonomy* would by 2001 have met with approval).

With the ceasefire of 6 September 1991, some of the political chickens came home to roost:

Domestic pressure emerged after Morocco and Polisario accepted a UN peace plan for Western Sahara.... Almost immediately the tacit political truce, observed more or less since the desert conflict began in 1975, was abandoned by the parties, particularly the Istiqlal and the USFP and their trade union federations. The king could no longer rely on them to soft-pedal demands in time of war, since the war was virtually over. They began agitating for political change or democratic reform, and backed up their demands by staging a string of strikes.[39]

With the death of Hassan II came the death of the king who had seized the nationalist agenda of Istiqlal, the political party most active in the struggle against the French protectorate, and wagered his own fate on his ability to take and hold the Western Sahara. Hughes cites him as saying he would have abdicated if the Green March strategy had failed.[40] Ostensibly, the succession presented the opportunity to cut the Gordian knot. But Mohamed VI did not slice the knot and permit the referendum to go ahead in the Western Sahara. Nor have he and his advisers come forward with any imaginative proposals that might satisfy the aspirations of Sahrawi nationalists and the honour of greater Moroccan nationalism. Rather he has chosen to pursue the grail of profitable economic exploitation of the territory combined with retention of political control. Indeed, it may be that the monarch believes the argument put forward by his emissaries that Morocco is an ethnic, tribal and regional patchwork only cemented by common obeisance to the king in his religious and secular capacities. By this logic, the whole edifice is weakened by loosening the bond to any constituent part and to grant the Western Sahara a measure of self-government over and above that of, say, the Rif, let alone independence, would open the way for a collapse of central authority.

There were soon doubts whether a more nuanced approach to opposition and criticism survived the first days of the new king's rule. The events of 1999 in the Western Sahara are dealt with in Chapter 8. Suffice it to say here that tentative openings to the development of civil society soon seemed to be closing and debate about alternative political futures became a sterile take-it-or-leave-it listing of local powers available under Rabat's vision of autonomy.

Inside Morocco itself the media remain constrained by repressive laws and the young king continues to belabour journalists about the 'responsibility' that comes with 'freedom'.[41] Indeed there are distinct signs of a tightening of restrictions on the press. In mid-2003, Ali Lmrabet, the editor of two satirical weeklies, was jailed for four years (later reduced to three years) for insulting the king and undermining the monarchy. The hunger strike that took him close to death drew international attention. In the wake of the Casablanca bombings, as his prime minister rushed to assure international investors that Morocco remained safe for business, the king gave a speech warning that the days of laxity were over for 'certain milieux making bad use of freedom of opinion'. Demonstrations by groups such as the unemployed continue to be banned[42] if deemed embarrassing. Scepticism over election results persists[43] and 'critical human rights activists – and they are not alone – openly declare that nothing has changed in the past 15 years'.[44]

Morocco continues to be routinely referred to as unstable and, to date, the political and economic gamble of moving into the Western Sahara over a quarter of a century ago remains just that.

Notes

1. 'Chirac, soutien de la transition marocaine', Jose Garcon, *Libération*, 30 October 1999.
2. Economist Intelligence Unit Country Profile 2002, p. 28.
3. IMF public information notice, 2 August 2001.
4. Economist Intelligence Unit Country Profile 2002, p. 42.
5. Reuters, 18 June 2002, citing Office des Changes statistics.
6. Ibid., p. 45.
7. 'Morocco in Figures 2000', Ministry of Economic Forecasting and Planning.
8. Mara A. Leichtman, 'Transforming Brain Drain into Capital Gain: Morocco's Changing Relationship with Migration and Remittances', *Journal of North African Studies*, vol. 7, no. 1, 2002.
9. Ibid., p. 126.
10. Ibid., p. 129.
11. *International Herald Tribune*, 27 February 2003.
12. Francis Ghiles, 'Deux ans après la mort de Hassan II: le pays entre dans la mondialisation par effraction', *Le Monde Diplomatique*, June 2001.
13. 'Morocco in Figures 2000', p. 19.
14. Reuters, 24 June 2002.

15. *Human Development Report* 2002, United Nations, New York, p. 143.

16. Maghreb Arabe Presse 14 October 2002.

17. 'Morocco in Numbers 2000', p. 132.

18. Anthony H. Cordesman, *The Military Balance in North Africa*, Center for Strategic and International Studies, Washington DC, 2002, p. 48.

19. Stephen O. Hughes, *Morocco under King Hassan*, Ithaca Press, Ithaca NY, 2001, p. 353.

20. Ibid., p. 344.

21. David Seddon, 'Morocco at War', in Richard Lawless and Laila Monahan, eds, *War and Refugees*, Pinter, London, 1987, p. 123.

22. Calculated from Anthony H. Cordesman, *Military Balance in the Middle East: North Africa – Country Analysis*, Center for Strategic and International Studies, Washington DC, 1998, p. 11.

23. International Institute for Strategic Studies, cited in Tony Hodges, *Western Sahara: The Roots of a Desert War*, Lawrence Hill, Westport CT, 1983.

24. Ibid.

25. Mohamed Abdel Aziz, leader of Polisario, spoke of 167,800 troops stationed on the wall in 1988 during a press conference 21 May 1988. Leo Kamil says there were over 150,000 troops on the wall in 1980 (Leo Kamil, *Fueling the Fire: US Policy and the Western Sahara Conflict*, Red Sea Press, New Jersey, 1987, p. 71). An Algerian diplomat with a knowledge of the Western Sahara issue referred loosely to 200,000 Moroccan military personnel in the Western Sahara.

26. Hughes, *Morocco under King Hassan*, p. 354.

27. Cited by Kamil, *Fueling the Fire*, p. 80.

28. Seddon, 'Morocco at War', p. 105.

29. Ibid., p. 123.

30. Cordesman, *Military Balance in the Middle East*, p. 11.

31. Akbarali Thobhani, *Western Sahara since 1975 under Moroccan Administration: Social, Economic and Political Transformation*, Edwin Mellen Press, Lewiston NY, 2002, p. 111.

32. 'Morocco in Figures 2000', p. 17 (the figure includes the Guelmime region of southern Morocco that has been amalgamated with Smara into a single province).

33. John Mercer, 'The Saharauis of Western Sahara', in Georgina Ashworth, ed., *World Minorities*, vol. 1, Quartermaine House, London, 1977, p. 133.

34. Hughes, *Morocco under King Hassan*, p. 230.

35. James Sater, 'The Dynamics of State and Civil Society in Morocco', *Journal of North African Studies*, vol. 7, no. 3, 2002, p. 105.

36. Hughes, *Morocco under King Hassan*, p. 251.

37. Ibid., pp. 254–7.

38. Susan Waltz, 'The Politics of Human Rights in the Maghreb', in John P. Entelis, ed., *Islam, Democracy and the State in North Africa*, Indiana University Press, Indianapolis, 1997, p. 79.

39. Hughes, *Morocco under King Hassan*, p. 325.

40. Ibid., p. 231.

41. For example, see *Al Hayat*, 17 November 2002.
42. For example, see *Al Hayat*, 16 November 2002.
43. For example, see Angel Perez, Gonzalez, 'La cuestion del Sahara y la estabilidad de Marruecos', Real Instituto Elcano de Estudios Internacionales y Estrategicos, 12 November 2002.
44. Sater, 'The Dynamics of State and Civil Society in Morocco', p. 115.

4

The Alchemist's Dream:
The Quest for Gold from
the Desert Sand

> Without its wealth, the Western Sahara would not perhaps have aroused the same covetousness and would already have been an independent country for years or even decades.[1]

Fadel Ismail recognised that the proven and the prospective natural resources of the Western Sahara are a blessing and a curse for the independence movement. On the one hand they promise an economic viability that was recognised by the visiting UN Mission in 1975 and more recently by James Baker. This gave rise to the now hackneyed description of an independent Western Sahara as a potential Kuwait of the Maghreb – resource-rich but low in population. On the other hand, of course, the mineral and fishing wealth of the territory has drawn the attention of others.

Exploration, evaluation and exploitation of resources run through the plot of the modern history of the Western Sahara. From the late 1940s the spotlight was on phosphates; from the mid-1970s fishing rights grew in importance; now oil – always in the wings – has taken centre stage. In future it could be vanadium. For Spain, maintaining a hold on the phosphate and fishing reserves was a key element when it considered its options as its occupation drew to a close. Though it protested at the time that it had no intention of holding on to control of the phosphate deposits and that it might even waive repayment of sunk investment, when push came to shove the Madrid Accords awarded it a healthy stake. For US and European business and governments, the prospect of oil and a range of strategically important minerals is always of interest, economic and geopolitical.

For Morocco, the natural resources of the area are of immense importance and they have a variety of functions. They enhance the kingdom's share of the world phosphate market. They allow it to maintain control over much of the rich and depleting fisheries of the North African Atlantic coast. They offer the tantalising prospect of reduced dependence on imports of oil. Indeed, even finds of a scale modest by international standards could turn Rabat from an importer to an exporter at a time when the US in particular wants to reduce its dependence on oil from the Arabian Gulf. In sum, they hold out the tantalising possibility that they could not only finance the costs of staying in the Western Sahara but could contribute to the development of Morocco.

The resources of the Western Sahara already provide Morocco with much needed employment, not only for settlers in the occupied territories but also for Moroccans living in Morocco. As projects to develop processing industries come to fruition, these benefits will grow. The longer the Moroccan presence in the territory continues, the more important Western Saharan resources, largely untapped so far, are likely to become. Officials point to the growing importance of fish landed in Laayoune and Dakhla. Oil, once discovered, would not be given up easily. And, if it is discovered, the associated natural gas would increase the potential value of local phosphates because ammonia and sulphur could be extracted for use in fertiliser plants. Assumptions about the volumes of fish and phosphates harvested from the Western Sahara are built into Morocco's five-year development programme.

The full potential of the territory is unknown – data are limited. In part this is because much work needs to be done – only about 20 per cent of Morocco itself has been properly prospected. But, as a meeting of jurists was told, there are other reasons why a full inventory of the Western Sahara's wealth does not exist:

> Evaluation of reserves is difficult in practice because of [Western Sahara's] history, marked by hegemonic impulses of one [party] or another. That is why serious prospecting work, carrying out studies of the terrain over large areas, does not exist.

Besides, some work has surely been sacrificed to strategic interests. Then, for reasons of political economy the results of research have not been published, and no more so by Morocco.[2]

Oil

'The Ottomans stopped at Algiers and so did the oil' is a Moroccan refrain. The economy of the kingdom is entirely dependent on imports and the cost of those imports is vast for an impoverished country. Running at 160,000 barrels a day in 2000, Morocco was the second biggest oil importer in Africa after South Africa. Per capita consumption rose 25 per cent between 1990 and 2001.[3] It receives 1 billion cubic metres of gas from Algeria each year in lieu of pipeline transit fees.

The kingdom's exports typically cover 70–75 per cent of imports, leaving a trade deficit of $2.5–3 billion a year. Oil and lubricants accounted for 13 per cent of the import bill in 1999 but some 18 per cent in 2000.[4] The volatility of the oil price – lows of $10 a barrel for Brent crude at the depth of the price crash of 1997–98 and highs of over $30 a barrel in 2001 – is reflected in Morocco's bill. In 1998, it paid MD5.4 billion (around $540 million) for crude oil imports but two years later it paid MD14.7 billion. The oil market is driven at least as much by geopolitics and war as by the fundamentals of supply and demand. This makes forecasting and economic planning difficult. But it is obvious that reduction of its dependence on oil imports would slash the trade deficit and enable better planning.

But in 2001, Morocco produced just 0.04 per cent of its oil requirements[5] from proven reserves, put by the US Department of Energy at a mere 1.8 million barrels and described by the same as 'insignificant'.[6]

However, onshore exploration in Morocco has continued in a desultory manner and in 2000 there was a flurry of excitement when the new king told a youth festival of a major find by Lone Star Energy, an affiliate of Texan company Skidmore, in the north-east of the country. The oil industry press cited reports of a find with a potential size of 100 million barrels of oil equivalent[7] but it was the abstract extrapolations of geologists that caught the popular eye and soon there was talk of 2 billion barrels. It all ended in humiliation. Little more has been heard of the Talsinnt discovery.

So onshore exploration has brought little. But that is not where the excitement is now. Improvements in exploration and production in deep offshore waters have transformed the oil industry. Expertise has grown and costs have come down. From waters offshore Angola to the Gulf of Mexico and the northern reaches of the UK Continental Shelf, oil is being drilled from reservoirs several kilometres below the sea surface. Oil companies have scrambled for acreage and as they have done so attention has eventually been paid to areas that were previously overlooked or deemed unpromising with earlier technology.

The north-west coast of Africa is just such a region. From the Gulf of Guinea all the way to northern Morocco exploration is under way. In the Gulf of Guinea the prospect of oil wealth set off a chain of territorial disputes. To the north, Dakar and Bissau, long at odds over the Casamance region of Senegal, nonetheless agreed a joint body to oversee offshore exploration and in 2002 Amerada Hess, a large US oil company, fresh from successes further south, farmed into licences held by a small Australian-based explorer, Fusion, offshore Senegal and Guinea Bissau, Gambia and Cameroon.

North again and we come to Mauritania, one of the poorest countries in the world, dependent for export income on the iron ore reserves at Zouerate (a source of employment over the years for many Sahrawis) and fishing agreements with the EU and others.

In 2001, a consortium led by Woodside of Australia and Agip of Italy but also including Fusion, among others, struck oil on the Chinguetti block offshore Mauritania. A second well disappointed but more drilling in the summer of 2002 demonstrated the find to be commercial. Analysts estimated the recoverable reserves of the Chinguetti area to be in the region of between 500 million and 1 billion barrels. Production was targeted to begin in 2005.

Even before the Chinguetti find, Morocco was successfully market-ing exploration licences in its own waters. In some three years Onarep, the state oil company, issued licences covering around forty offshore blocks and managed to attract some big names, including Shell, which subsequently also gained the interests in the area of Enterprise Oil. Part of the attraction to Morocco was undoubtedly the general rise in interest in the whole coast, particularly as geologists and exploration directors drew out the similarities between the rock formation of the Gulf of Guinea and that off the Atlantic coast of the Maghreb. Part of it was also a new petroleum law enacted in Morocco in 2000. The state's share in exploration and development concessions was cut back to a maximum of 25 per cent, royalties on production slashed, and tax exemptions introduced in the event of production.

Amina Benkhadra, head of Onarep, highlighted the success:

> Today, more than 14 oil companies are active in several regions of the country on reconnaissance zones or exploration permits onshore and offshore. They include majors such as Shell, Eni, TotalFina and Conoco, super-independents like Enterprise, Kerr–McGee, Energy Africa and Malaysian Petronas or emerging companies such as Vanco, Cabre, Taurus or MPE. These companies have signed nine petroleum agreements covering 47 exploration permits of which 38 are offshore, in addition to six reconnaissance licences, three of which are offshore.[8]

Yet Benkhadra's words disguised two other aspects of Morocco's rejuvenated quest for oil (which had already sparked a row with Spain over exploration rights around the Canary Islands), its determination to gain access to any reserves offshore the Western Sahara and its desperation to get major international companies to break the de facto embargo on operating in disputed territory.

Work done in the Spanish colonial era indicated the Western Sahara to be more prospective than Morocco, although no commercial reserves were discovered. Madrid issued forty-three concessions to eleven US and Spanish groups and the first onshore drilling equipment arrived in 1960. Some 10,000 to 12,000 workers are said to have arrived, mostly from the Canaries. But by 1964 while twenty-seven oil traces had been found, nothing commercial had come to light and the companies drifted away to more promising regions. Two years later offshore concessions were demarcated and some limited exploration work was done, culminating in 1974 when data gathered from a research vessel produced 'evidence of likely oil and methane gas zones in the continental shelf from Gambia to Spanish Sahara'.[9]

After Spain pulled out and Morocco marched in, exploration work ceased. The legal and diplomatic issues far outweighed any incentive to continue work in an area where there was no clear commerciality. And if that did not persuade the oil companies to keep away, a string of Polisario attacks against foreign fishing vessels working in Sahrawi waters did.

The Chinguetti find underlined the apparently greater chance of oil being found off the Western Sahara than further north. Chinguetti galvanised interest in the Western Sahara and vendors rushed to make available existing geological data on the territory, according to Jonathan Taylor, exploration director of Fusion Oil. Talsinnt had already shown the Moroccan establishment to be excitable when it comes to oil, and it may not have been just Fusion officials who wondered aloud if 'this could be like finding a new Gulf of Mexico'.

After a decade of ceasefire and consolidation of its presence, Rabat had concluded it was time to persuade oil companies from supportive countries to come to the territory and begin operations, economic interest going hand in hand with diplomatic stances.

In the autumn of 2001, it made its move, signing deals with TotalFinaElf, the oil major of France, and Kerr–McGee of Texas. The agreements parcelled out the entirety of the Western Sahara's waters, 90,000 square miles. The Kerr–McGee licence area is the size of 4,750 Gulf of Mexico blocks.

Total and Kerr–McGee professed innocence, saying they were neutral in the conflict. Yet Total then went a little further in a briefing note. Taking the lead from some highly contentious references to Morocco as the administering power (a precise and, here, misused term) by Kofi Annan, the UN secretary-general, Total asserted 'Morocco has an administrative mandate accorded by the United Nations.'

Some observers saw more in the nationality of the oil companies. The deals came against the backdrop of France and the US moving their diplomatic weight behind the Framework Agreement. An article in the Spanish newspaper La Razon argued:

> in the last weeks the United States has taken a new position to support the Sahara's autonomous solution, which envisages a regionalisation of the former Spanish colony under Moroccan sovereignty.

The key to the US change is the strong smell of oil oozing from the Sahara coasts – and even from the solid ground.

And:

From then on [i.e. after the licence deal], the French policy towards the Western Sahara issue changes. Not only does France become the leader of the Moroccan stance – 'the Sahara's autonomy within the Kingdom's sovereignty' – but the president himself, Jacques Chirac, talks of 'the provinces in the south' of Morocco when referring to the Sahara. TotalFinaElf, the fourth largest company of its kind, is the jewel of the gala crown, and its interests must be protected.

The US change is going to take a little longer, but it will eventually happen. The appeal of substantial oil profits has persuaded George Walker Bush's team to take a definite stance....

The Bush Administration is strongly associated with oil interests. The current president owes his fortune to juicy deals headed by Harken Energy Co. The National Security Adviser, Condoleezza Rice, was leading Chevron–Texaco; the Interior Secretary, Gale Norton, represents the interests of BP–Amoco; the Vice President, Dick Cheney, used to be the president of Halliburton, the primary company in the world to supply oil equipment.[10]

Others have noted that Kerr–McGee is a substantial donor to the Republican Party.

One oil industry source underlined the political context of the licences, saying they were not offered through the usual channels but rather awarded by fiat of the palace. Another said that the detail of the agreements signed with Kerr–McGee and Total illustrates the importance Morocco attached to drawing in international companies. Normally, an oil company has to pay 100 per cent of the cost of seismic data gathered in a licence area. If there is no further work done, then the data becomes the property of the licensing government. But in this case, the oil companies have been allowed to gather data on a 'semi-speculative' basis. Under this arrangement the seismic contractor will pay some of the cost. This reduces the outlay for the oil companies and means the data can be sold on to potential partners if further work goes ahead. However, the government loses ownership of data that it could have used to promote the area to other parties. The licences given to the companies were not technically exploration licences and this was to prove important in the subsequent row. They were what Morocco terms reconnaissance licences that permit survey work and the acquisition of seismic data but do not go as far as exploration drilling, for which another permit is required. In June 2002, Norwegian company TGS–Nopec Geophysical began gathering seismic data in the concession areas.

Of course, Polisario immediately condemned the agreements, writing to the president of the Security Council and saying the actions of Morocco and the oil companies could further delay the stalled peace process.

In February 2002, Hans Correll, the UN's legal counsel, presented his opinion[11] in a document hailed as a victory for Polisario but one that could yet be undermined. The opinion reaffirmed the principle of a people's 'permanent sovereignty over natural resources', referred to this sovereignty as an 'inalienable right' and asserted, 'The principle that the interests of the peoples of Non-Self-Governing Territories are paramount.' But, it then went on to outline a position that may prove as politically useful to Morocco as to Polisario.

First, it noted UN General Assembly recognition of 'the value of economic activities which are undertaken in accordance with the wishes of the peoples of those territories, and their contribution to the development of such territories'. Then: 'Where resource exploitation activities are concluded in Non-Self-Governing Territories for the benefit of the peoples of these territories, on their behalf, or in consultation with their representatives, they are considered compatible with the Charter obligations.' And, third, it noted that previous, comparable cases had dealt with the exploitation of resources, not prospecting.

Looking at the specifics of the contracts awarded to Total and Kerr–McGee, the opinion concluded that they were not illegal because 'oil reconnaissance and evaluation do not entail exploitation or the physical removal of the mineral resources, and no benefits have as of yet accrued'. If further exploration and exploitation proceeded in disregard of the interests and wishes of the Sahrawis, international law would have been broken.

What the opinion does is reaffirm a principle, but one the application of which begs the whole problem of the Western Sahara – who represents the Sahrawis? Who has the right to declare oil operations to be beneficial to the Sahrawis? Is it Polisario or the government of Rabat or the local government installed by Rabat, or could it be a tier of government introduced under an autonomy arrangement put in place either by the international community or by Morocco acting unilaterally?

Under the Framework Agreement, if it had gained Security Council approval, Morocco's provisional sovereignty would presumably have provided enough scope for reconnaissance to move smoothly on to exploration and exploitation.

Meanwhile, Morocco and its friends were not the only parties actively interested in the potential oil wealth of the territory. In May 2002, Fusion, the Australian minnow then with a 6 per cent stake in and big hopes of Chinguetti, called a press conference in London, where it is listed. There two senior company officials sat alongside Polisario diplomats and announced a technical cooperation agreement. Talks had been under way since 1999, they said. The area covered by the agreement was the same as that covered by the concessions given to Total and Kerr–McGee. Of course, unlike the latter two, Fusion could not gain direct access to Western Saharan waters and is barred from buying data gathered by TGS–Nopec. So it committed itself to a 12–16 month study of existing, available data, supplemented with new satellite data and the compilation of a report. For its part, Polisario is committed to giving Fusion an option to license up to three 20,000-square-kilometre exploration blocks within six months of the SADR becoming a member of the UN. The following year, another independent oil company, UK-listed Premier, joined the agreement through a wider deal with Fusion.

An interim report made to Polisario by Fusion confirmed that 'the main components of a working petroleum system have a high likelihood of being present' and that there was sufficient evidence to justify exploration work.[12]

Phosphates

Whether or not there is black gold at the end of the Western Saharan rainbow, a white gold has been scraped from the ground day in, day out for three decades.

Phosphate is a crucial component of some of the most widely used fertilisers and of detergents. It is also a valuable and vital source of exports for Morocco. Including the Western Sahara, where the output of the Bou Craa mine has been absorbed into that of the state company OCP, Morocco produced nearly 21.5 million tonnes of rock phosphate in 2000, exporting 10.3 million tonnes. That gave it more than a quarter of the world market and made it the third largest exporter. Its chemical industry is based on phosphoric acid and fertiliser production. It is the world's biggest phosphoric acid exporter, with a 50 per cent market share.[13] In 2000, phosphate and its derivatives comprised 17 per cent of Moroccan exports by value. Unlike agricultural production, which has suffered badly from drought in recent years, phosphate output can be planned, adding to its value to the government.

The immensity of the phosphate mining operation at Bou Craa is breathtaking. Mountains of spoil heaps surround the vast trenches, 15–30 metres deep, torn out of the scrub desert floor by giant draglines powered by colossal units that can move crab-like to the next patch of ground. Trucks the size of houses thunder around the opencast mine and a conveyor belt 100 kilometres long carries the phospate rock to the coast. There a massive, dedicated pier reaches out into the sea at Laayoune Port for bulkers of up to 60,000 deadweight tonnes to carry the phosphate to three continents. Some 560 workers working three shifts a day are employed at the mines and a total of 1,900 work in the whole phosphate industry in the Western Sahara.

The known exploitable reserves of the Bou Craa operation are 132 million tonnes. One story is that they were discovered in the late 1940s by Spanish geologist Manuel Alia Medina. When news of the find got to the Colonies Directorate he was sent out again and set up a laboratory in Laayoune. The new samples proved the deposit was worth mining. Another story is that the phosphates were found by oil prospectors.[14]

A state-of-the-art mining operation commenced in 1972 at a cost of perhaps £200 million, half of it from Spain.[15] Spain has kept much of its stake, owning 35 per cent of the Bou Craa operation to this day, a provision of the Madrid Accords. Production in those early years was between 2 and 3 million tonnes a year although the aim was to build up to 10 million tonnes a year. Morocco has not let that happen and additional investment has been minimal.

Average production still runs at around 2.4 million tonnes a year of high-quality processed phosphate, although in 2002 it was set for around 2.9 million tonnes with 500,000 tonnes to be stockpiled and the rest destined for the market. Moroccan and Western Saharan phosphate is sold on contracts ranging from one year's to ten years' duration. In late 2003, production was due to rise to 3 million tonnes a year.[16] Exports are divided equally between Australasia, the US and Latin America, and other destinations, principally in Europe.

As Hodges noted in the 1980s,

> It has often been said that Hassan's renewed interest in Western Sahara [in the 1970s] was motivated, in part at least, by a desire to control the territory's phosphate wealth.... Control of Bou Craa ... could have been anticipated, perhaps, to raise Morocco's share of world phosphate exports to more than 50 per cent. That, the king may have hoped, would have given Morocco as much leverage over world phosphate prices as Opec had over oil prices.[17]

Rabat argued in 1975 that Western Saharan deposits would be of only marginal significance to Morocco as its own deposits were large enough to maintain contemporary output levels for eight centuries.[18] The argument was disingenuous though, as control of Bou Craa would prevent a competitor from entering the market while enabling the Office Cherifien des Phosphates to increase its own market share. The tap controlling Western Saharan exports would be turned by OCP according to Moroccan economic interests. The prediction of the UN Mission that, 'eventually the territory will be among the largest exporters of phosphate in the world',[19] would be frustrated. The mission had calculated that an independent Western Sahara would become the world's second largest exporter, after Morocco with its 34 per cent share. At then prevailing world prices (which crashed the following year after a fourfold rise since 1973), Bou Craa would generate export income of $680 million[20] and give the population a per capita revenue equal to some European countries.[21] Morocco's phosphate exports in 1975 earned it just over $4 billion.[22]

Rezette, writing from an explicitly Moroccan standpoint just before the Green March, is worth quoting at length for his assessment evokes the strategic and economic considerations of the time:

It took the discovery of the phosphates to bring the Spanish Sahara out of oblivion and place it in the forefront of the international scene.... Spain, the mistress of all this wealth, was able to rig up as fruitful an operation as that of the great international oil companies who 'invented' the emirates of the Persian Gulf.

Morocco, master of the Spanish Sahara's phosphates, by adding them to its own reserves, was to become the first producer in the world and to play a determining role in setting the price of this raw material, assuring its 16m inhabitants of new jobs in which they were cruelly lacking.

If these phosphates were controlled by Mauritania, this country would, on the contrary, have means of bringing pressure to bear on Morocco, could threaten strong competition and price slashing in order to walk away with a larger share of the world market.[23]

He gives local, Sahrawi interests short shrift. 'It is only to be hoped that a population of 16m courageous and worthy [Moroccan] people will be able to profit by this wealth rather than see it transform specific notables of the Sahara into millionaires and assist, into the bargain, in transferring the excess yield of this production to Europe.'[24] This was apparently a dig at Spain's appointment of a clutch of favoured Sahrawi chiefs to the administrative board of the company formed to run Bou Craa.

If Hassan did have a dream of controlling the global phosphate market, its fulfilment proved as partial as Opec's. Moroccan phosphate earnings soared in the mid-1970s, providing a peak of 70 per cent of foreign currency income in 1974, but demand was trimmed and US producers undercut the kingdom and it saw its phosphate export revenues almost halved as quickly as they had increased.

Nonetheless, control of Bou Craa did increase Moroccan control of global reserves and allowed it to remove a potential competitor from the world market. Today, Bou Craa contributes something over 10 per cent of OCP's rock phosphate, rather than supplying an independent state with a volume around half as great as Morocco proper produces today.

It was actually Polisario that proved most effective at staunching the flow of Bou Craa product onto the market after guerrilla attacks on the conveyor belt shut the whole operation down for a considerable period. But the idea of limiting the impact on the market of Western Saharan phosphate occurred to Madrid as well as Rabat.

Mercer writes that 'in 1970, Morocco rejected a second time the Spanish offer of a common phosphate policy in exchange for the relinquishing of the former's claim to the Spanish Sahara'.[25]

Morocco's five-year development plan for 2000–04 notes that OCP is working to optimise production at Bou Craa and other mines and gear them more to the export market. Production of raw phosphates by OCP is set to rise some 14 per cent over the period but derivatives output has a target of over 24 per cent. The target growth for exports of phosphate rock is 9.3 per cent but for derivatives it is 22.6 per cent.[26] Whether processed or unprocessed, the exploitation of Western Saharan phosphates and their importance to Morocco is increasing.

Fisheries

Laayoune Port's fishing quay thrives even in the late morning when the peak of daily activity is over. A jumble of blue and grey spars, coils of rope and acres of netting stretches the length of the quay as trawlers crowd several deep while gangs of men and a few women unload box after box of catch. Some 10,000 people are seasonally employed in the fishing industry, offshore and on, in the Laayoune region, according to Moroccan officials. But the resources of the Western Sahara support fishermen and onshore workers in Morocco. The fleets that use the port come from Safi, Agadir and Essaouria as well as Laayoune. The catching and processing of squid and other cephalopods employ 95,000 people directly and indirectly according to one report.[27] Few of these jobs are in the Western Sahara.

In 2002 the current port was undergoing its third expansion since it opened in 1986. The fishing quay was being lengthened by 225 metres. At a cost of MD170 million, the capacity of the whole port was being doubled. Laayoune is now the biggest fishing port under Moroccan control. It accounts for 80 per cent of the sardine catch of Morocco and the Western Sahara although, as will be seen later, lack of economic infrastructure means much of this wealth has been squandered.

In 2001, over MD200 million worth of tidal fish (*poisons de marée*) was landed at Laayoune, up from MD110 million the year before. The value of the deep sea catch rose similarly, from MD296 million to MD355 million, almost of all of it accounted for by sardines, the bulk of which was destined for low-value fish-meal production, according to Moroccan statistics.[28]

The accents on the quay at Laayoune Port are Moroccan. Fishing has never been a mainstream Sahrawi occupation (and the diet reflects this). The coast has been worked by Iberian boats since the fifteenth century. By the eighteenth century, the fleet appears to have been based in the Canary Islands. By the nineteenth century there are reports of Canary vessels taking on Sahrawi crew[29] but by and large 'the inhabitants of the Western Sahara were not really involved in the exploitation of this resource and have not profited from the few businesses established along the coast'.[30]

As with phosphates, the wealth of the Western Sahara's fish stocks was well appreciated by Spain, and the Madrid Accords included an understanding that hundreds of Spanish vessels would continue to harvest them. As shoals have moved southwards[31] down the Atlantic coast of North Africa, so the Western Sahara has become more and more attractive and the catch has grown while the prospect of depletion, a danger well established and recognised in the 1970s,[32] has become a reality.

For the first years after Spain's departure, bilateral Moroccan–Spanish agreements maintained Spanish access to Western Saharan waters. Rabat also reached a deal with Lisbon. The agreements with Spain licensed and limited catch sizes in waters 'under Morocco's jurisdiction' and Madrid agreed to invest in the Moroccan fishing industry's development.

In 1986 Spain joined the European Union and negotiation of fishing agreements with Rabat became a responsibility of Brussels. In February 1988 the first EU–Morocco fishing agreement was reached. The waters covered were to be in 'Morocco's fishing zone', deemed to include 'all waters over which Morocco has sovereignty or jurisdiction'. The agreement did not mention the Western Sahara and the European Commission later refused to clarify the geographical boundaries of this area.[33]

That agreement gave the EU a total of 800 licences for four years at a cost of €282 million. The first renewal was delayed by European Parliament concerns over the territorial issue but in the event the new deal implicitly acceded to Morocco's presence in the

Western Sahara by naming Dakhla in the south of the territory as being one of the ports that the Moroccan authorities could oblige an EU vessel to put into.

The renewal cost €310 million for 650 licences − 636 of which went to Spain. In 1995, the cost went up again: €500 million and fewer licences as Morocco developed its own fishing industry and looked further afield for partners. That agreement expired in November 1999 and this time renegotiation proved impossible. As the process collapsed, the irritation was evident. By January 2001 Commissioner Fischler was saying, 'The unacceptable result of all this is that the latest offer from our Moroccan partners is substantially worse than the one that was on the table yesterday.'[34] A month later talks broke down with Fischler citing 'disproportionate financial demands of Morocco'.[35] To EU anger was added expense. In July 2001, the Commission put forward an aid package of €197 million for the conversion of 400 vessels, employing 4,300 crew, affected by the non-renewal. But underlining the importance of the wider region to the fishing industry, the EU in short order renewed agreements with Guinea Bissau, Senegal and Mauritania.

Exploitation of Western Saharan waters and use of Laayoune Port and Dakhla have been major factors in Morocco's development of its fishing industry into a major employer and provider of revenues. As noted earlier, little of the employment, put at 140,000 direct and up to 1 million indirect,[36] accrues to the Sahrawis. In 1996, the Moroccan fleet landed 616,000 tonnes of fish, of which 203,000 tonnes were exported. By 2000, 896,000 tonnes were landed and 317,000 tonnes exported. In 2000 exports of fisheries products accounted for MD10 billion of total foodstuffs exports of MD16.4 billion. The Bank al-Maghrib annual report for the year notes fisheries exports were up MD2.6 billion for the year, providing a cushion against drought-affected citrus exports. The following year, there was a slump in shellfish and crustacean exports but other fish and fish meal exports grew nearly 21 per cent to MD4.3 billion, according to the bank.

The Western Sahara contributes significantly to this growth. Figures issued by the governor of Laayoune put the proportion of Moroccan and Western Saharan-caught fish landed at Laayoune Port at 40 per cent of the total by weight.[37] The share by value was similar. Figures for Dakhla were unavailable. For the ports within the southern development zone set up in 2002 to take in the Western Sahara and the Goulmime and Tan-Tan area to the north of the international border, the share of the total catch rose from 20 per cent in 1990 to 54 per cent in 2000, with a forecast of a massive 90 per cent by 2007.[38] With port development steaming ahead and plans to increase both the fleet size and the value added to the catch through processing, Western Saharan fisheries will become increasingly important to the Moroccan economy and an increasing block to consideration of a withdrawal.

Morocco hopes to be one of the fifteen top fishing nations by 2004 with an annual catch of 1.5 million tonnes.[39] As the port developments at Laayoune and Dakhla attest, the Western Sahara will play an increasing role in the drive to realise this ambition. But the drive to raise catches runs up against attempts to ensure the sustainability of the resource. A report released by the UN Environment Programme in March 1992 on Mauritania noted that catches of cephalopods had halved in four years while some other species had disappeared entirely. Cephalopods are the principal catch of the 'artisanal fleet' of Morocco and Western Sahara and are particularly important for Dakhla. Morocco has introduced a quota system but Gorez reports that in 2001 it took one month for coastal and artisanal fishermen to catch over 90 per cent of their ceiling. After a drastic fall in sardine stocks was noted in 1997, closed periods were instituted along the coast of the Western Sahara. By 2003, there were further alarming indications that fishery management was failing. The closed season for octopus was extended as it became clear that stocks were continuing to decline. Furthermore, only the coastal fishermen were catching up to their quota limits; the deep-sea and artisanal branches of the industry were unable to find sufficient catches to reach the limits.[40] Attempts at managing stocks continue but there is a recognised problem of illegal fishing. In May 2002, an association of owners of small fishing boats in Dakhla alleged there were more unregistered than registered vessels operating in the area, and that they did so with the connivance of the authorities.

Just as commercial and political pressures have failed to stem decades of depletion of North Sea fishing stocks, so the resources of Western Sahara are under threat.

Iron and other ores

The potential of the Western Sahara as a producer of minerals and metals apart from phosphate is unquantifiable but assumed to be good. One expert said: 'The subsoil of the Western Sahara is rich in exploitable resources. Among the minerals are phosphate, iron, uranium, titanium and precious stones.'[41]

Just south of the border with Western Sahara are the Mauritanian iron ore workings at Zouerate. To the east at Gara Djebilet are more iron ore deposits, within Algerian territory. In 1947, Alia, the same geologist who is credited with discovering Bou Craa, reported ferrugineous enrichment in the Smara Arc. In 1961, after the Algerian deposits were found, a Spanish survey of the north east of the Western Sahara was carried out but was inconclusive. Mercer writes: 'Soundings were to be taken next, but there is no further information either because the results were negative or for political reasons – to avoid exciting nationalist and neighbouring claims.'[42]

Further work was carried out in the early 1970s, and taking account of that Brenneisen estimates the territory has exploitable reserves of 2.4 billion tonnes of iron ore. And he is upbeat about its commerciality. The quality is excellent and would find a market not far away, in Europe. Infrastructural investment could be minimised if an agreement could be reached with Mauritania to use the railway that transports ore to the coast at Nouadhibou.

Theoretical reserves of titanium are estimated at 271 million tonnes. Titanium metal is used in the military and civil aviation industries but 95 per cent of the mineral is used to make titanium oxide, which is used for paint making. There is a market for titanium as the US is highly dependent on imports, mostly from Canada and Australia.

Again by extrapolation, Brenneisen argues the Western Sahara could have some of the world's largest reserves of vanadium, a strategic metal used to strengthen titanium alloys used in jet engine and high-speed airframes as well as automobile and machine making. The US government estimated in 2002 that known global reserves amounted to 63 million tonnes, with China, Russia and South Africa being the major producers.[43] In theory, the Western Sahara could have exploitable reserves of over 23 million tonnes, a quantity that would give anyone controlling it both market share and market influence.

Uranium can be extracted from phosphate, and Brenneisen goes so far as to argue that the 320,000 tonnes that could theoretically be extracted from the Bou Craa reserves 'could have had a certain importance in the birth of the conflict over the Western Sahara', a decade and a half before the end of the Cold War. While a long-term collapse in the price of uranium might preclude its extraction, its control could remain of strategic importance with Morocco, Algeria and Libya all interested in nuclear research. In 2002, the vague assertion that 'there is intelligence that Iraq has sought the supply of significant quantities of uranium from Africa'[44] in the build-up to launching war against Iraq underlined the sensitivity of Washington and London to access to the mineral by states of which they do not approve.

Parts of the Western Sahara where the desert is sandy have been exploited, largely for export to the Canary Islands. The volumes exported have risen from 4,450 tonnes in 1988 to 754,579 tonnes in 2001, according to Moroccan statistics.

Morocco is moving ahead with pre-prospecting work. There is a programme to map the territory it controls over ten years and a regional unit will be established in the Western Sahara.[45] In August 2002, Morocco and China signed an agreement on the financing of a project to map the geology of the Goulimin–Smara province, suggesting Rabat is preparing to prospect in the area and has begun a quest for overseas partners.

Notes

1. Ismail Sayeh (nom de plume of Fadel Ismail), *Les Sahraouis*, L'Harmattan, Paris, 1998, p. 107.
2. Afifa Karmous, 'Les resources naturelles d'un territoire non autonome: le Sahara Occidental', paper given to Colloque des jurists sur le Sahara Occidental, 28 April 2001.
3. *World Oil and Gas Review 2002*, ENI, Rome, 2002–09–13.
4. Economist Intelligence Unit, 'EIU Country Profile 2002: Morocco', 2002.
5. ENI, *World Oil and Gas Review 2002*.
6. Morocco section in Arab Maghreb Union pages on www.eia.doe.gov.
7. 'Lone Star Fires Up Moroccan Optimism', *Upstream*, 25 August 2000.

8. Speech to MIOG conference 2002, Onarep website, www.onarep.com.
9. John Mercer, *Spanish Sahara*, George Allen & Unwin, London, 1976, pp. 189–92.
10. *La Razon*, 1 May, 2002, reproduced in English on www.wsahara.net/02/razon/050102.html.
11. Opinion delivered to Mr Jagdish Koonjul, president of the UN Security Council, 29 January 2002.
12. Private correspondence, March 2003.
13. 'EIU Country Profile 2002: Morocco'.
14. Mercer, *Spanish Sahara*, pp. 184–7.
15. Ibid.
16. *Le Matin*, 3 April 2003.
17. Tony Hodges, *Western Sahara: The Roots of a Desert War*, Lawrence Hill, Westport CT, 1983, p. 174.
18. 'Report of the UN Visiting Mission to Spanish Sahara', UN Document A/10023/Rev 1, 1975, p. 81.
19. Ibid., p. 38.
20. Ibid., p. 53.
21. Ibid., p. 52.
22. Cited by Hodges, *Western Sahara*, p. 175.
23. Robert Rezette, *The Western Sahara and the Frontiers of Morocco*, Nouvelles Editions Latines, Paris, 1975, pp. 32–3.
24. Ibid., p. 164.
25. Mercer, *Spanish Sahara*, p. 187.
26. Ministry of Economic Forecasting and Planning, *Le plan de développement economique et social 2000–2004*, vol. 2, 7-2.1–2.
27. Beatrice Gorez, 'Les ressources halieutiques du Sahara Occidental – Une richesse fragile à preserver', paper given in March 2002 to a conference in Brussels on the natural resources of the Western Sahara.
28. ONP Delegation Régionale de Laayoune, statistics provided to author.
29. Mercer, *Spanish Sahara*, p. 177.
30. Gorez, 'Les ressources halieutiques du Sahara Occidental'.
31. Ministry of Economic Forecasting and Planning, *Le plan de développement économique et social 2000–2004*, vol. 2, section 3-1-5.
32. Mercer, *Spanish Sahara*, p. 179.
33. Gilonne D'Origny, 'Rights over Western Sahara's Natural Resources', LLM paper for University of London School of Oriental and African Studies, July 2000, unpublished.
34. Speech by Commissioner Fischler, Rabat, 9 January 2001, issued by European Commission as Speech/01/4, 10 January 2001.
35. European Commission press release IP/01/241, 21 February 2001.
36. Ministry of Economic Forecasting and Planning, *Le plan de développement économique et social 2000–2004*, vol. 2, section 3-1-5.
37. *Plan de développement integré de la province de Laayoune*.
38. Interview with Abdellatif Guerraoui, governor of Laayoune and head of the southern development agency, *L'Économiste*, 19 December 2001.
39. 'EIU Country Profile 2002: Morocco'.

40. *L'Économiste*, 29 January 2003.

41. Christoph M. Brenneisen, 'Les ressources exploitables du Sahara occidental', *L'Ouest Saharien* 1, L'Harmattan, Paris, 1998.

42. Mercer, *Spanish Sahara*, p. 188.

43. US Geological Survey website, www.usgs.gov.

44. *Iraq's Weapons of Mass Destruction: The Assessment of the British Government*, HMSO, London, 2002, p. 25.

45. Ministry of Economic Forecasting and Planning, *Le plan de développement économique et social 2000–2004*, vol. 2, section 8-2-1–8-2-3.

5

Sahrawi Society

under Occupation

Hamed grew up in Goulmime, one of the towns in southern Morocco with a large Sahrawi population, cleaved from the Western Sahara as France and Spain carved up that corner of the Maghreb. Work with the state phosphate company took him to Laayoune. In 1999 there was an upsurge of protest in the towns of the Western Sahara. Activists say the wave of demonstrations and prison protests reunited Sahrawis who had never left the territory with those transferred to Laayoune and Smara for the referendum from places like Goulmime and Tan Tan. It also provided the impetus for families of the disappeared to speak out and contact human rights groups. And it brought forth and united individual activists, who formed a new civil rights movement.

Hamed was one of those activists and he became a core member of the Sahrawi section of the Truth and Justice Forum. In the summer of 2002 there was a crackdown on civil rights activists and Hamed's employment was summarily transferred to Casablanca, a peculiarly bureaucratic form of punishment used by the Moroccan authorities. Others were arrested.

Hamed's life in Laayoune before his transfer exemplifies the personal and political complexities created by the division of the Sahrawis between those living in areas now acknowledged even by Polisario as being part of Morocco and those living under occupation since 1975 (let alone those in the camps around Tindouf or in exile further afield).

After the death of his parents Hamed brought his younger siblings – the family had nine children – together to live with him in his flat in Laayoune. As he campaigned for the 'Disappeared' and for the release of political prisoners, he faced harassment from the security forces and so did his family. He spent time in detention, where he was tortured. A younger brother was severely beaten in the street by security forces, in front of one sister, 'as a message to me'.

Meanwhile, another brother worked as a policeman in the town, conscientiously doing his job but concerned about some of the things he saw and heard. In 2001 he was transferred to a police unit inside Morocco. He is convinced this was not because of anything he had done but because as a Sahrawi he was not to be trusted and, presumably, because of his brother's activities.

Fatma, another sibling, is in her early twenties. English speaking, well educated, she has worked briefly in the United States and is engaged to a junior doctor, of Sahrawi origin, who lives in Agadir. She feels uncomfortable in Laayoune. She says she finds the Hassaniya dialect of the Sahrawis difficult to speak and the Moroccan dialect comes more naturally to her. She has no time for Hamed's aspiration for independence. The family is tight-knit and affectionate, yet the one small flat contained Hamed the activist and Fatma who is not just neutral but integrationist.

Yet if a half-century of integration into Morocco has produced this *mélange* of attitudes within families outside the territories occupied by Morocco in 1975, a quarter of century after the Green March the division between the indigenous and Moroccan populations of towns like Laayoune and Smara is sometimes subtle, sometimes striking, always present.

Laayoune has spacious new mosques – used by Moroccans, largely avoided by Sahrawis. In the courtyard of Sahrawi-inhabited housing blocks there may be a small mudbrick-walled enclosure where Sahrawis pray in the open, on the sand, as they did before they settled.

Walking through the main street of Smara after nightfall the visitor could just as well be in a town in central Morocco. The cafés echo with chatter in Moroccan accents as men sit drinking the mint tea typical of the north. In the central area of the souk lock-up shops sell Moroccan clothing and the earthernware for cooking cous cous and tajine. Then, at one end of the market, the dress code changes in preference for the billowing wraps of Sahrawi women and the blue *deraa* of Sahrawi men.

Needs must the communities interact at a commercial level but there is little sign of integration. As one Moroccan newspaper reported from Laayoune:

> The integration between Moroccans from the provinces of the north and those of the south [Sahrawis] is superficial. Here, whether in the cafés or in houses, it is rare that a group comprises both Moroccans originally from the north and the south. Twenty-five years after the regaining of the Sahara, integration is feeble..... 'To all intents and purposes I don't spend time with any Sahrawis. All my friends are people from the interior. Perhaps it's because of different clothing and traditions', says a taxi driver originally from Meknes, living in Laayoune for 14 years. Perhaps. But as Mohamed Salem Dahi, local representative of the Moroccan Human Rights Organisation in Laayoune, explains it: 'The administration is in large part responsible for the situation. It has neglected to invest in Sahrawi human capital.'[1]

In the small coastal town of Boujdour, where there are perhaps 5,000 Sahrawi adults and the Moroccan population outnumbers them three or four to one, the separation of the communities is even clearer and the surveillance of the Sahrawi community more explicit than in Laayoune. Here pedestrian visitors are tailed by informers and their cars openly followed by security forces' vehicles.

Both Sahrawi and Moroccan political players are often keen to downplay tensions between the Sahrawi and settler communities, referring to each other as 'our brothers'. And, by and large, the very lack of social integration means conflict is not intercommunal in the broader sense but is between Sahrawis and the Moroccan authorities. However, this is not always the case. There are reports of attacks by settlers on the indigenous minority in Dakhla after the death of Hassan II, for example, because Sahrawis were deemed not to be displaying public grief. In a back street of Smara a middle-aged Sahrawi, unexpectedly attired in a tweed jacket, says of the Moroccan inhabitants of the town, 'They are all soldiers and thieves.'

Education is an interface for Sahrawi and incomer. It is also an area of cultural contest. The curriculum is Moroccan, as are most of the teachers. An educationalist said that of 300 teachers in Boujdour just three are Sahrawi. Although the languages of the classroom are modern standard Arabic and French, given the demography of the territory there is the danger of the Hassaniya dialect of the Sahrawis being diluted by exposure to Moroccan dialect. Some older Sahrawis are resentful about the replacement of Spanish by French as the second language. Sahrawi responses to the exposure of their children to Moroccan peers is mixed. One Sahrawi activist said she could not and would not prevent her children from mixing with Moroccan children at school but that the contact should stop there – no social mixing outside of the school gate. Another said she had nothing against individual Moroccans and would not prevent her children making friends with them. The educationalist said the differences between Sahrawi and Moroccan school students became clearer as they grew up, celebrating different occasions by wearing distinctive national dress, the Sahrawis noticing the divergence between curricular history and the oral history they heard at home.

School enrolment is put at 96 per cent by the authorities, although Sahrawis maintain that the dropout rate for their children is very high because of the peripheral expenses of nominally free schooling. However, there are signs of nationalism in the schools – students at one Laayoune school announced they were renaming the institution after Fadel Ismail, the Polisario diplomat and writer who died in 2002. At another school Sahrawi students declined to take part in a collection in honour of a Moroccan teacher, saying no such collection was allowed after Fadel Ismail's death.

There is no university in the Western Sahara. Officials say this is because there is a wide choice available in the north and that students from the Western Sahara receive grants and preferential access to accommodation as well as free travel. Supporters of independence are cynical about the official line. They argue that poverty weeds out many potential Sahrawi students well before tertiary education. Benefits such as free travel were won by student protest, they say. Often cited is the case of 6,000 young Sahrawis promised employment in a speech of Hassan II in July 1988. The account of an activist maintains that following the speech young Sahrawis were rounded up and pressed to accept employment. In October the 6,000 youngsters were assigned to low-status and low-wage jobs inside Morocco.

The activist maintains that once transferred the Sahrawis were then encouraged not to turn up for work and so gain experience but rather to run up debts and get into bad habits. Then, in 1991, they were returned to the Western Sahara, having lost the opportunity to try for tertiary education or gain professional training.

At the same time activists also assert that Sahrawi students are forced to attend universities in Agadir and Rabat and elsewhere inside Morocco in order to Moroccanise them. As Sahrawi students in Rabat and elsewhere have shown their mettle through numerous protests since 1999, if that is a Moroccan policy it is one that may backfire by increasing awareness among Moroccans of Sahrawi grievances.

Yet the division of the population in the Western Sahara is not a simple split between Moroccan and Sahrawi. There is a three-way differentiation in the population of Laayoune and Smara. Apart from northern Moroccans and Sahrawis long settled in the Moroccan-occupied territories, there are also many thousands of ethnic Sahrawis brought to the towns by Rabat for the referendum. These are not individuals like Hamed who moved of their own volition but tens of thousands of people bussed in from 1991 to live first in tents and then in more permanent versions of the Wahda (Unity) camps as voter registration dragged on. These are the people Morocco believed would win the referendum for it but who, according to Polisario, proved to have retained nationalist sentiments, this persuading Rabat to undermine the process. Some maintain that the transfer of ethnic Sahrawis from towns like Tan Tan is also part of a policy to Moroccanise the area known as the Tarfaya Strip.

The Wahda camps are rigorously organised into tribal units and subunits with a tight administrative structure that feeds into the government administration and security apparatus. A walk through the camp in Laayoune with a camera quickly results in an invitation from a policeman to visit the camp administration office before proceeding on an authorised and accompanied tour that is nonetheless interrupted by small children shouting 'Sahara, Sahara' and waving victory salutes.

In Laayoune the Wahda camp stretches over a large area on both sides of the main road leading out of town towards the interior. It is a clearly distinguishable sea of breeze-block and mudbrick houses once on the edge of town but now being surrounded by modern buildings. According to Hamid Chabar, a senior Moroccan official whose office overlooks it, Laayoune Wahda camp has a population of around 50,000. At Smara, the smaller Wahda camp is a mile or two outside the historic town. In Laayoune, a decade after the Wahda camp arose, the first tranche of its inhabitants was due to move into purpose-built permanent housing on the edge of town in June 2002 but had not done so in February the following year. In Boujdour where the camp inhabitants are largely from northern Morocco, the population growth in the camp is prodigious, with the number of primary schools rising from two to eight in just a few years. The majority of the inhabitants of the camps depend on state handouts for their subsistence although much of the aid is said to be siphoned off by corrupt officials.[2]

In the late 1970s Sahrawi householders were forced to take in Moroccan lodgers, and in some cases were then ejected from their own homes, according to some.[3] Most of Laayoune, whether inhabited by Sahrawis or Moroccans, is unremarkable in terms of housing conditions, but for a Sahrawi underclass there remain the *barraque*. Tucked away in neighbourhoods like Dir Yeddak the *barraque* are corrugated iron and scrap-built shanties constructed before the Spanish left and comparable in deprivation to those of sub-Saharan Africa. Some of the original inhabitants arrived in search of work when drought forced them to abandon animal husbandry and some arrived in search of medical attention. They remain, still without running water or electricity and still sweetening their tea with sugar loaves from Mauritania, showing visitors faded ID cards from the 1970s. They tell of a son living abroad, another believed to have died in the Tindouf camps, and another in Rabat. Grandchildren are growing up in the shanties, their mothers complaining bitterly that the cost of books and clothing means they will have to abandon education before secondary school.

The demographic fog

The most fundamental element of the proposals for the Western Sahara drawn up by James Baker over the last few years is the stipulation that the final decision on the long-term future of the territory would be taken by residents rather than indigenes. For supporters of independence this is wholly unacceptable because it turns the referendum process on its head. For all the confusion caused by population movements, omissions, incomplete data and the passage of time, not to mention deliberate obfuscation, using 1974 Spanish census data as the basis of an electoral register, as agreed by the parties in 1991, was clearly an attempt to ensure that it was Sahrawis alone who decided the fate of the Western Sahara.

Enfranchisement of Moroccan residents would massively weight the result towards integration with Morocco, for the Sahrawis are now a minority within their own homeland. The numbers are imprecise and variable. By the logic of its integrationist position, Morocco has no political interest in statistical differentiation between Sahrawis and Moroccans. There has not been a census since 1994 and the current administrative boundaries, which for example marry Smara and Goulmime (the former in the Western Sahara and the latter not), complicate extrapolation of data.

In 1970, the Spanish put the number of Sahrawis in the territory at 76,425.[4] Five years later, the UN Mission mulled the complexity of counting a people with a nomadic tradition and communities established outside of the territory in question. Spain, it noted, reckoned there were no more than 9,000 Sahrawis living outside of the Western Sahara, while Rabat said there were 30,000 to 35,000 living as refugees in southern Morocco. Polisario estimated the total number living outside the territory at 50,000 and put the potential population of an independent state after an ingathering at an improbable 750,000.[5]

The Wali of Laayoune said the region he administered had a population of around 200,000 in 2002, while the governor of Smara said the town and surrounding areas had 50,000 inhabitants.[6] Dakhla and the smaller communities in the Oued–Eddahab–Lagouira region had a population of 44,000 according to 1998 estimates.[7]

Sahrawis have no accurate means to gauge their own numbers inside the Western Sahara as opposed to those of the settler community. A report in Le Monde in 2002[8] put the total population of the Western Sahara at 400,000, saying three-quarters were non-Sahrawis. The overall figure seems too high unless notional figures for the area controlled by Polisario are added. But it seems likely that the Le Monde figures assumed all of the residents of the Wahda camps to be non-Sahrawis. In fact, tens of thousands in Laayoune are ethnic Sahrawis.

Certainly Morocco claims more Sahrawis live under its rule than under Polisario's. The commission responsible for registering voters for the referendum found 46,255 eligible voters inside the territory and in Morocco during the first phase of counting and added another 2,135 in the second phase.[9] The overwhelming majority of the 46,255 would have been in the territory while the bulk of the smaller group, from 'contested tribes', may have been in Morocco. Sahrawi nationalists suggest the total number of Sahrawis is probably twice the number of voters, taking into account those too young to vote. That would give roughly 90,000 indigenous Sahrawis living inside the Moroccan-controlled bulk of the Western Sahara.

Though the five-year economic development plan for Morocco makes no mention of settler migration into the Western Sahara, disparities in population growth rates hint at it continuing at a very rapid rate in some parts of the territory. The annual population growth rate in Morocco is put at something over 2 per cent. Yet in the Oued–Eddahab–Lagouira region of the territory, between 1982 and 1998 it was 4.8 per cent, from 21,000 to 44,000 inhabitants.[10] The incentive to settle in the Western Sahara is strong. Moroccans, who account for almost the entire payroll of government and state agencies, are, according to the US State Department, paid 85 per cent more than their counterparts outside the territory, exempted from income tax and value added tax and receive subsidies on many basic goods and services.[11]

Ask someone from a long-settled society where they are from and they will name a region, a town, even a street. Ask the same in a recently settled society like that of the Sahrawis and you cause confusion because many adults' earlier lives were nomadic, the circumstances of urbanisation being a landmark in their lives. A drought in the late 1960s and early 1970s pushed very many to abandon nomadism, with the Sahrawi population of Laayoune, for example, increasing three and a half times over between 1960 and 1970.[12] 'By making the state-subsidised life in the towns more attractive, this drought is the Spaniards' crucial ally in their attempt to sedentarise the nomads and thereby bring them to depend on the colonial administration.'[13]

Now, some 80 per cent of the population of Oued–Eddahab–Lagouira live in towns, for Laayoune region it is about 95 per cent, and for the Smara part of the Goulmime–Smara region it is over 60 per cent.[14]

Sahrawis under Moroccan rule, like former nomads elsewhere, strive to retain some connection with their recent past. Families return to the desert if they can for a few weeks a year. Skills are passed on. A driver recounted how he took his son from the age of 7 into the desert to camp and learn, and would leave him in the night to find his own way home. This was more than nostalgia or even father–son bonding. As a youth Mohammed knew boys who died having missed their bearings and run out of water.

Economic development: grand plans, grim reality

Economic development of the Western Sahara is vital to Morocco both to unlock the value inherent in the natural resources of the territory and to defray the civil expenses of occupation, let alone the military expenses. But foreign private investors and, indeed, Moroccan private investors have been chary about putting money into the Western Sahara. World Bank money does not – officially at any rate – go to projects in the territory and there is scant evidence of overseas aid money because of the political and legal situation. Polisario sources say the main source of private-sector investment is a group of five wealthy Sahrawi families that have been willing to accommodate the Moroccan administration whilst not necessarily closing off other, future political options.

Abdellatif Guerraoui, Wali of Laayoune and head of the southern region development agency that takes in the Western Sahara, said Morocco has spent $1 billion on infrastructure in the territory since 1976,[15] although some other estimates are much higher. Over 90 per cent of the households have electricity and 80 per cent have drinking water, much higher rates than Morocco's national average, according to Moroccan figures.

The cost of keeping settlers from the north in the Western Sahara is high. In Laayoune province, excluding seasonal fishing activity, the number employed in the private sector was just 2,620 against

20,000 in the public sector[16] at the beginning of the decade. The 20,000 included those on Promotion National or PM.

PM is a workfare scheme used to trim the unemployment figures and supposedly lead to training and proper employment. Sahrawis complain about it bitterly. They say it is wholly inadequate, giving a family some MD1,000 ($100) to MD1,500 a month, and that it is distributed through favouritism. It is also said to be used as an additional subsidy to keep the Wahda camps quiet. Guerraoui said there were 8,092 PM recipients in Laayoune in 2001. The number dropped to 7,245 in the first months of 2002 as training programmes kicked in, he said,[17] but remained more than two and a half times the number employed in the private sector.

Nonetheless, unemployment in Laayoune province officially stood at 25 per cent in 2001/02 and 27 per cent in Smara – although a local in the latter town said he believed it to be more like 45 per cent – against a national average for rural and urban Morocco combined of between 12 and 13 per cent.[18] In 2000, the official unemployment rate for the Western Sahara was 25.2 per cent, the highest for any recorded region. Noticeably, in rural areas it reached over 17 per cent, three and a half times the average for all regions. The economic activity rate for the Western Sahara was the lowest for any region.[19]

Sahrawi activists say employment generation is geared towards settlers from the north in order to attract them and then keep them in the Western Sahara. For Sahrawis, unemployment is rampant and Sahrawis are all but excluded from state jobs with responsibility or higher salaries, they say, mirroring the situation during Spanish rule. The economy of the territory is so underdeveloped that there are few possibilities for employment, said one campaigner. He estimated there to be ten factories in the Laayoune area, nine of them processing low-value-added fish meal and each employing just 20 or 30 workers. The tenth, he said, was a canning factory with a workforce of around 200 to 300. He estimated that of the total salaried workforce only 2 or 3 per cent were Sahrawis.[20] The Association of the Sahrawi Unemployed says Moroccans occupy 86–88 per cent of available jobs.[21] Moroccan figures note some fifteen fish-processing units in the wider Laayoune and Boujdour region, employing 1,200 workers.[22]

The fishing industry employs up to 10,000 people on a seasonal basis in Laayoune province and several thousand more around Dakhla. But anecdotal evidence, supported by accounts from the Spanish period, is that few Sahrawis are involved in fishing, for the present at any rate. In Boujdour, for example, Sahrawis said that they had no experience of fishing as a way of life and that they could afford neither boats nor licences. With no traditional or modern system of micro-credit, there is no obvious means of raising capital necessary for small enterprises.

The phosphate industry is a major employer with some 1,900 staff at the Bou Craa mines and others at the treatment plant at Laayoune Port. Around 50 per cent of the total are manual workers, 30 per cent are skilled workers, and 20 per cent are technicians. There are ten engineers. A Bou Craa manager said 60 per cent of employees are Sahrawi, the rest having come in from Morocco. Sahrawis dispute the numbers and say their compatriots are for the most part limited to manual labouring jobs. Activists said the number of Sahrawis employed in the industry was now no more than 200, a fall from 567 in late 1976 and 1,600 in 1968.[23] The remaining Sahrawi workers have been edged into lower-grade jobs. In many cases their wages have been cut without explanation. The average salary for a Sahrawi worker is around MD3,000 a month (although some earn more than twice this amount).

A news report in May 2002 said sixty workers for Bou Craa were recruited in Agadir the previous month, 'whereas the Moroccan authorities are encouraging Sahrawis to emigrate to the Arab emirates to work as waiters and baggage porters'.[24] An activist said Rabat wanted Sahrawis to go and work on cruise liners, a reference to the Al Najat scandal in which a UAE-based company was allowed to extract money from thousands of people in Morocco and, apparently, the Western Sahara on the promise of jobs afloat. The International Transport Workers Federation condemned the practice as fraudulent, pointing to similar exercises by Al Najat in Kenya, Pakistan, Syria, Tanzania and Vietnam. But, in the cases of Morocco and Kenya, it said, 'the key to the success of the fraud was the active participation of those countries' employment ministries in promoting the scheme'.[25]

Lack of employment opportunities is an incentive for young Sahrawis to leave their homeland, adding to the demographic pressure.

France Libertés identified over forty cases in 2002 of Sahrawis from Dakhla trying to enter Spain illegally via the Canaries.[26] But the high level of unemployment and state subvention is costly and politically dangerous. Nationalist Sahrawi activists agree in part with the Moroccan analysis of incidents such as the demonstrations and rioting in Smara in November 2001, saying they are sparked by social grievances, unemployment being the most important. For the Moroccans, these incidents are exploited by Polisario. For Polisario they are an expression of wider popular discontent with Moroccan rule. The French newspaper Libération noted that the announcement of job-creation schemes and employment opportunities for Sahrawi graduates, plus house-building programmes in December 1999, followed hard on the heels of violent protests three months earlier.[27]

The Moroccan authorities believe some 15,000 to 20,000 jobs need to be created to eradicate male unemployment in Laayoune province.[28] In 2002 the Moroccan government had plans to create 13,600 jobs in the Western Sahara.

Apart from minimising social unrest, mobilisation of the human capital available in the Western Sahara is necessary for the development of its economic potential. A geologist who has worked in cooperation with Polisario to evaluate the potential of the Western Sahara noted: 'But in the case of the development of the mining sector it would be necessary to expect important movements of people from neighbouring countries, the indigenous population being so small in number.'[29]

For the meantime, the fishing industry is where Morocco sees the opportunity for rapid growth. There are several good reasons for this. The natural resources are concentrated there. Employment and added value can be achieved quickly and without the foreign investment that eludes Moroccan projects in the Western Sahara while the territory is contested – although technology transfer is an issue. Then, it also feeds into a national Moroccan plan to boost fishery exports. According to the regional investment centre for the Laayoune and Boujdour region, 90 per cent of applications it dealt with between November 2002 and mid-March 2003 concerned fish processing.[30]

There are several strands to the strategy. The ports of Laayoune, Dakhla and Boujdour (along with Tarfaya and Tan Tan in southern

Morocco) are being upgraded. Expansion of Laayoune Port was set to cost over MD200 million while a new harbour and associated work at Dakhla were costed at over MD480 million. On top of that, the fisheries agency was set to spend MD240 million on fleet modernisation, improved onshore facilities and new fishing villages. There is also the stated intention to develop local processing industries, away from fish meal and towards processes that add value. Guerraoui notes that 65 per cent of fish landed in the Western Sahara is turned into fish meal. In Europe, he said, Norway and Iceland multiply tenfold the value of similar catches through canning. Foreign governments such as the South Koreans and Japanese have been told the granting of fishing licences to their fleets is conditional on them building processing plants.[31]

The project to build six new fishing communities aims at creating 6,000 jobs. Between them the villages, to be built by 2004, will have 1,000 small boats. A training centre has been built, and by the end of April 2002 well over 7,000 enrolment requests were registered. The design of the villages was to allow for small hotels for foreign tourists.[32] Sahrawi activists are unimpressed, saying the jobs generated would prove to be for Moroccans. They are convinced that Rabat's intention is to limit Sahrawi access to work as a way of pressuring them into emigrating to either the Canary Islands, where there is a sizeable Sahrawi community, or to other parts of the Arab world.

House building is another major area of planned job creation and one that serves a dual role in damping down popular discontent – providing jobs and better accommodation. One of the bigger projects is the replacement accommodation intended for the residents of Laayoune's Wahda camp. The first phase of the attractive and sympathetic development was approaching completion in April 2002 and would house perhaps 15,000 people.

In the medium to long term, tourism is seen as a potential money-spinner by the administration. Some hotel development has taken place at Laayoune Plage, although at present it remains a windswept and unprepossessing location with little to attract the holidaymaker. Guerraoui notes that 12 million tourists visit the Canary Islands – just a half-hour flight away – yet only 6,000 Spaniards visit the Western Sahara each year. (Ironically, the Western Sahara exports sand to the Canary Islands to replenish its beaches. And, in a twist to the irony, most of it blows back on the prevailing wind.) If even a small proportion of visitors to the Canary Islands then travelled on to Laayoune the earnings could be worthwhile. Currently, the only foreign tourists are a few north European motor caravanners and some fishing enthusiasts, plus the odd group of curious Germans flown in from Las Palmas.

Niche tourism is the way forward, according to the governor of Smara. It is higher value, exploits the natural facets of the area, and makes fewer infrastructural demands. The Smara area has features that would certainly attract the well-heeled European – cave paintings, acacia forest, a famous *zawiya* (religious centre) and desert scenery more attractive than that near the coast.[33]

Yet it will take more than the current hotel provision plus the planned auberges in the planned fishing villages to attract patronage. As far back as 1988, there were notions of drawing in tourists[34] and even during Spanish rule there was 'a small but growing tourist industry'.[35] Some Moroccan officials have been keen to suggest negotiations are in train with European travel companies. Club Med of France was named in the Arabic press as planning a tourist village near Dakhla,[36] although the company said it was doing nothing there 'for the moment'.[37] One London-based travel company also denied any current plans for the Western Sahara although, like Club Med, it is active in Morocco. The political situation is not conducive, said a manager. Again, even after a quarter of a century in the Western Sahara and a decade of ceasefire, overseas Morocco requires more time or some form of legitimisation before it can attract foreign capital to fund its plans to exploit the Western Sahara. Legitimation was what the Framework Agreement promised.

The Sahrawis have always needed to trade, exchanging camels and goats for manufactured goods and comestibles in the markets of Tindouf or Goulmime. Traditionally, they worked as guides on the trans-Saharan caravan route. In the nineteenth century the iconic marabout known as Ma el Ainin, whose heritage of resistance to European colonialism is claimed by both sides in the Western Sahara conflict, wanted to establish Smara as a centre for trade between Morocco and sub-Saharan Africa. That never happened and, of course, since 1975 cross-border trade has been limited to the informal and risky. The conflict and resultant minefields, the lack of infrastructure and rocky political relations prevented official trade, although Sahrawis living in the areas of the Western Sahara under Polisario control have been able to move in and out of Mauritania.

After a decade of ceasefire Morocco moved to open the border with Mauritania to sanctioned traffic. Route 41 now runs down the coast to the border south of Dakhla.

Despite the war, the sand walls and the minefields, the pull to the south has remained strong in the Smara area. The governor said in April 2002 that trade with Mauritania could again be important with carpets, kitchenware and fresh food exported from Morocco and traditional (Sahrawi) clothing coming north.[38] A few months later, the Moroccan government announced plans to open a second border crossing, this one south of Smara.

Volumes traded over the border are likely to be low for now but the opening of the crossings serves other purposes. At the regional level it is a move towards the economic and infrastructural integration promised by the Maghreb Arab Union yet never delivered. It emotionally and physically re-establishes Morocco as the country with roots in Africa that Hassan II once described. And it serves in the competition with Algeria: one of the reasons given by Moroccan diplomats for continued Algerian support for Polisario is a contest to become the transit country for trade with sub-Saharan Africa – whilst there was war in the Western Sahara, Morocco's traditional trade routes to the south were closed.[39]

Yet, more than anything, the opening of the frontier is an assertion, a statement for local, regional and international consumption to the effect that Rabat controls and can maintain control of the territory, that the conflict is over.

Notes

1. 'Chomage et habitat insalubre, ici aussi', *L'Économiste*, 19 December 2001.
2. Ibid.
3. Interview with refugees, May 1998.
4. John Mercer, *Spanish Sahara*, George Allen & Unwin, London, 1976, p. 124.
5. 'Report of the UN Visiting Mission to Spanish Sahara', UN Document A/10023/Rev 1, 1975, pp. 46–7.

6. Interviews with the author, April 2002.
7. Ministry of Economic Forecasting and Planning, *Le plan de développement économique et social 2000–2004*, vol. 1, section 2, p. 2.
8. 'Au milieu du desert, El Ayoun voit vivre les deux communautés', *Le Monde*, 22 February 2002.
9. Correspondence with United Nations.
10. Ibid., p. 2.
11. US Department of State Bureau of Democracy, Human Rights and Labor, 'Western Sahara: Country Report on Human Rights Practices – 2001', March 2002.
12. Mercer, *Spanish Sahara*, p. 124.
13. Ibid., pp. 35–6.
14. Ministry of Economic Forecasting and Planning, *Le plan de développement economique et social 2000–2004*, vol. 1, section 1, p. 2; section 2, p. 2, section 3, p. 176.
15. Interview by author with Guerraoui.
16. 'Chomage et habitat insalubre, ici aussi'.
17. Interview.
18. Reuters, 24 June 2002.
19. Ministry of Economic Forecasting and Planning, Rabat, 'Morocco in Figures 2000', pp. 17–21.
20. Interviews with author, April 2002.
21. El Mundo, 8 May 2002.
22. 'Chomage et habitat insalubre, ici aussi'.
23. 'International Mission of Investigation in Western Sahara', France Libertés–AFASPA, January 2003, p. 27.
24. Cited on www.arso.org, 10 May 2002.
25. ITF media release, 27 September 2002.
26. 'International Mission of Investigation in Western Sahara', p. 34.
27. 'Creation d'emplois au Sahara-Occidental', *Libération*, 7 December 1999.
28. Interview with Guerraoui.
29. Christoph Brenneisen, 'Les ressources exploitables du Sahara Occidental', *L'Ouest Saharien*, vol. 1, 1998.
30. *L'Economiste*, 21 March 2003.
31. Interview.
32. 'Plan de développement integré de la province de Laayoune', presentation to author by officials of Laayoune government.
33. Interview.
34. Attilio Gaudio, *Guerres et paix au Maroc*, 1988.
35. 'Report of the UN Visiting Mission to Spanish Sahara', p. 51.
36. *Al Hayat*, 19 June 2002.
37. Correspondence with the author, July 2002.
38. Interview by author with Governor of Smara.
39. Interview with Mohammed Belmahi, Moroccan ambassador, London 2002.

6

The 'Years of Lead'

El Qateb el Hafez fills a cool, bare Laayoune house with his absence. Around the walls of the reception room sit women family members and visitors. A toddler giggles at the flame of a cigarette lighter flicked on and off for her amusement. Young men − sons, cousins, in-laws, family friends − come and go.[1]

The face of El Qateb gazes without expression from a black-and-white passport photograph. It freezes the life of a young man, attractive but unexceptional, typically Sahrawi with dark curly hair, fine-boned and dark-eyed with a thin moustache. The memento is handed round the circle as Sahrawi tea is prepared on a low brazier. It is relinquished to visiting journalists in the hope that giving away this fossil fragment of the man may help to bring back the living son, husband, brother, cousin.

The neighbourhood of the quiet house, just to the west of Laayoune's teeming Wahda camp, maintains a reputation as a bastion of Sahrawi nationalism. Reminiscent of the north of Ireland or the West Bank, pre-teenage boys cheerfully lob stones at a foreigner with a camera on the grounds that they 'don't know who the photographs are for'.

On 6 November 1992 there was a nationalist demonstration in these streets. El Qateb, aged 19, was not on the demonstration but had helped prepare banners. Hours later he became one of the 'Disappeared'. Security men arrived at the house and took him away. That is simply the last that has been seen of him. His father died four months later, said to be tortured by remorse at opening the door to the men who stole his son.

The family went through the motions, using the few channels open to them in a heavily surveyed society. They asked at barracks and police stations. A letter was deposited at the court of first instance. They contacted the state-sponsored human rights monitor, the Conseil Consultatif des Droits de l'Homme and were told there was no information. Human rights activists believe El Qateb was put under the charge of an officer of the CMI, or Mobile Intervention companies, who is alleged to be responsible for at least four deaths under torture.

Under surveillance, hearing news of other disappearances in the area, deprived of two central figures, avenues exhausted, the family finally found help. In the hopes and the turmoil of 1999, they decided to contact the Saharan section of the Truth and Justice Forum – since closed down – one of the civil rights groups that surfaced in that year. They have no news of El Qateb but they know his case has been pursued, that documentation has been sent abroad, and they are now part of a network of families of the Disappeared.

In Sahrawi quarters of Western Saharan towns there are security force patrols, there is a policeman in every corner café. Here, even after the liberalisation and prisoner releases in Morocco of recent years, Sahrawis may be swept up by agents of any of an alphabet soup of security forces: FAR, GR, FA, DGSN, DST, CMI or DGED. The number of Moroccan troops who would have been permitted to stay even during the referendum process under the 1991 Settlement Plan was a massive 65,000.

Days before El Qateb's abduction, 27-year-old Kerouan Mahjoub was taken. The story is similar: the same part of Laayoune, a demonstration in which the victim had not taken part, a knock at the door at four in the morning, five men from the DST. And the same round of enquiries, hopefully proferring the registration number of the car that took Kerouan away.

The families of El Qateb and Kerouan hold on to their hopes. After all, people have emerged from Moroccan detention centres after two decades. But an extra twist of the knife is that their relatives, as of the time of writing, were probably among the very last to disappear long term.

One of Kerouan's relatives said, prior to the knock on the door, there had been no indication of interest in the family on the part of the security forces. For him, this was the point of disappearances. They told all Sahrawis they were at risk, that they might be next. And the documentation bears this out. Among the Disappeared are women as well as men and children as well as adults. The horror of these abductions for the families left behind is that the wound constantly festers. There is no release date. There is no grave. Wives do not know if they are widows and so cannot remarry, and that has financial as well as emotional implications. It is 'constant mourning' said an activist working with the families.

El Qateb's and Kerouan's families have the bitterness of knowing their loved ones may have been among the last to disappear. The family of Faraji Mohamed Salem Beih Oubarkh have the pain of a quarter of a century of the 'constant mourning'. Faraji was disappeared on 4 June 1976, one of the first victims of the policy. Still there is no news, no body. Still Maimouna bint Baha, his wife, hopes he will return. Faraji's case highlights that the selection of victims has often been random. This is underscored by the confusion of the events, not least the confusion of the security forces.

In 1976, when the conflict was in its early stages, Polisario was able to operate with impunity throughout the Western Sahara, northern Mauritania and southern Morocco. Maimouna recounts that there had been a guerrilla attack on Laayoune. Hours later a dozen men barged into the house and searched and left. An hour later there was another knock and Maimouna's mother was told to call Faraji and tell him he was wanted for questioning. He was taken away. In the early hours of the morning another jeep full of security men arrived and trashed the house, while Maimouna, her crying baby of five months, and mother looked on. The women were then beaten as the security men demanded to know where Faraji was. He had been snatched by one agency and then sought by another. In the following weeks Maimouna herself was summoned frequently for interrogation.

Faraji had or has Spanish nationality, according to his family, and indeed had served in the Spanish forces in the Western Sahara. Prior to his disappearance he had given serious consideration to joining the Moroccan army but had been dissuaded by the family. Perhaps his decision not to join up was cause for suspicion. Otherwise the family can see no reason for him to have been selected. They say a neighbour, Mrabbi Ould Bennu, was taken a fortnight after Faraji, and he had served in the Moroccan 'sand army'.

Maimouna recalls that for years the repression was so intense that she could not even talk about Faraji's disappearance outside of the family. Over the years she came to know other families of the Disappeared. But, again, it was the 'Laayoune events' of 1999 that convinced her to make wider contacts. She was hesitant and afraid but she did get in touch with Sahrawi human rights activists, and hopes exposure of her husband's case may yet bring some closure.

Sahrawi activists say 500 cases of disappearance are outstanding, a hundred of them are documented and witnessed. On top of that are another 321 released from detention centres inside Morocco in 1991 and 57 known to have died in detention. Of these 378, there were 73 women, of whom 19 had babies when taken. Periods of detention ranged from four to sixteen years. Another 1,000 or more have been held for periods ranging from a few weeks to four years.[2]

For a community already traumatised by war, with families torn between the camps in Tindouf, the Moroccan-occupied territories, the Polisario-controlled zone, southern Morocco, northern Mauritania, the policy of disappearance heaped fear on fear. In tight-knit family and tribal units in a wider community as small as that of the Sahrawis, disappearance on this scale even, or especially sustained over a period of decades, ensured suffering was spread as widely as possible.

Amnesty International called the issue of the Disappeared, Moroccan as well as Sahrawi, 'one of the most painful unresolved human right issues'.[3] While acknowledging that a number of the Sahrawi and Moroccan Disappeared have been accounted for, the Amnesty report also roughly concurs with Sahrawi activists over the number who remain unaccounted for.

It also said that 'Rather than turning the page on past human rights violations, the measures which the Moroccan government have taken on this matter are tantamount to them turning their back on the victims of "Disappearance".'[4] Its report noted that the CCDH, the official human rights organisation of Morocco, only acknowledged 112 Disappeared, none of them Sahrawi. Three years later the Moroccan authorities were still saying the issue was being investigated and the relatives were still saying nothing was happening.

Moroccans who survived the years of solitary confinement, the deprivation of sunlight for as much as eighteen years, whole 'sentences' passed unable to get up from the floor, do receive discretionary stipends from the authorities. But as the Amnesty report said, released Sahrawis have not been offered this token of recompense and, moreover, remain subject to intimidation and rearrest.

Yet, with scarcely comprehensible courage, some of the released Sahrawis have engaged in activity in Rabat, working with Moroccan former detainees and issuing joint communiqués. This, as the Amnesty report noted, has contributed to raising awareness of their plight and chipping away at the taboo of discussing the Sahrawi Disappeared.

The taboo may be dented but it is not broken yet. Fifteen Sahrawis died at the detention centre at Qalat Mgouna and the majority of the prisoners who passed through were Sahrawis. In the summer 2002 a three-bus convoy of former detainees, Moroccan human rights activists and attendant relatives and journalists held a vigil outside the camp. Bar one, there were no Sahrawis present because it was deemed their presence might politicise the event.[5]

Mid-morning one day late in April 2002 the court at Laayoune is packed with Sahrawis. Plainclothes and uniformed security men mill around the entrance and foyer. A van arrives with the first batch of the accused. A young man is taken from the back of the van and accompanied up the steps of the building. Some hesitation and then an older man is extracted from the van. He is unable to walk unassisted and slumps and sways as warders haul him into the court. Covering the back of his head is a large dressing drenched in blood. During the proceedings the defence lawyers will say the prisoners, held on remand for the past six months, have been tortured.

The court sits until late at night. The following day judgment is passed and fourteen of the sixteen accused are jailed for between six months and two years for a variety of public order offences during demonstrations in Smara the previous November.

These are Morocco's official Sahrawi prisoners, convicted in open court of specified charges after events that all sides attest were riotous. There have been numerous such trials in courts and military tribunals of groups of Sahrawis, particularly over the past decade as use of disappearance has waned under international criticism and as reformists in Morocco have attempted to moderate the state's activities. The problem the authorities have in bringing Sahrawis to open trial after demonstrations is that it highlights both the events and, by implication, the views of the charged, contradicting the assertion that the locals are happy under Moroccan tutelage. In the case of the Smara detainees, the circle was squared by arguing that the demonstrations were over economic demands that the administration was in the process of addressing.

Human rights activists report trials of groups, primarily of young Sahrawi men, from the towns of the Western Sahara and also from Sahrawi areas of southern Morocco. Sahrawi students in Marrakesh and Rabat have also been held. Nine at the university of Marakesh were jailed for between two and five years in May 2000 and thirteen studying in Rabat were arrested at the same time but acquitted after six months on remand.[6] Sentences passed in the 1990s ranged up to twenty years, as in the instance of a group of eight men picked up after a demonstration in Laayoune in 1995.[7]

An indication of the number of Sahrawi prisoners who consider themselves something other than 'common criminals' is given by participation in prison protests. In 2002 in the jail in Laayoune, known as the Black Prison, over 140 detainees took part in hunger strikes.[8] The US State Department refers to 'A number of other Sahrawi [who] remained imprisoned for peaceful protests supporting Saharan independence.'[9] The number of longer-term prisoners still being held is unknown. Morocco denies holding any. Polisario says there are several hundred political prisoners and 300 prisoners of war. Campaigners list twenty-five list forms of torture used against prisoners by the Moroccan authorities.

The courts also hand out sentences of banishment to Sahrawis. In October 2002, a group was convicted of instigating protests against discriminatory employment practices. Among them, Nigro Mohamed and El Belaoui Hamadi were jailed for two years and banned from entering towns in the Western Sahara for five years.[10]

The longest serving Amnesty-defined prisoner of conscience held by Morocco was the Sahrawi Mohamed Daddach. He joined Polisario in 1973, was captured and held for two years before being press-ganged into the Moroccan forces. In 1979 he and an associate took a car and tried to flee Moroccan-controlled territory. He was recaptured and spent the next twenty-two years in prison, convicted of desertion, having initially been condemned to death. A shoulder broken during his escape attempt was never treated and he was severely tortured in Kenitra prison. A total of fifty-six Sahrawi prisoners were released in late 2001, but it was Daddach's release after a campaign driven largely from inside the Western Sahara that marked a high point of the local human rights campaign.

It may be that it was *the* high point, for just months later the boundaries of the regime's tolerance seemed to have been reached. The limited space allowed since 1999 to those working to establish the basis for Sahrawi civil society began to be closed off. Those who had spoken out began to be stifled once more.

By autumn 2002, Sahrawis were fearing a return to the 'years of lead':

> After the police raid of 24 September, using methods thought abandoned once and for all, the Moroccan occupation authorities are again using the most barbarous methods of torture on Sahrawi activists abducted on this occasion. Salek Bazaid, after having been interrogated and tortured by the judicial police brigade was taken to the headquarters of the Mobile Intervention Companies in Laayoune, a secret jail infamous as a place of torture and which was thought to be out of use.[11]

In March 2003, three activists, Salek Bazaid, Moussamih Bab and Bourhil Mohamed Lamine, were handed down ten-year prison sentences.

Going from person to person in a room full of Sahrawi activists in a Laayoune flat soon evinces a litany of petty suffering and harassment piled on top of the periods of detention, long or short, that many have endured. Short-term arrest and interrogation are frequent. Daddach[12] says everyone he has associated with since his release has been intimidated as a result. Some are called in for interrogation, one lost his job at a canning factory, another had his car confiscated. El Hadaoui M'barek's dyeing workshop in Assa was ransacked.

Passports are difficult for activists to obtain and several in the room say they have been prevented from travelling to international forums where they could air their grievances. Meeting or planning to meet those international delegations permitted to enter the Western Sahara also attracts harassment. Families are threatened with reprisals if activists continue their work.

Sudden transfer of employment to towns inside Morocco is used to isolate individuals and break up networks of contacts. Four civil rights campaigners were sent variously to Casablanca, Taounate and Meknes[13] after the Saharan section of the Truth and Justice Forum was closed down. Teachers' unions reported that several Sahrawi members had been told they were to be transferred to Moroccan towns at around the same time. In 1999, there were reports of a campaign to press many Sahrawi youths into the Moroccan forces.[14] Other forms of social control include long-term house arrest, as in the case of former political prisoner Roukaibi Sidi Mohamed.[15]

When campaigns around civil rights are constricted, public expressions of Sahrawi nationalism are, of course, rapidly quashed. After the death of Polisario diplomat Fadel Ismail, who was greatly respected inside the Western Sahara, a public memorial event was prevented from taking place at the planned venue and those who managed to get to the hastily rearranged location were harassed.

In May 2002 mentally handicapped Driss Bilal Khatri Sidi Barra was beaten and then detained for wearing pro-independence tattoos,[16] an offence that has also resulted in teenagers being threatened with removal to northern Morocco for 're-education', according to human rights activists. In April 2003 a blind and disturbed old Sahrawi woman arrived in Laayoune Camp in Algeria via Mauritania, saying she had been imprisoned by the Moroccan authorities for shouting political slogans.

The case of Ali Salem Tamek[17] illustrates the extent of persecution of one nationalist and trade unionist working most recently with the Forum and the campaign over the Disappeared. Tamek was born in the southern Moroccan town of Assa where he worked in the local administration. Aged 20, in 1993 he was jailed for five years, reduced to two, on charges of trying to join Polisario. He was re-arrested in the Western Saharan town of Dakhla in December 1997 and released ten days later in Laayoune. In April 2002 he was told to leave Assa for Meknes in the north. He refused and his salary was suspended. He has consistently been refused a passport. He receives no family allowance for one daughter because the authorities refused to register her name – Athawra (Revolution).

In August 2002, he attempted to register at a police station in Rabat as an election candidate in Assa and was arrested and taken to Casablanca. After questioning there he was taken for further interrogation in Agadir in the south and remanded on charges of participation in a Polisario spy ring. He denied the charge but said he favoured Sahrawi self-determination. The following month he was sentenced to two years' imprisonment and a fine of MD10,000 (around $1,000 when GDP per capita for Morocco is some $3,400). Once imprisoned he embarked on a series of hunger strikes, one of which brought him close to death.

As harassment of activists was ratcheted up again in late spring 2002, after a Moroccan charm offensive during which some foreign journalists were invited into the Western Sahara and several made contact with Sahrawi groups, so one of the most prominent organisations was shut down.

In February the Saharan section of the Truth and Justice Forum signed up to a document on human rights abuses in the Western Sahara since 1975. This was presented to a European Parliament delegation and to the UN human rights commission in Geneva. Among the allegations to outrage the Moroccan press was one of genocide and mass executions. The Moroccan executive of the Forum ran for cover, saying the document had no official sanction and was the work of individuals.[18] The activists who ran the section were expelled, soon to face arrest and dispersal. The Sahara section of the Forum was officially wound up by the Moroccan courts at the end of June 2003 and named activists were banned from working together in future.[19]

Just as Sahrawis had been excluded from the vigil at Qalat Mgouna for fear they might politicise the event, so the publicity around the document – which was no stronger than that issued when the Saharan section was inaugurated – raised fear in the executive that it would be tarred with the brush of tolerating separatist sympathies. Discussion of the Western Sahara conflict remains a taboo in Morocco and one that is backed by sanction.

In April 2000, *Le Journal* and its sister paper *As Sahifa* were promptly banned after the former ran an interview with Polisario leader

Mohamed Abdelaziz. The editor of Le Journal, a proponent of the integration of Western Sahara into Morocco, was accused of associating with foreign interests hostile to Morocco. A government newspaper accused him of being a fifth columnist.[20] When the television channel 2M reported the ban and showed a copy of the offending publication three editors were sacked.[21]

Attempts to establish an independent newspaper in the Western Sahara have been rebuffed and Moroccan journalists run risks attempting to report events in the territory. Darif Noureddine was held in detention for six months before acquittal, having been picked up in the wake of the Smara unrest of November 2001. L'Économiste has conscientiously reported on social conditions in Laayoune and Smara, has even tackled the lack of integration between settlers and Sahrawis, but it has been careful to meld this with the government line on protest and separatism – the protests are economic and Polisario has little support. But for the most part the Moroccan press runs sanitised propaganda on the territory, indistinguishable in tone from the reports of the government mouthpiece, the agency Maghreb Arab Press. Indeed, with some obvious justification, Sahrawi nationalists say much of the Moroccan press is actively engaged in the suppression of debate and the falsification of facts concerning the Western Sahara.

Foreign publications sold in Morocco are not immune to government displeasure either. In its 2002 end-of-year report on the country, Reporters sans frontières said, 'During the year, no less than nine newspapers – seven of them foreign – were censured for having dealt with subjects such as the Western Sahara, corruption or, above all, the person of the king'.[22] At one of the court hearings against the Truth and Justice Forum's Sahara section, the police offered as evidence reports that members of the group had met with named foreign journalists from publications such as the Financial Times and Daily Telegraph who had been invited to the territory by the Moroccan government.

Notes

1. The following accounts are based on the author's interviews with relatives of the Disappeared.

2. 'Situation des droits de l'homme – Sahara Occidental', paper issued under the name Defenseurs des droits de l'homme Sahraouis, Laayoune, 11 February 2002.

3. Amnesty International, 'Morocco/Western Sahara – Turning the Page: Achievements and Obstacles', January 1999.

4. Ibid.

5. Eileen Byrne, 'Letter from Qalat Mgouna', *Middle East International*, 12 July 2002.

6. 'Situation des droits de l'homme – Sahara Occidental'.

7. Ibid.

8. Sahara Press Service report, 6 September 2002.

9. *Western Sahara: Country Reports on Human Rights*, US Department of State Bureau for Democracy, Human Rights and Labor, March 2002.

10. ARSO website, www.arso.org, 2 September 2002, pp. 10–11.

11. ARSO website, news for week 40, 2002, report from a correspondent.

12. Interview with the author.

13. 'Letter ouverte aux ONG de defense des droits humains', in the name of Defenseurs des droits de l'homme sahraouis, 5 September 2002.

14. ARSO website, 7 October 1999.

15. ARSO website, week 41, 2002.

16. ARSO website, 22 May 2002.

17. Compiled from reports of ARSO and Defenseurs des droits de l'homme sahraouis.

18. *Al Bayane*, 13 June 2002; *Le Reporter*, 13 June 2002; Sahara Press Service, 10 June 2002.

19. Among the evidence offered by the prosecution was that members had attended meetings where separatist statements had been made, that they had associated with leaders of overseas groups supportive of Polisario and met with names members of the international press, including the author of this book.

20. Jose Garcon, 'Maroc: un avertissement à la presse', *Libération*, 18 April 2000.

21. Nick Pelham, 'Press Clampdown', *Middle East International*, 5 May 2000.

22. Reporters sans frontières, *Maroc Rapport annuel* 2002, Paris, December 2002.

7

An Identity Forged by Resistance

'Before, the combat was military, but now, it is here', says Mohamed Daddach, adding 'We will continue and have continued to struggle with our modest means, under the leadership of our representative, the Polisario Front.'[1]

Since the guns fell silent in 1991 in a ceasefire that has been breached by neither side, the role of the Polisario fighters has become marginal in practical terms. With the collapse of the referendum process almost a decade later, the population of the refugee camps in Tindouf was disarmed of its most powerful weapon, the vote that would win the struggle. 'This no war, no peace situation has been very bad for us and cannot continue for too much longer', remarked a Polisario representative in late 2002.

In the diplomatic arena Polisario continues to claim representation of the Sahrawis and has been remarkably successful in resisting the powerful triumvirate of the US, France and the UK in the Security Council. From bedsit offices in modest terraced houses and flats, Polisario's emissaries have lobbied against trilateral delegations of these three permanent members of the Security Council, convincing countries like Norway and Ireland to stand firm, reminding Spain of its historic responsibilities, but suffering attritional losses as a number of countries withdrew recognition of the SADR.

But on the ground, it is the Sahrawis under Moroccan adminis-tration who have taken centre stage, particularly since 1999. Then the shutters that had hidden the bulk of the Western Sahara from scrutiny budged, raised in part by the increased level of resistance that year, in part by the fact that activity around the referendum process increased contact with people from outside, and in part by the knock-on effects of a modest liberalisation in Morocco after the death of Hassan II. As a wave of arrests in mid-2002 demonstrated, shutters that have been opened can also be slammed shut. Yet, in the history of the information technology and telecommunications industries there should be a footnote on the contribution of the mobile phone and personal computer to sustaining the visibility of struggles made remote by distance or inaccessible by government fiat.

When Daddach was released he addressed a rally in Laayoune where his words were conveyed to the refugee camps and to supporters in Europe by mobile phone. That rally and another in Smara were recorded on video camera and distributed through the occupied territories and shown to visitors. Of course, they were also filmed by the Moroccan security forces. To some small extent, the years, the desert miles and the minefields dividing family members between the occupied territories, the camps and further-flung exile have been crossed by the mobile phone too. And email not only allows news to be transmitted quickly out of the area but also throws up the unexpected on occasion. 'Zahrat Isahara', or Desert Flowers, may be an individual or a group, may be genuine or not, but this name pops up from time to time at the bottom of pro-independence letters and statements, yet the identity of the sender is known by neither Laayoune-based activists nor Polisario representatives.

The means of resistance and expression available to the Sahrawis under Moroccan rule are modest and fragile. The most basic but most enduring level is simply the maintenance of their collective identity. For Sahrawi nationalists their identity is forged in a history of struggle. Repression has radicalised the Sahrawis, says Daddach. He adds that the Sahrawis have a history and identity expressed through long years of struggle: 'They struggled against Spain and have never changed the struggle although the aggressor has changed [from Spain to Morocco].'

A necessary but not a sufficient condition of this 'resistance identity' is maintenance of cultural and ethnic signifiers – use of the Hassaniya dialect, diet, wearing traditional clothing, teaching desert skills to children, preferring to pray outside rather than in a mosque, the phrase often slipped quietly into an innocuous conversation, 'I am a Sahrawi'. These and many other expressions of ethnic identity are shared, of course, by Sahrawis who are firmly in the Moroccan camp, the shioukh presented to visiting delegations to vow allegiance to Rabat and the Sahrawis who say they have fled the Tindouf camps. They are also shared by a group of professional women of varying political persuasions who run valuable nongovernmental organisations in Laayoune.

That these cultural and ethnic tokens are so widespread makes identity politics a necessary but treacherous battleground for both sides. Is the officially sanctioned collecting of oral histories in the Sahrawi Hassaniya dialect politically neutral? Does it build a culture of separation or of integration? On the other side of the sand wall, Polisario has encouraged archaeological study of the areas under its control. In passing, it is worth quoting a party to another struggle for identity affecting Morocco. Professor Salem Chaker writes: 'To be Berber today – and wish to remain so – is necessarily an act that is militant, cultural, eventually scientific, always political.'[2]

Just as it has moved to appropriate and integrate Saharan natural resources into its own economy, so Morocco is moving to co-opt Sahrawis and their identity. Among instances typifying this were the announcement that several key defectors from Polisario were to be posted to Moroccan embassies abroad to voice support for integration, the appointment of a Polisario defector to the administration of the occupied territories, and the announcement that Sahrawi music would henceforth be included in a major Moroccan cultural festival.

Depoliticisation of Sahrawi actions – describing them as criminal or as motivated by economic rather than political factors – is a part of Morocco's strategy of minimising support for independence both to its own citizens and to outsiders. *L'Économiste*, a Moroccan daily newspaper, argued: 'The separatists are a small minority, their method of recruitment only functions when its get results from the absence of universal standards (human rights and the right to development), but they have no socio-economic alternative to propose.'[3] Earlier in its suite of articles on the Western Sahara, the paper cited an official of the OADP, a Moroccan political party then in the governing coalition, saying that the 'separatists' exploit social conditions to build support. He argued there are few who share Polisario's political project but many who have lost faith in the administration because of its repeated political and economic mistakes. From this perspective, the battle is for hearts and minds.

This line of argument, propounded by Moroccan officialdom, points to the rallies in Laayoune and Smara to welcome Daddach after his release, saying they were small and largely made up of bystanders. Of the near contemporaneous confrontations in Smara, the official line is that protest over understandable economic grievances that the reforming government was addressing was exploited by a small number of agents provocateurs, leading to a spate of criminal acts.

Through the optic of the independence movement, those two events look very different. The rallies for Daddach were a triumph, they say: the first open, fully public exposition of a nationalist political position, made under the very eyes of the Moroccan security forces. They claim 3,000 people attended the smaller Smara rally – the Moroccan party official cited by *L'Économiste* said 600 and the video footage suggests some figure in the middle. What is plain from the footage is that despite the legacy of fierce repression, a sizeable body of Sahrawis, many of them young and many of them women, turned out to cheer every word of Daddach and echo them with shouts of 'Timor sharqiya, Sahara ghrabia' ('East Timor, Western Sahara').

That was on 13 November 2001. Four days later, they agree, the demonstration that ended in rioting was over unemployment, but the security forces, they say, sought revenge for the Daddach rally and attacked the crowd. The implication of this is that the security forces at least do not share the official view that a Sahrawi with a social grievance is distinct from a Polisario supporter. A witness cited by *L'Économiste* makes the point: 'That day, I regretted being Moroccan. The forces of order spared no-one. Sahrawi and non-Sahrawi, women and children and old people were passing by. In their eyes [the police], they were all separatists.'[4] The witness goes on to say that a demonstration that began with pictures of the king being held aloft ended with pro-Polisario chants. Activists emphasise that for weeks before these two events there had been persistent activity in Smara, agitation over economic issues, petitioning for prisoner releases, hanging out of Polisario banners. Indeed a planned visit by Mohamed VI to the town was postponed.

As Sahrawi nationalists argue that Moroccan rule has entailed all-encompassing marginalisation of the indigenous population, they see protest over economic issues as a valid expression of their struggle. Indeed, like human rights advocacy, it has been one of the few areas where any form of open activity has been possible, given that open support for independence has been an invitation to arrest for spying. As activists explain, it is a matter of finding and operating in whatever space is available. Resistance may take the form of graffiti, distributing nationalist leaflets, hanging out flags at night, demonstrating for jobs, campaigning for the release of prisoners, working with human rights groups, supporting victims of landmines.

This being the case, many of the demonstrations and protests that are reported in the territory and in Sahrawi towns inside Morocco present superficially as demands for social reform. Closer reading of the demands and the reaction of the security forces to such expressions makes clear the underlying nationalist nature of the incidents. To take an example, in late August 2002 the Association of Unemployed Sahrawis organised a demonstration in boulevard Alkayrawan in Laayoune. Half an hour later it was broken up by riot squads and several arrests were made. The office of the Association was then raided. Four of those arrested were fined and jailed for six months, whereupon they joined a hunger strike of Sahrawi prisoners. A statement issued by the Association referred to jobs being given to 'Moroccan settlers' (sic) in preference to Sahrawis.[5] In a flat in Laayoune, a group of old former nomads discuss their twenty-year campaign to win restitution for camel herds slaughtered by Moroccan troops. For these old men the issue is a simple matter of justice yet their demands carry political baggage – for Morocco to admit its troops butchered the herds, whether for the fun of it or to deprive Polisario of provisions, would open the floodgates to calls for recompense for property, lives and rights forgone. In February 2003, a group of victims of landmines prepared to request official permission to operate but were unsure whether they would receive it, knowing Morocco would be sensitive to anything that raised consciousness of the issue.

Despite the levels of surveillance in the towns of the territory, militant, overtly pro-Polisario protests do occur. In May 2002, there were reports of twenty young men, wearing hoods and carrying petrol bombs, waving flags in the Skikima district of Laayoune and handing out leaflets.[6] Later in the year, there were reports of a similar sized group attacking a police station with petrol bombs.

Prison plays an important role in the struggle of Sahrawi nationalists. The imprisonment and the disappearance of individual Sahrawis stands as a cipher for the perception of a nation that has been imprisoned and denied an existence. Released prisoners achieve a certain social status. Two women former detainees said their standing in the community had risen and that the community supported them. In contrast with a certain social diffidence which some other Arab women political prisoners have found themselves subject to, one of the women said she had married shortly after her release.[7]

In the case of officially acknowledged prisoners (as opposed to the Disappeared) there is also a dynamic in struggles around imprisonment in that the incarcerated and their supporters can work together and also draw in external support. In the so-called Black Prison in Laayoune, Sahrawi prisoners have used the hunger strike as a means of pressing their demands.

In mid-June 2002, over a hundred Sahrawi prisoners were reported by Polisario's Sahara Press Service to have gone on hunger strike for a week in solidarity with one El Keinan who was refusing food after being tortured.[8] Three months later the same source said 141 prisoners in the same prison had declared a hunger strike against their conditions. The men, whose sentences ranged from one year to thirty-two years, had called on Amnesty International to look into their situation. A few days later they used their platform to broadcast the nationalist message, calling for a boycott of the Moroccan general election and saying that all attempts 'to tame our people failed thanks to our unity around the objectives of the Polisario Front'.[9]

The release of Daddach and a number of other Sahrawi political prisoners was a major fillip to Sahrawi civil rights activists, not least because they were able to claim it as a victory for a campaign they had initiated and a campaign that seemed to bring success quickly. The Action Committee for the Release of Daddach was only inaugurated two months before the release in November 2001 but quickly drew support and signatories locally and from abroad.[10]

Sahrawi students and teachers in Moroccan universities and schools have played a courageous role in supporting their compatriots in the Western Sahara as well as pressing their own sectional demands. In 1999, it was their example that inspired the biggest upsurge of resistance to date. As mentioned earlier, this has not been without cost – a number have been arrested. A few examples of their activity will suffice. Students at Rabat received Daddach after his release from Kenitra prison.[11] Two years earlier Sahrawi women students marched to the Moroccan parliament protesting about attacks on demonstrators in Laayoune.[12] In June 2002, around one hundred young Sahrawi teachers declared themselves to be on strike and set up a picket outside the Ministry of Education in Rabat, demanding to be posted back to the Western Sahara and parity with Moroccan colleagues.[13] In early 2003 a meeting organised as part of three days of events around Agadir university drew crowds of up to 1,500 and, significantly, the portrait of the founder of Polisario was displayed.[14] 'When I saw that meeting, I knew we would win in the end', said a human rights activist and former prisoner.

Notes

1. Interview with the author, April 2002.
2. Salem Chaker, *Berberes aujourd'hui*, L'Harmattan, Paris, 1989; cited in David Crawford, 'Morocco's Invisible Imazighen', *Journal of North African Studies*, vol. 7, no. 1.
3. 'Enjeu: Passer vite à une économie auto-entretenue', *L'Économiste*, 19 December 2001.
4. 'Chômage et habitat insalubre, ici aussi', *L'Économiste*, 19 December 2001.
5. ARSO website, www.arso.org, 22 August 2002; Sahara Press Service 14 September 2002.
6. ARSO, 17 May 2002.
7. Interview with the author, April 2002.
8. Sahara Press Service, 16 June 2002.
9. Sahara Press Service, 1 and 6 September 2002.
10. *El Karama* 21, Bureau Européen pour le respect de droits de l'homme au Sahara occidental, Geneva.
11. Ibid.
12. Newsletter of Western Sahara Campaign UK, December 1999.
13. Sahara Press Service, 16 June 2002.
14. Videotape recorded by participant.

Smara camp, Tindouf region, 2003

Polisario fighter returned to Laayoune, 2002

Sahrawis caught in sandstorm, Tindouf region, 2003

Boy entering a tent in the desert, occupied territories, Morocco

Child herding goats, Smara camp, Tindouf region, 2003

Sahrawi women attend a wedding, Laayoune, 2002

Moroccan fishing vessels in Laayoune Port, 2002

Phosphate mine, Bou Craa, 2002

Polisario fighters scout the Moroccan berm, Western Sahara, 1988

Polisario fighters approach the Moroccan defensive berm, 1988

Lemsid ancient Sahrawi cemetery, occupied territories

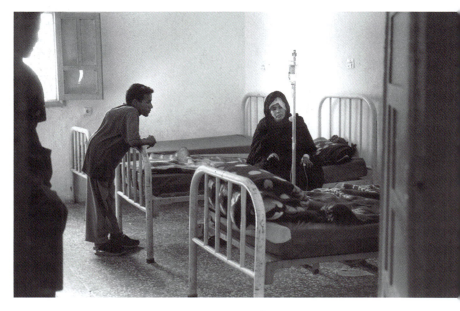

Polisario hospital, Tindouf region HQ, 2003

Sahrawi shepherds, Western Sahara, 2002

Polisario fighter, 1988

Mohamed Daddach, released political prisoner and iconic figure, Laayoune, 2002

Polisario fighters attend Congress parade, Laayoune camp, 1988

8

1999: Civil Society
and Breaking Down
the 'Wall of Fear'

The year 1999 was one of drama in the Western Sahara and trauma in Morocco. The referendum process was crippled and the struggles of the Sahrawis living in Moroccan-controlled Western Sahara and in Morocco itself came to the fore. This was partly because of increased activism; partly because political uncertainty in Morocco provided more, albeit very limited, opportunity for protest; and partly because with no fighting and no voting the population of the refugee camps had lost its two weapons.

In the towns of the Western Sahara, the second half of 1999 was a period of sit-ins, demonstrations and confrontation with the security forces in which the Sahrawis inside the territory were supported by their kin in southern Morocco and by Sahrawi students in northern Morocco. Out of this unprecedented level of activity came the project of developing a semi-public oppositional civil society, drawing in not just activists but also people like the families of the Disappeared. Organisations like the Saharan section of the Truth and Justice Forum were born out of what inevitably became known as the Sahrawi intifada. There is a certain glibness to the comparison but there are underlying similarities. As in the case of the first Palestinian intifada, the activities of the Sahrawis in 1999 extended beyond the 'usual suspects' and were widespread enough to cause real concern at the heart of the ruling regime (though some say the events were permitted and exploited to allow interior minister Basri to be removed). Perhaps more crucially in the long run, the perceived and actual centre of resistance was relocated in both cases from the guerrilla liberator in refugee camps abroad to the demonstrator on the streets of the homeland. The potential political consequences of that shift are profound.

In Morocco, the death of Hassan II removed a pillar that supported the entire political edifice. True enough his son Mohamed VI inherited the religious credentials of the Alaouite monarchy but Hassan had personally shaped Morocco over four decades. He had appointed ministers. He had managed relations with France, often using his personal understanding with key figures there such as Jacques Chirac. He steered Morocco through the Cold War, always playing to the US yet placating the Soviet Union. All major policy initiatives − not least the Green March − were his. And, of course, his patronage dictated who controlled, formally or informally, what economic resources. A Polisario diplomat described the transition from Hassan to Mohamed as being from a man who, though loathed, was a decision-maker with the authority to see through policy changes, to an untested, unconfident, perhaps unwilling monarch of little standing.[1] Variations of this view were widely held by observers and remain so.[2] In the longer term the judgement may prove harsh on Mohamed − his father's accession was greeted by comparable concerns − but certainly in 1999 the trauma of Hassan's death was deep.

It was not until 2001 that James Baker formally presented the Framework Agreement, outlining autonomy for the Western Sahara under Moroccan sovereignty. But it was 1999 when Morocco decided the existing referendum plan was too risky. Paris and Washington acquiesced, apparently because they too doubted the new king's authority at home and believed loss of the referendum, which looked increasingly likely, would destabilise Morocco.

Brahim Buseif was a Polisario observer with the UN voter identification commission as it worked in the Western Sahara and in Morocco. He reports the change of atmosphere as it sunk home to Moroccan officials that attempts to register thousands of their nominees as bona fide Sahrawi voters were not going to succeed and that the referendum would be in favour of independence.[3]

The Polisario leadership had instructed its observers to establish good relations with their Moroccan counterparts and Sahrawi 'collaborators' during the registration process. Confidence building now would facilitate a referendum they believed was going to take place and, after the appointment of James Baker, take place with the weight of the US behind it. Some of the Moroccans reciprocated and a certain openness developed as long as there was no one to overhear conversations. The Moroccans too believed there would be a vote. Over time, though, they became increasingly glum, said Buseif. They too thought the registration process was going against Morocco and feared it would be pushed through by a US with no more Cold War rationale for supporting Rabat.

One summer Friday, Buseif had been with the commission in Assa in south-eastern Morocco. As usual, he said farewell to his counterparts for the weekend and was driven to Goulmime and then on to the airport at Tan Tan for the UN flight to Tindouf. On arrival in the camps he found mobs of children shouting, 'The dictator is dead!' The era of Hassan II had passed.

In the camps in 1999, family contacts with relatives in the occupied territories had been re-established. Until Morocco cracked down and forbade all but small groups of would-be voters from going to the registration centres, the process had been accompanied by crowds of Sahrawis come to meet the delegations from the camps and exchange letters and parcels. Buseif recalls a UN official commenting wryly that 'Identification is easy – those who bring letters for relatives are clearly Sahrawi.'

For the population of the Tindouf camps, confidence in the imminence of the referendum took practical, ultimately poignant forms. After years under canvas many refugees had managed to build more permanent housing. With a return home just around the corner, many refugees stripped the metal roofs from their houses and beat the sheets into containers for their possessions. Others began to sell off their camels and goats, herds patiently rebuilt to replace those lost during the exodus.

In the refugee camps, among Sahrawi nationalists inside the territory and indeed among foreign powers providing diplomatic support for self-determination, the prospect of a vote on the future of the Western Sahara looked brighter because of a beacon many thousands of miles away. In August 1999, the people of an East Timor ravaged by Indonesian militias and security forces finally went to the ballot box in their own referendum on self-determination after two decades of an occupation Jakarta had sworn would never end. Three days before the Timorese vote, the president of the East Timorese National Resistance Council, Xanana Gusmao, sent a message of support to the tenth Polisario congress, one of many dispatched over the years.

It would not be until the meeting in Berlin in September 2000 that Rabat made clear that it would not permit a referendum it could not be sure of winning, but the decision was taken in 1999. According to an Algerian diplomatic source, informal sounding out of Algeria and Polisario about autonomy began in 1999. Other reports suggest the frustration of the voter registration had brought 'third way' ideas out of the woodwork even earlier. Ironically, it may be that the death of the architect of the occupation of the Western Sahara sealed the issue, removing the last hopes that occupation could be reversed by referendum – Hassan II had the prestige at home to declare a 'peace of the brave' but his untested son did not. A report to the French Senate in October[4] clearly came out against a 'winner takes all' end to the conflict, while the government in Paris was doing all it could to shore up Mohamed VI with high-level visits and plans for formal military cooperation.

And by the autumn of 1999, shoring up was what Mohamed VI needed. To the overall crisis of succession was added an explosion of protest in the Western Sahara. The national question aside, for the new king there was the danger of Sahrawi discontent contaminating Morocco's impoverished population, bringing on to the streets the crowds that threw the country into riot and repression in 1984.

There had been protests in the first half of the year.[5] In late February and March there was trouble between Sahrawi and Moroccan students at Souissi 1 university campus in Rabat. Sahrawi students in Casablanca, Marrakesh and Agadir staged solidarity actions. Then on May Day in Casablanca, Sahrawis carried banners calling for justice for the Disappeared and other Sahrawi prisoners. A few days later, postgraduate Sahrawis threatened a strike over unpaid bursaries. In June a small group of Sahrawi graduates demanding jobs was broken up in Laayoune.

Participants in the later events agree that increased activism among Sahrawi university students provided the impetus for the upsurge in protests inside the territory. That activism was made possible by two factors. First, after the experience of seeing a generation of senior school students deprived of higher education and moved to take up purported jobs in Morocco, Sahrawis had determined to secure university places, and the Rabat authorities, in a change of policy, facilitated this as a means of integration. Numbers built rapidly: in 2003 there were 800 Sahrawi students at university in Rabat alone and greater numbers in Marrakesh and, particularly, Agadir, where they numbered several thousand. That gave them the mass they needed to organise and protest. A student organiser in Rabat estimated that up to 50 per cent of Sahrawi students participated to some degree in activities. Second, the relatively more liberal atmosphere of Moroccan university life, as compared with daily life in Laayoune or Smara, provided space for organisation around social issues. Later human rights issues would be raised and by 2003 explicitly political images and slogans were beginning to appear, as was evident at a three-day series of events organised at Agadir. In the universities, Sahrawi students again came into contact with the left-wing Moroccan group Ila el amam, with which some of Polisario's founders had been involved three decades earlier, while their social and human rights-related demands have also attracted the interest of a wider constituency of the Moroccan student body.

It was September when things flared in Laayoune. As usual, the protests were peaceful and targeted social and economic discrimination.[6] On 10 September some forty students began a sit-in protest outside the administrative headquarters in Laayoune. After a few days former Bou Craa mine workers joined them, along with groups of unemployed, representatives of professional associations and of disabled Sahrawis, some two hundred people in all.

After almost a fortnight, riot police, having prevented food from reaching the protestors, surrounded the encampment and attacked it under cover of dark. By all accounts it was a bloody affair with over sixty demonstrators injured, half of them seriously and one believed killed. Some managed to escape to hospitals only to find the doors barred to them. Others were arrested and others dumped in the desert.

The initial sit-in had been organised. What followed had not. Indeed it was the very spontaneity of the Sahrawi population that forced activists to begin thinking about how to take things forward as they realised to their regret that they had no mechanism by which to harness the popular energy that had been unleashed.

Four days later, youths staged a demonstration march around Laayoune, with some splitting off and attacking commercial property. Students returned to the administrative headquarters to protest against the attack on the protestors' encampment. Three days and nights of clashes commenced. Initially the violence was centred around the poor Sahrawi areas of Maatallah and Moulay R'chid but also, worryingly for the authorities, around the sprawling Wahda camp, enforced home to the very people Rabat hoped would win the referendum for it. At times, the police were forced back under a hail of stones and Molotovs.

By 28 September the security forces had regained control; in order to maintain it they adopted a new tactic. They recruited settlers from a lawless quarter of the town to put down the Sahrawis. The reprisals were drawn out and vicious, with security forces aided by settlers rampaging through Sahrawi areas.

The repression of the Laayoune demonstrations sparked protests among Sahrawi students in Marrakesh, Casablanca and Agadir. Some three hundred youths staged a sit-down protest outside the government buildings in Tan Tan. Then, at the end of October, clashes resumed in Laayoune over a period of days with up to one hundred arrests made. Property was damaged and individuals deemed to be collaborators with the Moroccan authorities attacked. There were more solidarity protests throughout the autumn inside southern Morocco, suggesting that the unrest was spreading. Inside the occupied territories the major towns were under sporadic curfew and the security-force presence was overwhelming.

The events of September and October were dramatic but just as important was the evidence of support for the people of Laayoune from the Sahrawi population of southern Morocco and the network of Sahrawi students and others inside Morocco. The pace of violent confrontation with the authorities was clearly unsustainable but it brought forth a long and continuing stream of protests. For example, in late February 2000, students organised marches in solidarity with political detainees; in Smara a sit-in demanding jobs and better working conditions as well as the release of political prisoners began on

21 February and ended in a riot in which a number of demonstrators and police were injured; in early March in Laayoune a school students' march in solidarity with Sahrawi students in Morocco and calling for the release of prisoners ended in a confrontation.

Rabat's reaction to events in the Western Sahara was schizophrenic, highlighting the uncertainties of power post-Hassan II. On the one hand there were the beatings, the arrests, curfews, unleashing of the worst elements among the settlers. On the other was a more conciliatory approach that sought to calm rather than crush. For many Sahrawi nationalists this was just a 'soft cop, hard cop' ploy, for others a demonstration that after the death of Hassan II the rigid power structure in the Moroccan establishment was fracturing into competing fiefdoms.

Some observers saw it as an expression of the struggle within Rabat between the old guard of Hassan II's interior minister Driss Basri and Mohamed VI and his advisors. According to the French daily *Libération*,[7] containment of the Western Sahara was at the heart of talks between President Chirac and the young king that October. The idea was to increase Sahrawi representation in local government, reduce social inequalities between Sahrawi and Moroccan in the territory and so, in theory, avoid a repetition of the uprising. By November the decision had been taken to rejuvenate the Royal Consultative Council on Saharan Affairs, which over the last eighteen years had become 'a springboard for tribal notables to become members of the local makhzen'.[8]

In November 1999, *Jeune Afrique l'Intelligent* devoted several thousand words to a diary of Driss Basri's fall from grace, largely played out through his ousting and that of many of his placemen from control of the Western Sahara.[9]

In late September 1999 a royal commission was announced to follow Saharan affairs. Local representatives would sit alongside military and civil appointees. Basri was on the commission but alongside military men not answerable to him. The commission sat in Laayoune on 3 November and there Basri shuffled his papers while the chairman – once a role Basri would have assumed automatically – publicly regretted the 'errors' committed by the security forces in the previous weeks and spoke of the need to hold to account those responsible. Less than a week later Basri was dismissed.

The commission continued its work, listening to the complaints of Sahrawis about the repression of their protests and their social conditions. Several commanders of the security forces were transferred, units were withdrawn (but replaced). Some of the students' demands were met – free transport and supplementary loans – although four years later students said these concessions were being clawed back. Some sentences of those convicted after demonstrations were reduced. In December, plans to employ some 1,200 unemployed Sahrawi graduates were announced as part of a major new job creation scheme.[10] Requests for access to tiny percentages of the export earnings from Bou Craa to set up projects for the unemployed were rejected.

Driss Basri's fall from grace left in place many of his creatures, and their influence has probably been an important determinant in the day-to-day control exerted over the population. It may even be that the wave of repression of 2002 was their riposte to events of 1999, a reassertion of power.

But certainly there were changes of personnel. For instance, pushed to the fore was Hamid Chabar, appointed as point man in relations with the UN force on the ground, Minurso, and a senior man in the administration of the Western Sahara. Educated at Louvain University in Belgium, he is a convinced advocate of the development and democracy model for the territory:

> Since the accession of Mohamed VI we have initiated a new
> approach of which I am a symbol. This new approach consists
> of broadening democratic space and space of public liberty. We
> are determined to go forward with this. We are part of the new
> king's view that democracy is the future of Morocco.... We are
> determined to establish real democracy, to be a model for Arab
> countries.[11]

Moroccan officials and Sahrawi supporters of integration with Morocco point to the presence of Sahrawi members of parliament. There is, for example, Ali Salem Chagaf, the youthful member for Dakhla, who claims that to allow the Sahrawis to rule themselves would be to invite tribal warfare, adding that as a member of the Ould Delim he would never consent to be ruled by a Reguibat.

'Moroccan democracy is interesting for us because it may allow us self-determination', said a nationalist activist in Laayoune in

April 2002, his remark caveated by his companions' remarks that greater political freedom in Morocco was not being replicated in the Western Sahara whatever the official rhetoric of development and democracy.[12] Continuing harassment and limitation of organisations without clear Moroccan sponsorship, and the decision to deal with unrest as criminal activity stemming from economic conditions, point to a policy of tight control of Sahrawi society rather than its elimination.

Yet there was a dynamic relationship between the wave of protests in 1999, with the following creation of Sahrawi activist networks, and the change of control in Rabat. Even if reform was on the agenda of the new king, the prime minister and a layer of younger technocrats, the events that began in September 1999 certainly forced the pace of change, however modest. That in itself proved the Sahrawis could have some political influence. The release of Daddach and other political prisoners two years later seemed to make the same point – even if Mohamed VI had other reasons to continue the clearing out of his father's dungeons, the reality was that the releases came after Sahrawis organised and campaigned for them.

What 1999 did was reformulate the challenge to both sides. To Morocco it was restated as a question of whether Sahrawi discontent could be bought off with development and a democratisation that nonetheless ruled out of bounds the issue of national identity. To nationalist Sahrawis it posed the question of what their role could or should be. In 1975 virtually the entire Polisario cadre decamped to Tindouf. Those who remained were quickly picked up by Moroccan security forces, allegedly using lists provided by the Spanish government. The Sahrawis in the territory were left without a local nationalist leadership. Given the extent of the repression, Polisario was unable to organise that population and decided instead to simply give permission to whatever autonomous activity small, unconnected groups could organise while concentrating on the military and diplomatic battles waged out of Tindouf. The activists of 1999 are still confronting the downsides of this survival strategy.

Among those downsides is a lack of self-confidence among seasoned activists, who worry about not having a local leadership to guide them and are as yet unwilling to assume that role themselves. Daddach is a revered figure who represents the historic conscience of the nationalist struggle, but after decades of imprisonment and isolation he cannot be expected to formulate new strategies for new times. Tamek is of a younger generation and is talked of as being a charismatic leader. His arrest was a major factor in derailing a move to stand four Sahrawi activists in Laayoune and Assa in the Moroccan parliamentary elections of September 2002, piggybacking on the list of a Moroccan leftist party. (Tamek was detained as he tried to lodge his candidacy papers.) Another of the downsides is that the lack of structure to low-level nationalist expression has disenfranchised the ordinary Sahrawi. They have had no way to connect to the struggle. A school student interviewed in Laayoune exemplifies this. He talked of minor acts of rebellion at school, of persuading Moroccan friends of the justice of the Sahrawi cause, but said there was little more open for him to do. He saw no means to confront the discrimination of everyday life of which he complained and so aspired to emigration.

The project of building Sahrawi civil society, in the eyes of its proponents, is aimed at addressing these two problems and at breaking the climate of fear. Self-organisation will throw up cadres, and at the same time will provide channels of activity for the Sahrawi population in general, whether schoolboys forced to contemplate a life of exile or the crowds who, to the surprise of committed militants, took to the streets in 1999. In the spring of 2003, activists were continuing the painstaking task of building and linking networks after a string of setbacks in 2002, including renunciation of the Sahrawi section of the Truth and Justice Forum by its Moroccan sponsoring organisation and closure of an association of the unemployed that claimed a membership of 700. The section of the Forum was being reconstituted; there was a move to establish a new Sahrawi human rights organisation with no ties to Moroccan counterparts; and victims of landmines were about to constitute themselves formally into a group. As if in response, in mid-March three members of the Forum section arrested the previous September were jailed for ten years, the most severe sentences handed down since 1999.

The activist nuclei expounding the civil society project see themselves pursuing a parallel course to that of Polisario. Their political orientation is nationalist and they do not believe that the Sahrawis can live freely under Moroccan rule. For instance, a former activist with the association of the unemployed remarked that job discrimination would only end when the Western Sahara was independent. But while Polisario does have its agents inside the territory and some may work in the emerging groups, the stratum of activists is not Polisario-run or Polisario-inspired in the way that, say, Palestinian organisations in the West Bank and Gaza in the 1980s were fronts for PLO factions. Indeed, there is an implicit recognition in some activist circles that building Sahrawi civil society will help to compensate for some of the shortfalls of Polisario. One former prisoner and current activist remarked that the leadership of Polisario has devoted itself – through need – to military and diplomatic struggle but its skills may well not extend to building a society or a state in an independent Western Sahara.

It was incumbent on the minister in Polisario's SADR government holding the occupied territories portfolio to assert that Polisario had expected an uprising and that it had been inspired by resolutions at the movement's congress. But he conceded that until the mid-1990s the portfolio had been inactive and it was only after the events of 1999 that attention had really been turned on the territories. Other senior members more candidly admitted they were as surprised as anyone by the upsurge of unrest. Since then links between the political activists in the occupied territories and Polisario outside have increased, 'from the carrier pigeon to the Internet'.[13] Polisario leader Mohamed Abdelaziz is well informed about a number of activists inside the occupied territories. Tamek was even telephone-interviewed from his prison cell by Polisario's radio station.

Polisario cannot and will not dictate the activities of the civil society movement inside the Western Sahara and, indeed, for it try to limit the autonomy of its compatriots would probably cause the movement severe harm.

Abdelaziz said in an interview for this book:

> What we have seen in the Sahrawi struggle in the occupied territories and even inside Morocco gives the Sahrawi struggle a new dimension, even though it is a very low, very simple struggle. What is happening now makes it impossible for anyone to blockade the struggle. So, nowadays we can say our struggle is inside and outside. What happens there and here provides guarantees our struggle will continue.[14]

For Polisario, the events of 1999 and since have shifted focus from the war of position in the UN Security Council and the stasis in the refugee camps. But the movement still views the activity inside the territory as defensive – protesting against Moroccan abuses – and not politically oriented enough to be able to take the lead in the struggle. According to the minister for the occupied territories,[15] an important role that can be carried out by activists in the territories and inside Morocco is to link up with Moroccan trade-union and student organisations, to 'infect Moroccans' and encourage them to struggle against their own government. This chimes with the broader Polisario strategy that re-emerged after Hassan II's death of persuading the international community that Morocco is dangerously unstable.

At the same time, the minister said Polisario would not encourage violent action such as that taken occasionally by groups of masked youths in Laayoune. While frustration might increasingly breed frustration that could express itself violently or in the growth of Islamism inside the Western Sahara, Polisario advocated peaceful political struggle against the occupation, he said.

Notes

1. Interview with the author, October 2002.
2. See for example, Abdeslam Maghraoui, 'Political Authority in Crisis', *Middle East Reports* (Merip) 218, Spring 2001.
3. Interview with the author, November 2002.
4. Rapport d'information, French Senate, 30 September to 3 October 1999.
5. Weekly reports, www.arso.org; and Sahrawi Press Service.
6. The following account of events draws on interviews by the author with participants as well as reports carried by ARSO and SPS, a report by the Moroccan human rights organisation OMDH and Ahmed R. Benchemsi, 'Tout commence par un sit-in, place Dcheira…', *Jeune Afrique l'Intelligent*, 19 October 1999.
7. Jose Garcon, 'Chirac soutien de la transition marocaine', *Libération*, 30 October 1999.
8. Ahmed R. Benchemsi, 'Mohammed VI et la logique securitaire', *Jeune Afrique l'Intelligent*, 2 November 1999.
9. Ahmed R. Benchemsi, 'La longue descente aux enfers de Si Driss', *Jeune Afrique l'Intelligent*, 16 November 1999.
10. *Libération*, 7 December 1999.

11. Interview with the author, 20 April 2002.
12. Interviews with the author, April 2002.
13. Mustapha Mohamed Ali Sidi Bachir, SADR minister for the occupied territories, interviewed by the author, 12 June 2003.
14. Interview with the author at Rabbouni, 13 June 2003.
15. Interview with the author in Smara camp, 12 June 2003.

9

Zero-Sum Game:
The Western Sahara and
the UN Process

Braheem's father is in his sixties. He can point out the first house built in Laayoune, and the second and third, because he predates them. The nearest town was Tarfaya, over a hundred miles to the north. The first contact he remembers with the Spanish was trading for sugar and clothing. Then they hired camels and drivers to move supplies to the site that became Laayoune. Years later, as pressure from Polisario attacks built up to the extent that Spaniards could not move around without Sahrawi companions, and international pressure to decolonise grew, he expected the Western Sahara to gain first autonomy under Madrid and then independence.

Reminiscing to his sons and to visitors, he says he had no inkling that Spain would hand the Western Sahara to Morocco and Mauritania. His contact with his northern neighbours was minimal, first when his father took him to Tarfaya and later when a small detachment of Moroccan troops in the Spanish forces was transferred from the Ifni enclave to the Western Sahara.

Braheem well remembers being told by his parents to remain very quiet as he watched armed men move into Laayoune – his first contact with Morocco. For this family, international politicking delivered them from the hands of one set of strangers to another.

The Western Sahara – then the Spanish Sahara – was fed to the wheels of the UN machine in 1964 when the committee on de-colonisation first determined that the right of self-determination applied to the people of the territory. Under the terms of General

Assembly resolution 1514 of 1960, they could opt for an independent state, association with an independent state or integration with an independent state.[1]

The next year, a General Assembly resolution called on Spain to begin the process of decolonisation in the Sahara and in the enclave of Ifni to the north. Another year on and another resolution, this time asking Spain, in consultation with neighbouring countries, to make arrangements for a referendum of self-determination. Importantly in the light of future events, the resolution specified that only native inhabitants should participate. And, ironically, given Rabat's manoeuvring three decades later, Rezette, who argued the case for integration with Morocco, wondered, 'Wouldn't there be a massive rush of the populations of adjacent powers toward the Western Sahara to influence the results of the referendum?'[2]

The resolutions were solemnly recalled every year. Ifni dropped out of the text from 1969 because Spain had returned it to Morocco. In 1973, the year Polisario was founded and began its military campaign against Spain, a new tone was injected, saying the current situation threatened the stability of the subregion, expressing solidarity with the people of the territory, and discouraging investment just as Madrid was developing the Bou Craa phosphate mine.

In Madrid it was clear which way the wind was blowing. The major colonial powers were well on the way to divesting themselves of their colonies and establishing new political and economic relationships. The era of the Iberian dictators was also drawing to an end. In 1974, the Portugese Revolution would result in a hurried withdrawal from African colonies that bequeathed, in the cases of Angola and Mozambique, years of carnage. Franco's days were clearly numbered and Spain would have more to worry about than overseas possessions, hitherto held more for prestige than real profit. (Ironically, the potential for making Western Sahara a profitable possession was just being realised with the development of the Bou Craa phospate deposits.)

In August 1974, Madrid informed the UN it would conduct a census in the Western Sahara, ahead of a referendum to be held in 1975. The census was carried out but only of Sahrawis within the territory. It excluded the thousands who had fled repression after an armed uprising in 1957. Often they had gone to the Tarfaya Strip (handed to Morocco by Spain in 1958) and surrounding areas but some went to Tindouf, forerunners of the tens of thousands who would follow. As the UN Mission of 1975 would discover, there were widely differing estimates of how many refugees lived where, but assessments ranged into the tens of thousands. The flaw in the scope of the 1974 census would be crucial in later arguments.

Madrid's intention had been to devolve powers to a reconstituted local assembly in the territory and nurture selected political forces in the territory with a view to securing a friendly and amenable government in an independent Western Sahara. The referendum never happened.

Morocco failed in initial attempts to secure the handover of the territory in return for military bases and a share of mineral and fishing wealth. Hassan II then resorted to thinly veiled threats and said Morocco would not accept a referendum that included the option of independence. Spain put troops on alert and war looked likely. But in September 1974, Hassan II said he would go to the International Court of Justice for a ruling on Morocco's claims of sovereignty to the Western Sahara, thus delaying the referendum. Mauritania then announced it would also go to the ICJ to test its own claims.

The nub of the Moroccan argument was that it had been able over the centuries before Spanish colonisation (taken as 1884 by the court) to appoint officials, obtain pledges of fealty and gather taxes from communities in the territory, as well as coordinate resistance to foreign penetration. It argued that its sovereignty was demonstrated in these ties between communities and the Moroccan Crown, rather than on notions of territory. These ties reflected the special (quasi-religious) nature of the Moroccan monarchy and state. Additionally, it was argued that a number of treaties signed with foreign powers demonstrated the latter's acceptance of Moroccan sovereignty as far south as Cape Boujdour. For its part, Mauritania argued that the Sahrawis fell within the Bilad Chinguetti, a nation or people closely tied by language, race, religion and culture that had stretched from the Senegal river to the Wadi Saguiet el Hamra prior to 1884.

In October 1975 the court rejected both claims to sovereignty.[3] The Western Sahara had not been *terra nullius* (land belonging to no organised society) prior to the declaration of the Spanish protectorate over the Rio de Oro and had not been treated as such by Spain. But Morocco could not demonstrate that it had displayed effective and exclusive state activity in the Western Sahara. There was evidence of legal ties of allegiance between the Sultan and some of the people of the territory through the *caids*, or leaders of the Tekna tribal grouping, but that was it. So far as Mauritania went, the court recognised legal ties 'which knew no frontier' between people living in what became Mauritania and the Western Sahara. It also recognised the cultural ties but declared that the Mauritanian entity at the time of colonisation of the Western Sahara had no 'corporate' identity.

Joffe has argued that the case for Morocco (and that for Mauritania) was bound to fail 'because the underlying principles of the Moroccan case could not and did not coincide with those of territorial sovereignty under the precepts of international law'.[4] Morocco was trying to describe a historical situation under Islamic law, based on notions of community not on the notions of territory that international law relies on. This same jarring of historical notions of sovereignty and those derived from the colonial era were behind Morocco objecting to the Organisation of African Unity's declaration of the principle of inviolability of inherited borders.

While the ICJ deliberated, the UN had dispatched a mission to the territory to review progress towards decolonisation. Its report was published one day before the ICJ opinion. It pronounced the explicit and much-quoted view that 'the majority of the population within the Spanish Sahara was manifestly in favour of independence'.[5]

The mission clarified the attitudes of the various actors towards the proposed referendum. Polisario, clearly the ascendant political force in the territory in the view of the Mission members, said a referendum was unnecessary but if one was held it should be under UN auspices after a Spanish withdrawal and the return of refugees. The question – ambiguously – would be, 'Do you wish to be free or remain under Spanish rule?'[6] A Spanish-sponsored grouping, PUNS, wanted voters to be asked if they wanted independence or not. If they declined, there should be another vote to determine what they wanted. Morocco said it would only countenance a referendum that followed a Spanish withdrawal and asked, 'Do you want to remain under the authority of Spain or to rejoin Morocco?'[7] In words redolent of Sahrawi nationalists in the following years, the Moroccan government questioned how a fair referendum could be held under a military occupation in a territory with a tame local government.

Yet it was Spain's comments to the Mission that signalled what was to happen. Madrid was becoming more and more rattled. With the delay to its referendum plans, the struggle between the various political elements in the territory had become more intense and threatened to become violent. The military threat from Polisario was growing and tension on the border with Morocco was increasing. 'If the situation on the border deteriorated, or if internal opposition to its continued presence … became such that it could no longer administer the territory … the Spanish government might consider withdrawing completely from the territory without waiting for the referendum.'[8] As these views had been expressed in May 1975, it is inconceivable that Rabat had not divined them by October, encouraging Hassan II to increase the pressure.

That is exactly what he did do. Within hours of the ICJ report being published, Hassan II turned reality on its head and declared the opinion to vindicate Morocco's claim to sovereignty and announced the recruitment of 350,000 of his subjects who would stage a Green March across the border into the Western Sahara, a project that had been under preparation for weeks or months.

Initially, Spain looked set to resist Morocco. Indeed, there were meetings with Polisario to prepare for Western Saharan independence. Polisario leaders travelled to Laayoune to prepare for government, according to Hodges.[9] PUNS joined Polisario in declaring it would resist Morocco. But then Franco's health failed for what would prove to be the last time and Madrid's resolve weakened. Within days Spanish–Moroccan–Mauritanian talks began, first to find a way to accommodate the Green March without bloodshed and then on the terms of capitulation. Even as the UN tried to cobble together a team of civil servants and peacekeepers, a Spanish evacuation programme got under way and Moroccan troops, harassed by Polisario fighters, began to move across the border to the east of Tarfaya where the multitudes were regimented for a Green March that would prove to be no more than symbolic. Tripartite talks continued in November as Franco's health deteriorated and the Spanish government agreed to partition the Western Sahara between Morocco and Mauritania. Ostensibly, this was for a three-month interim period, but the only provision made for self-determination by the Sahrawis was a vote by the local assembly of tribal leaders. A rump of this *jema'a* was convened in Laayoune by Morocco to ratify the so-called Madrid Accords. Many members were absent and a second vote was taken when some voted against ratification.[10]

Under the terms agreed, Spain would retain a large stake in the Bou Craa phosphate project, sign a fishing accord, and gain the right to establish three military bases in the Western Sahara. Morocco would soft-pedal its claims to the *presidios* on its Mediterranean coast and cut supplies to Gibraltar.[11]

Sixteen years of war between Polisario and Morocco had begun. Mauritania would soon prove incapable of withstanding the pressures of the conflict. Polisario declared the formation of the Sahrawi Arab Democratic Republic on 27 February 1976 and progressively built up the number of states that recognised it to between seventy and eighty, while Morocco's sovereignty over the Western Sahara was not formally recognised by a single country. UN votes came and went but the focus of diplomacy shifted largely to the Organisation of African Unity (now the African Union).

Hassan II feigned dismissiveness of the diplomatic advances made by the SADR in Africa, yet in 1981 it was at an OAU summit in Nairobi that he effected the clever move of calling for a ceasefire followed by a referendum under international supervision. Morocco's isolation in Africa had become more and more evident since 1976 when the OAU's Liberation Committee recognised Polisario as a liberation movement. Morocco (and Mauritania) resisted the pressure for a while but once the war had brought the downfall of the government in Nouakchott, the need to address the issue was clear. A five-member committee of heads of state was established. After sending a delegation to the subregion, it called for a ceasefire and a referendum of self-determination offering independence or main-tenance of the status quo. Rabat continued to resist but concern was growing among its allies, and both Paris and Washington applied pressure on the king to bend with the wind.[12]

A twelve-point plan was drawn up by the OAU, allowing for confinement of Moroccan troops, international peacekeeping, prisoner releases, return of refugees and so forth. The question to be put to voters would be whether they wanted integration with Morocco or independence. Morocco accepted the plan but Hassan II went on to say he expected the referendum to approve integration, characterising it more as an act of confirmation than of self-determination.

Argument broke out over the positioning of troops, with Algeria maintaining that Moroccan forces should be withdrawn, pointing out that Rabat held the same view vis-à-vis Spanish forces in 1974. As voters, Polisario fighters should remain in the territory, said Algiers. On 10 February 1982, the seven-member heads of state committee of the OAU dealing with Western Sahara met to iron out details. Twelve days later an OAU committee meeting accepted the SADR as a member of the organisation. The Moroccan delegation walked out with allies from nineteen other states.

The dispute meant the next summit, planned for later that year, was postponed and could only take place in 1983 when the SADR agreed not to attend. But a new resolution was passed, approving the peace plan but calling for direct negotiations between the parties, something Hassan II rejected. In November 1984 the SADR was formally admitted to the OAU and again Morocco walked out, arguing that the admittance of the putative state had not been voted in the assembly and suggesting, with some logic, that the move prejudged the results of a referendum the OAU was supposed to be supervising.

The OAU push for a referendum to bring about a settlement was not the only game in town. According to diplomatic sources, Algeria had made advances in 1982 but they foundered. In 1984, Morocco rejected a union des états proposal. Later it also rejected a move to find a solution based on that found for New Caledonia. It was to be several years after Morocco stormed out of the OAU before there would be visible progress towards a resolution.

The Settlement Plan: from ceasefire to deadlock

On 6 September 1991 a ceasefire came into effect in the Western Sahara. A year after Namibia achieved independence, Africa's last non-self-governing territory looked to be moving towards a future of its own making. The UN dispatched its Mission for the Referendum in Western Sahara (Minurso) to supervise both the ceasefire and the referendum that was to follow in January 1992.

Between the guns being muzzled and the announcement of the result of the vote, Minurso was to identify eligible voters, using 1974 Spanish census data as a basis, supervise a withdrawal of all but 65,000 Moroccan troops, ensure Polisario units remained in designated areas, and organise a prisoner exchange. Then the refugees were to return from Tindouf, after which there would be three weeks of political campaigning, followed by voting over a period of several days on whether Western Sahara should become independent or integrate with Morocco.[13]

The Settlement Plan, under the auspices of the UN and the OAU, was five years in the negotiating. It was accepted in principle by Morocco and Polisario at the end of August 1988 after proximity talks in Geneva, and signed off by the Security Council at the end of April 1991.[14]

UN and OAU resolutions had called for direct negotiations between the parties to smooth the path of the referendum. Polisario was insistent on this, apparently seeing it as a way to discuss relations between a Sahrawi state and Morocco after a vote and, probably, to sweeten the talks with assurances of close ties and economic cooperation. Polisario hoped for an outcome similar to the Evian Accord that settled the terms of French withdrawal from Algeria.[15] Hassan II was reluctant, knowing it could bring further accusations of weakness from the major Moroccan political parties. But the air of rapprochement with Algeria as the Maghreb Arab Union was signed into being and the bilateral border settlement was ratified sweetened the atmosphere. In December 1998, Hassan II signalled in a French magazine interview his willingness to talk with Polisario members as Polisario members and not, as previously insisted, as Moroccan citizens.

In early January 1989, three senior members of Polisario met with Hassan II in Marrakesh. The meeting was significant although the two sides inevitably put very different spins on the talks. Morocco maintained the king had granted an audience and had simply listened to what Polisario had to say. Polisario said it was the start of negotiations and announced a one-month unilateral ceasefire[16] but made it clear that more meetings must follow.[17] Indeed, it was clear Polisario had expected another meeting in February. It did not happen, and by June Polisario fighters were back in action, attacking the berm near Amgal. Morocco refused to accept 200 prisoners of war released by Polisario, and the political and military climate deteriorated with the independence movement claiming to have launched seventy six attacks in September[18] alone.

Over the next weeks there were four major battles in the Guelta Zemmour, Hawza and Imgall sectors.[19] But no more talks ever took place with Hassan II, and Polisario had to settle for proximity talks and behind-the-scenes meetings between officials ahead of the Security Council's adoption of the Settlement Plan. In the same period, the movement suffered several high-level defections. Once signed, the ceasefire remained intact but the Settlement Plan, while cruelly raising the hopes of the refugee communities, became what one of the regular UN Secretary General reports called 'a zero sum game'.[20] As the same report noted, 'each side felt it had to win since, owing to the nature of the agreement that the United Nations was trying to implement, the referendum would produce one winner and one loser and the stakes were therefore extremely high.'

In early 2000 the population inside the Western Sahara drew breath after a sustained period of protest. Activists galvanised new organisations and confidence grew that a referendum was doable and winnable. Even as the voice of the Sahrawi nationalists under Moroccan rule became louder, the last rites were being read over the referendum. In a glum assessment of the Settlement Plan and one of a number of precursors to the démarche planned to replace it, the February 2000 report of the secretary-general abandoned the increasingly farcical game of setting a target date for voting (2002 was the last date hazarded). 'The developments during the past nine years, and particularly over the last months, constitute a real source of concern and raise doubts about the possibility of achieving a smooth and consensual implementation of the settlement plan',[21] the report stated, adding that, 'if the result were not to be recognised and accepted by one party, it is worth noting that no enforcement mechanism is envisioned by the settlement plan, nor is one likely to be proposed, calling for the use of military means to effect enforcement.'

The latter point is very important. Not only was Kofi Annan saying the referendum looked impractical without a change of strategy by one of the players; he was also saying that if the vote did take place, its outcome could not be upheld. Given the imbalance of forces, the subtext was surely that he was conceding that Morocco could hold on to the Western Sahara if it lost the vote and there was no obvious likelihood of the UN doing anything to eject it. On the one level, this may be interpreted as a simple statement of fact – there is no provision for enforcement in the Settlement Plan. Or it could be a statement of legal nicety, the process of decolonisation falling under Chapter VI of the UN Charter, which deals with the pacific settlement of disputes and makes no provision for enforcement. In fact, the groundwork for this declaration had been laid at least as early as May 2000. Then, according to a source present at the time, the secretary-general's personal envoy, James Baker, had told Polisario and Algeria in London that 'Western Sahara is not Kuwait. There is no army going to go in.'

In the final paragraph of the February 2000 report, the secretary-general reached his conclusion and announced his intention to ask Baker 'to explore ways and means to achieve an early, durable and agreed resolution of their dispute, which would define their respective rights and obligations in Western Sahara'. That May, the Security Council announced its 'expectation' that the parties would offer not only concrete proposals to resolve the problems surrounding implementation of the Settlement Plan but also would 'explore all ways and means to achieve an early, durable and agreed resolution to their dispute'.[22] The meaning was clear to participants: the public project to ditch a referendum of the Sahrawi people, born in February, was baptised in May, having been conceived some time earlier, as will be seen.

The Security Council meeting in May was, by the admission of the US delegate, 'very difficult'.[23] Namibia voted against the resolution, with its delegate saying, 'My delegation cannot endorse observations which seek to diverge from the United Nations settlement plan.'[24] The Netherlands expressed reservations and Jamaica and Mali abstained in the vote. By contrast, the US was evidently clearing the decks for the new project, arguing for the secretary-general and his envoy to have 'full leeway and authority to work with the parties ... in order to find ways that are acceptable to the parties – and I stress the need for such acceptance – to peacefully resolve their dispute'.[25]

The frustrations and the costs (way in excess of the originally budgeted $200 million, substantially diluted from initial assessments) of the Minurso operation and the wider process of the Settlement Plan show through in the succession of reports to the Security Council. And sometimes the human costs of the 'zero-sum game' have been reflected in the documents. As one of them reminded the council:

> Twenty-six long years have elapsed since the outbreak of this conflict. It took five years to negotiate the United Nations settlement proposals and plan and 10 more years to try to implement that plan. In the meantime, an entire new generation of Saharan refugees was born and grew up in the Tindouf camps, while many among the first generation have already died without being able to return home.[26]

A litany of disputes racked the Settlement Plan process from the start. Marrack Goulding, one of the senior UN Secretariat figures of the time, paints a picture of diplomatic duplicity, bureaucratic incompetence and grudge fights paving the way for delay and failure.[27] Months before the ceasefire came into effect and shortly after Minurso was formed in April 1991 there was a major disagreement over where Polisario fighters would be located during the transitional period. This issue was not resolved for another six years. The issue of prisoner exchanges was never resolved. Though some 1,300 had been released over the years, over 900 Moroccan prisoners of war were still held by Polisario after a September 2003 handover, while Morocco continued to deny knowledge of disappeared Sahrawis.[28] A pilot project to return some refugees was not implemented, 'because of the concerns expressed by the Government of Morocco'.[29]

However, far and away the most fundamental problem lay in disagreements over the electoral base. From the point at which the Settlement Plan was agreed until 2000, both Morocco and Polisario insisted on the 'winner takes all' formula for the referendum, independence or integration, although both insisted at various times that they were open-minded on ways to ensure the pill was sweetened for the loser. Morocco said at times it would consider taking Polisario leaders into government if they accepted Moroccan sovereignty, and Polisario representatives talked of an independent Western Sahara granting long-term economic concessions to Morocco. But for both sides the non-negotiable issue remained determination of sovereignty and both sides believed they would win. Hassan II had said as far back as 1981, when he proposed a referendum at an OAU summit, that he was convinced a vote would go in favour of integration.[30]

Yet just as historic, fluid communitarian understandings of allegiance and colonially imposed, territorially based notions of statehood created a mismatch of perceptions of the Western Sahara's place in the world, so the nomadic and essentially borderless inheritance of the Sahrawis, plus the legacy of Spanish and French military repression, meant there were very different ideas about who should have the right to vote. And both sides thought they knew that the composition of the electorate would determine the result. In consequence, both fought tooth and nail to influence the roll.

At the outset of the Settlement Plan, Polisario had maintained that only the 74,000 people registered in the Spanish census should be eligible to vote. On the contrary, Morocco argued, there were many thousands of Sahrawis who were not included in the census and who should be allowed to vote. These included people in the territory at the time but not counted by the Spanish; people whose nomadic lifestyle had placed them outside the territory at the time of the census; refugees from the fighting of the late 1950s; and residents of the strip of Saharan territory that Spain had handed over to Morocco in the 1950s and 1960s and had been incorporated into southern Morocco.

Then UN secretary-general Javier Perez de Cuellar proposed a set of conditions of eligibility designed to bridge the gap, including family and residential links to the territory. Johannes Manz was so convinced Perez de Cuellar's methodology would corrupt the referendum process that he resigned as special representative to the secretary-general.[31] The US, too, 'felt his work was unacceptable' but was too taken up with Latin American affairs in the last days of Perez de Cuellar's term to address the issue and settled instead for the weakest of possible diplomatic acknowledgements of the recommendations, a 'welcome'.[32] Needless to say, Polisario was unconvinced by the set of conditions and the consequent deadlock was not broken until 1994, so voter identification did not begin until two years after the referendum was initially supposed to have taken place.

Just one year later the process was thrown back into crisis. The Rabat government announced its intention to present 100,000 residents from outside of the territory for identification as voters.[33] Polisario said it would suspend its participation in the identification process in protest at that and at the jailing of a group of Sahrawis by Morocco. A month later, Polisario leader Mohamed Abdelaziz complained of Moroccan attempts to insert a 'substitute population' into the electoral roll but seemed to agree to continue participation, and arrangements were made for some forty new identification centres to be set up inside Morocco. Again, Polisario's reservations were more than matched elsewhere. The US government had estimated the total number of voters to be around 80,000–85,000 and the UN had budgeted on those estimates. The Moroccan moves 'raised, as they say diplomatically, a problem'.[34]

Then, another month on, in August 1995, the issue of the 'contested tribes' caused Polisario to say it would not assist in the identification of persons from the Chorfa tribal grouping or the Tribus del Norte (Northern Tribes) and Tribus Costeras y del Sur (Southern and Coastal Tribes). Again, the movement's fear was that Morocco had identified a crack in the identification process and was levering it open to allow in people with little or no connection with the Western Sahara. The 1974 census identified eighty-eight tribal grouping categories. All but three of these related to specific groups but the remaining three caused the problem. They lumped together members of various miscellaneous tribal groups only sparsely represented in the territory. What Morocco wanted to do was allow all members of these tribal groups to apply to be voters, tens of thousands of people, comprising 50 per cent of all applicants from southern Morocco. Polisario argued that the plan clearly meant that only tribal subfractions the majority of whose members were resident in the territory at the time of the census could be voters, and the wider spread tribal communities were beyond consideration. It would, however, agree to the participation of individuals from these groupings who were included in the census and their immediate family.[35] Frank Ruddy, a former US ambassador who served as deputy chairman of the Identification Commission of Minurso in 1994, called Morocco's position 'another laughable attempt by Morocco to hold off the referendum'.[36]

On the ground in the Western Sahara, according to Ruddy, Morocco was doing all it could to ensure control of who was registered as a voter. The UN had allowed a system to develop whereby Sahrawis living under Moroccan rule had to register not with the UN but with the Moroccan authorities, who then 'lost' many registrations. Indeed, there were allegations of Minurso documentation being passed on to the Moroccan authorities from very early on.[37] Sahrawis were barred (as they still are) from direct contact with Minurso. The mission's headquarters in Laayoune is watched by Moroccan plainclothes security men who prevent anyone without accreditation from walking past the building, let alone entering. Requests for interviews with officials are met with lack of cooperation. During the process Sahrawis were only permitted to travel to registration centres in Moroccan security buses. On arrival they were filmed by Moroccan security agents and on departure had their registration receipts confiscated.[38] At the same time, a Polisario observer to the registration process recalls aged applicants unable to speak Hassaniya, confusing place names with tribe names, deeply troubled by being obliged to try to pass themselves off as Sahrawis during Ramadan, the holy month of Islam when lying is particularly shameful. Needless to say, Morocco has claimed that Polisario has pressured voters living in its jurisdiction, and official visitors to Laayoune are introduced to batches of tribal elders keen to vow allegiance to the Moroccan monarchy and accuse Polisario of holding the refugee population hostage.

By September 1996 the secretary-general had decided to engage in some brinkmanship of his own. The report of that month recommended the suspension of the identification process, withdrawal of associated staff, closure of offices, pullout of all but a handful of civilian police and a 20 per cent cut in the military component to 230 men. By this point some 60,000 voters had been identified.[39] But another 164,000 files awaited evaluation.

The delays were also fraying the nerves of the military. Polisario conducted live fire exercises in August. Morocco also carried out live fire exercises, re-equipped ammunition dumps, reorganised units on the berm and conducted air drills.[40] Resumption of hostilities looked possible. Polisario commanders had begun expressing the opinion that 'they would have no option but to return to war, since a ceasefire in the absence of a political agreement acted to their disadvantage'.[41] That fear that idle time is a powerful ally of Morocco has dogged Sahrawi nationalists ever since.

In 1997 a new vitality appeared to be injected into the Settlement Plan process. There was general surprise that Washington appeared to have moved the Western Sahara up its priority list with the nomination of former secretary of state James Baker as personal envoy to Kofi Annan. The general expectation had been that the job would go to a much less prestigious figure. Polisario and Algeria believed the appointment meant the US would put its weight behind implementation of the referendum.

Mr Baker declined to be interviewed about the Western Sahara while still in post, but there are at least two competing accounts of his expectations of the parties when he came to the job. The first is that he accepted the assurances of Morocco and Polisario that they were both fully committed to the Settlement Plan and to the simple formulation of the question to be put to the voters,[42] and he proceeded to do his best to further the process through a series of face-to-face meetings between the two sides. The other account is that he accepted the job having been persuaded that Algeria was ready to pressure Polisario into a compromise. Algiers did not then make the expected move (although in the following two years there were rumours it was about to dilute its support for Polisario), spawning a further suspicion that its renowned diplomats had lured Baker into the post in order to raise the profile of the conflict on the international stage. Certainly, Baker was encouraged to think by Kofi Annan that a solution other than those proposed by the Settlement Plan should be sought. Goulding says that his penultimate task in the UN Secretariat was to go to Houston for Kofi Annan, 'to persuade James Baker III to accept an appointment as special representative and try to negotiate a deal based on enhanced autonomy for Western Sahara within the Kingdom of Morocco'.[43] But Goulding also said in correspondence with the author that 'I don't recall that Mr Baker was led, by me or anyone else, to believe that Polisario or Algeria had given any indication that they might accept an enhanced autonomy solution.'

A March 1997 letter from the UN secretary-general to Baker as the latter was being wooed into post at the very least blurs the focus of the mission and could be construed as dangerously undermining the integrity of the Settlement Plan by demonstrating a less than wholehearted commitment to its implementation. The letter states: 'if ... you judged that there was an alternative and more promising possibility, you would endeavour to negotiate a deal on that basis either through direct negotiations or, more probably, through shuttle diplomacy.'[44]

Confusion over whether a 'third way' had already been part-brokered or was the desired outcome of his boss may explain why Baker, on his initial meetings with the parties, asked each repeatedly whether they were committed to the winner-takes-all formula. Both said they were. In any event, Baker did force the pace after the years of stagnation when the UN was headed up by Boutros Boutros-Ghali. Direct, UN-brokered talks between the parties had been envisaged when the plan was being drawn up but had not taken place. In London in June 1997 he told representatives of Polisario, Morocco, Algeria and Mauritania that he wanted the first two to hold direct talks, with the last couple as observers. That meeting took place two weeks later in Lisbon, and Baker submitted a proposal to break the deadlock over voter identification. A month later there was a second round of talks in London where a deal was reached on that issue and on preparations for a return of refugees. More talks then took place in Lisbon, again at the end of August where troop containment and prisoner releases were discussed along with a code of conduct for the referendum campaign.

With the process looking firmly back on track, a fourth round of talks was held in mid-September in Houston. The location – Baker's home base – was seen as a sign that he, personally, expected the talks to succeed. It was also thought to signal that Washington was watching closely – after all, two former assistant secretaries of state were working with Baker at this point – and neither side would wish to embarrass the US by provoking a failure on its turf.

The Houston meeting produced an agreed code of conduct for the campaigning period, guaranteeing freedom of expression and movement, assuring equal access to radio broadcasts, detailing the permissioning of rallies, in sum detailing all the paraphernalia of a free and fair referendum. Furthermore, as the agreement was that nothing was agreed until everything was agreed and Houston dealt with the last outstanding issues, with the deal done there the whole process was back on the road – or so it looked.

Gone was the gloom from the September report to the Security Council, which referred to the 'goodwill and spirit of cooperation shown during the talks'.[45] Identification was to restart with a view to a vote taking place 'within a year'. The compromise on the 'contested tribes' was that Morocco would not sponsor anyone from the groupings apart from individuals on the census list and their immediate kin. At the same time there would be no barrier to anyone from these groupings putting themselves forward for assessment. The UN High Commission for Refugees would begin work to prepare for repatriation of refugees. The location of Polisario fighters during the transition period was settled and both sides said they would release prisoners.[46]

Identification resumed in December involving 130 Minurso personnel, 60 observers from Morocco and Polisario (ferried weekly between Tindouf and Morocco), and 160 tribal leaders nominated by the two sides as expert witnesses for or against candidate voters.[47]

The first phase of the identification process – excluding the 'contested tribes' – produced 46,255 eligible voters in the Western Sahara and Morocco, 33,786 in the Tindouf area and another 4,210 in Mauritania, a total close to the initial US estimates adopted by the UN. But Morocco's attempt to widen the electoral base and increase the number of voters living under its rule did not stop. While a second phase of the process assessed applicants from the 'contested tribes', no fewer than 79,125 appeals were lodged. That is to say, the number of appeals amounted to 94 per cent of the number of certified voters. Of these, 95 per cent were from areas under Moroccan rule and only 5 per cent from the camps and from Mauritania. Some 63,000 of the 65,000 that were appeals against exclusion were from areas under Moroccan rule and almost all appellants intended to present witnesses to support their cases. It would take 10–12 months for a beefed-up Minurso to assess the appeals.[48] The workload and expense this implied for Minurso was daunting and the prospects for the referendum again waned. Meanwhile, the

Moroccan authorities had for months been holding communications equipment needed by the mission at Laayoune airport.

When the second phase of identification was completed, of all the 65,000 people Morocco had initially proposed as potential voters from the 'contested tribes', just 2,135 were found to be eligible. Rabat expressed 'surprise and dismay'[49] and again invoked the appeal process. By late February 2000, a total of 54,889 appeals were lodged, 53,327 against exclusion and 49,138 of them lodged from areas under Moroccan control. That brought the total number of appeals to some 130,000.[50] Again the vast majority opted for time-consuming appeals based on witnesses rather than documentation. For good measure and perhaps with an element of conscious or unconscious irony, Rabat also raised the issue of registering voters who had come of age over the years since the registration process began.

The costs mounted at Minurso and the mission's mandate was now being extended piecemeal by periods of just a few months at a time. There was no progress on prisoner releases or on return of refugees.

Baker reverted to his policy of banging heads together at meetings between the parties, the first since the Houston meeting three years before. A meeting in London on 14 May 2000 was described as 'frank' and 'inconclusive'.[51] A follow-up meeting in June 'moved things backwards'.[52]

The referendum process was in a deeper crisis than it had ever been. The electoral chickens had come home to roost. After all the years of wrangling and redefining the universe of potential voters, the numbers were on the table and from its behaviour it was quite clear that Rabat did not like them enough to risk a vote. Although the figures showed a majority of eligible voters to be living under Moroccan control, the authorities in Rabat assessed they could not ensure a sufficiently high proportion would vote the way it wanted. Of the 48,390 living in Morocco and the Moroccan-controlled bulk of the Western Sahara, how many could be relied upon not to vote for independence or abstain? The towns of the territory were going through a sustained period of unrest that even drew comment from the UN secretary-general. During that unrest it was clear that not only local Sahrawis were involved – the Wahda camp in Laayoune, full of voters and nominated voters shipped in from southern Morocco, was also turbulent.

Would there be any significant vote for integration with Morocco from the nearly 34,000 voters in the camps or the 4,000 or so in Mauritania? Rabat would have been prudent enough to assume Polisario could ensure the camps voted solidly for independence. Then the evidence from UN High Commission for Refugees workers strongly indicated that the people in the camps were suspicious and frightened of the Moroccan authorities, declining to return to the territory without safeguards.

The assessment of observers was not propitious for Rabat either. A delegation from the Nato Parliamentary Assembly was told by Minurso officials in May 1999 that, 'if the number of voters does not rise significantly the odds were slightly on the [SADR/Polisario] side'. With some prescience, the officials went on to say that Morocco might decide to extend the development and democratisation process to the territory as a means of persuading Sahrawi refugees to vote for integration. 'It seems fair to say that Morocco will probably never allow a referendum to take place which it is not sure of winning', the delegation report concluded.[53]

Ruddy, who by his own account came to his Minurso job with a bias against Polisario, said:

> If the Moroccans had any doubts where Sahrawi sympathies
> lay, they were dissipated once Sahrawis came together as the
> referendum formalities got under way…. As far back as 1975, a
> UN fact-finding mission … concluded that the Saharans were
> overwhelmingly in favour of independence. Nothing had changed.
> The referendum would still be about whether the Saharans would
> be one people again, and that would not happen if they remained
> separated by Morocco's occupation.[54]

Things had not yet gone far enough for Morocco to be able to renounce openly the Settlement Plan (although it would in time) without causing diplomatic offence and being seen to be unconvinced of its own case. Obstruction of the process was the only viable option, still leaving open the small possibility that brinkmanship would persuade the UN to change the rules again in Rabat's favour, allowing the numbers to be reconfigured. Obstruction also bought time, and time allowed for new policies, just as the Nato visitors had been told.

Sidelining the Sahrawis

In fact the negotiations of 2000, the meetings between Baker and the parties in that year, and political debate in Paris were pregnant with a new plan, one that threatened to destroy utterly Polisario's established political and diplomatic tenets.

In December 1999, the UN secretary-general said there was little possibility of holding the referendum before 2002. Three months later, having been told that Morocco had lodged the second batch of tens of thousands of appeals, he openly said there must be doubts whether the referendum could ever go ahead or the result followed through. Baker would be asked now 'to explore ways and means to achieve an early durable and agreed resolution to their dispute'.[55] With the deadlock at the London meeting in May, Baker asked Polisario and Morocco if they would be prepared to consider a 'third way'. He fleshed this out in June as the deadlock over the referendum continued: 'There could be a negotiated agreement for full integration of Western Sahara with Morocco, or for full independence, although in his view, neither prospect appeared likely. Alternatively, a negotiated agreement could produce a solution somewhere between those two results.'[56]

Then, at a meeting in Berlin in September of 2000, Baker told the two sides he had heard enough pledges of sincerity since 1997 and did not believe them any more. Although formally stating that the Settlement Plan would remain as one track of a twin-track negotiation, in fact at this point he was shunting it into a siding. He asked if Polisario and Morocco had thought about alternative solutions. Polisario said it was 'not ready to discuss anything outside the Settlement Plan'.[57] But the Moroccan delegation, led by the reformist foreign minister Mohamed Benaissa, said it would explore every avenue to work out a solution 'that would take account of Morocco's sovereignty and territorial integrity, and the specifics of the region, in compliance with the democratic and decentralisation principles that Morocco wished to develop and apply, beginning with the Sahara region'.[58]

According to participants at the meeting, Morocco said it would have a proposal to put in three months' time. But already Kofi Annan had sketched the parameters, urging Morocco 'to offer or support some devolution of governmental authority, for all inhabitants and former inhabitants of the Territory, that is genuine, substantial and in keeping with international norms'.[59] In fact, the secretary-general had gone over this ground with Baker two years before when, in the letter quoted earlier, he suggested that an alternative to the Settlement Plan could be 'agreement by Morocco to give the Western Sahara a greater deal of autonomy than the country's other regions, together with a special status for the Polisario leadership, in return for which Polisario would agree to the territory being part of Morocco'.[60]

With Morocco alone in expressing interest in a new approach, the secretary-general was already delineating for the kingdom the minimum it needed to do to escape from the referendum and still secure the sovereignty it wanted. The terminology used was significant. He referred, not for the last time, to Morocco as the 'administrative power'. This caused outrage among legal observers, who pointed out that the designation, as Annan surely knew, carried with it precise rights and obligations that still rested with Spain. But his use of the term 'inhabitants' was also important, foreshadowing the formulation of a power structure for the Western Sahara that would guarantee it remained in Moroccan hands.

On 5 May 2001, Baker presented to Algerian president Bouteflika a draft 'Framework Agreement on the Status of Western Sahara', which, he said, he was 'confident the Kingdom of Morocco would support'.[61] That confidence was well founded according to one source, who maintains that after the Berlin meeting Morocco had faxed a proposal to Baker, who had rejected it as insufficient but after two revisions had accepted it as the basis for his Framework Agreement.

The document[62] proposed that the 'population' of the Western Sahara (not the Sahrawi people) would have competence over: local government administration; territorial budget and taxation; law enforcement; internal security; social welfare; culture; education; commerce; transportation; agriculture; mining; fisheries and industry; environmental policy; housing and urban development; water and electricity; roads and other basic infrastructure. Morocco would have exclusive competence over foreign relations; national security and external defence; all matters relating to weapons; and 'the preservation of the territorial integrity against secessionist attempts'. The flag, currency, customs, postal and telecommunications systems would be Moroccan.

The territory would be run for four years by an executive elected by voters eligible to vote in the abandoned referendum. But after the four-year term, the executive would be replaced by one elected by an assembly. That assembly would only be permitted to pass laws that complied with the Moroccan constitution and moreover would be elected not from the referendum roll nor from any other definition of the Sahrawi people but anyone over 18 who had lived in the territory since 31 October 1998 or was on the October 2000 list of refugees to be repatriated.

Then, within five years of the agreement coming into effect, there would be a referendum on the status of the Western Sahara of devastating simplicity. Out for ever went the notion of Sahrawi national identity or self-determination, or of addressing the business left unfinished by Spain's overhasty withdrawal from its former colony. To vote on the status of the Western Sahara, one would simply have to have been a full-time resident in the territory for the preceding one year. In other words, settlers would vote alongside Sahrawis, and Morocco would have the incentive to boost their numbers over a period of four years.

President Bouteflika was diplomatic and said his government's response would follow. When Baker took his plan to Tindouf, he received short shrift. It is said that Polisario leader Mohamed Abdelaziz ended the meeting after twenty minutes and walked out, leaving Baker to return to the airport. Abdelaziz said: 'anything other than independence meant integration with Morocco and that he did not want to consider or discuss the framework proposal'.[63] In its written response, Polisario reiterated that the Settlement Plan was the only way forward in its view and proposed modest steps to move it forward.

Later, lengthier ripostes to the Framework Agreement were issued by the independence movement. A memorandum dated June–July 2002 does not dwell on the powers offered to an autonomous territory but notes that the voters for the Assembly and in the referendum would include Moroccans. The Framework Agreement constituted 'an obvious attempt to satisfy Morocco's aspirations and legitimise its illegal occupation of Western Sahara', it said, identifying what it argued were three inconsistencies in the adoption of this approach. First, the appeals process under the Settlement Plan would take two years, after which there could be a vote, whereas there would be no vote for five years under the Framework Agreement – the UN would be lumbered with the issue for a longer not a shorter time. Second, lack of enforcement mechanisms for the Settlement Plan had been raised as an obstacle, yet two permanent members of the Security Council (the US and France) were ready to 'guarantee' the implementation of the Framework Agreement. Third, whilst sacrificing the principles of the UN decolonisation process, the Framework Agreement, far from circumventing a winner-takes-all approach, would enshrine it in a policy only one party had accepted.

Bouteflika's promised response from Algeria was damning,[64] arguing that, contrary to assurances, the dual-track approach had been abandoned. It majored on the way the Framework Agreement undermined the notion of self-determination by substituting the notion of 'population' for that of a people. It rejected the proposed administrative and legislative structures as unbalanced and bound to lead to Moroccan dominance. The executive would be a hostage deprived of proper authority. In an excoriating concluding page, the response describes the Framework Agreement draft as violating international law, not being in compliance with Security Council resolutions, and deliberately favouring integration with Morocco.

The Framework Agreement was far from the first time the autonomy kite had been flown. Hassan II had maintained on occasion that everything but the 'stamp and flag' was negotiable once Moroccan sovereignty was secured, just as Polisario had said it would negotiate everything except the act of self-determination through a referendum on sovereignty. In 1999, there were informal talks about autonomy but they failed when Morocco would offer no more than the regional autonomy it planned for the kingdom. It drew parallels with the German *Länder* system – an Algerian sceptic pointed to the Basque country.

In Paris, autonomy was drawing approval in the Senate in 1999. A report following a mission to Morocco at the end of September noted a 'new method' of managing the Western Sahara question and said that alternative ways to the referendum might be found to satisfy the aspirations of the populations concerned. Such a new approach might also save the international community from a failure that could send out the wrong signals. Rabat had begun to approach the right issues, the report argued. The methods of governing the territory would have to change, and that was already being addressed by the new king, said the report, pointing to the commission set up in the wake of the civil disturbances of the autumn. Social, cultural and religious concerns were being addressed and a local government system devised that would give a role to the young elite of the territory. With increased regionalisation, it asked if one could conceive of the project for a referendum to confirm the Moroccanness of the territory being replaced by the idea of an autonomy that confirmed its Sahrawi nature but under Moroccan sovereignty, eventually sanctioned by a referendum.[65]

Everything seemed to be going Morocco's way. Baker and Annan had formally proposed a solution that would virtually guarantee sovereignty over the Western Sahara within five years, and in the intervening period it would have the legal and diplomatic cover to increase settlement activity and press ahead with economic exploitation of the territory. French and US guarantees would prevent outside interference from Algeria. And then, not only did the UK government come on board too but these three permanent members of the security council began, as a troika, actively lobbying for the proposal. In the autumn of 2001, Rabat was confident enough of its position to make the first serious moves towards attracting foreign capital to the Western Sahara, issuing licences to Total of France and Kerr–McGee of the US to begin looking for oil offshore. In early 2002, Morocco embarked on a charm offensive with the European press, inviting selected journalists on official visits to Laayoune ahead of a vital Security Council vote at the end of April.

The Security Council was asked to consider four options and adopt one. The first of the four was to continue attempts to implement the Settlement Plan without the concurrence of the parties. But the secretary-general had already indicated he believed the Settlement Plan could not be rescued, and, anyway, how could the plan be imposed with no suggestion an enforcement mechanism would be put in place? Second was adoption of a clarified Framework Agreement, which had the support of the US, France and the UK. Baker later denied reports he had threatened to resign if this option was not adopted. Third was the idea of partition. This option arose unexpectedly in early 2002 and its provenance remained unclear for some time. Morocco asserted it was an Algerian suggestion that was designed to muddy the water while exposing an alleged hypocrisy in its talk of the principles of self-determination and inviolability of inherited borders. An Algerian source said the proposal was from Washington and was put to Bouteflika at a meeting at the Baker Institute. A later Sahrawi version was that in order to deflect Baker from the Framework Agreement, Algeria had allowed him to think partition might be acceptable. Polisario appeared to have been caught out by this option becoming public. At least one of its senior representatives declined to rule it out immediately and the movement took some time before formally rejecting it. Two years later, the UN secretary-general said the option had been favoured (though not necessarily proposed) by Algeria and Polisario. Partition is not dead as an option. Morocco and Spain accepted the principle in 1975 through the Madrid Accords and France suggested it in 1978 as Mauritania prepared to leave the fray. A senior Polisario figure said in mid-June 2003 that 'It is not a matter of discussion because we have not received a proposition.'[66] A Sahrawi state on less than the entire territory would require approval of the Sahrawi people and would have to be viable in terms of security, economics and demography, he added. The fourth option was for the UN mission to be declared a failure and wrapped up. Kofi Annan said he opposed this.

Morocco approached the 30 April meeting with increasing confidence. Foreign journalists were assured there would be 'dancing in the streets'. In the event the kingdom suffered a knock-back, with the Security Council deciding more time was needed and postponing a decision to the end of July. Russia had made clear it was not ready to accept the Framework Agreement. Moroccan diplomats tried to put a brave face on it, saying the meeting had come as Moscow and Algiers were negotiating a major arms deal and Russia wanted a delay in order to conclude the sale without upsetting its customer.

But come the end of July, the Framework Agreement was in more trouble. Supporters of the Polisario cause in lobby groups and solidarity organisations were advised that things looked bleak. But again the Security Council provided respite, albeit temporary. The majority of non-permanent members of the council joined Russia in calling for another deferral. But this time Polisario and Algeria not only impeded the implementation of the Framework Agreement, they forced a partial retreat on its backers. The resolution adopted[67] called for a political solution 'which will provide for the self-determination of the people of Western Sahara in the context of arrangements consistent with the principles and purposes of the Charter of the United Nations'. The stress on self-determination, seeming to underline that the Western Sahara issue was rooted in an incomplete decolonisation, was repeated in the resolution. Further, Baker was asked to go back to the parties and rework his proposals, 'taking into account the concerns expressed by the parties'.

Yet the diplomatic victory for Polisario and Algeria was tactical rather than strategic, for once more the zero-sum nature of the conflict had come to the fore. The objection to the Framework Agreement was fundamental in nature – it would, quite clearly, deliver the territory to Morocco through an electoral roll that was massively stacked in its favour. Morocco and others had judged that a vote under the Settlement Plan would probably deliver a vote for independence and the risk was not acceptable, but there was never the stark inevitability that the Framework Agreement presented.

In the months between the end of July vote and Baker's next trip to the region in January 2003, the official Moroccan position hardened in an entirely predictable way. In a tradition that stretched back at least as far as Hassan II's portrayal of the ICJ determination as a vindication of Moroccan claims, Rabat declared itself satisfied with UN Resolution 1429, citing mention of the prisoner issue and the regional context of the dispute.

Then, in a speech on the twenty-seventh anniversary of the Green March, Mohamed VI reiterated the development and democracy approach, saying 'I have always wanted these provinces to become a focal point of investment and model of regional development' and arguing that 'we have provided our loyal subjects in these provinces with a precious, indeed invaluable, asset, namely the freedom that enables them to lead a decent life.' But now he went further, saying that the 'regional democracy option' had won domestic and international support, making 'the proposed referendum, provided for under the UN Settlement Plan, obsolete because it would be unrealisable in practical terms'.[68]

Thus, as Ramadan started and the pace of work in the Islamic world slowed right down, Baker was faced with Polisario maintaining its position and a hardening of the Moroccan position to the point where Rabat had declared the Settlement Plan process agreed in 1988 to be dead.

Baker tries again

In mid-January, Baker returned to the region with his reworked proposals. With another US-led war against Iraq looming, Kofi Annan warned,

> At a time when the United Nations is facing many other pressing concerns regarding the maintenance of international peace and security, the parties should demonstrate statesmanship and seize this new opportunity to provide the people of Western Sahara with a chance for a better life.[69]

The meeting with the Polisario leadership was not as brief as it had been in 2001 but it only stretched to one hour and was no more productive. Perhaps naively, many Polisario representatives were genuinely taken aback when Baker presented the Framework Agreement, and a year and a half later there was still a residue of goodwill towards him. That evaporated when the reworked proposals were read. 'It is very clear now, the complicity between Baker, France and Morocco', said Mohamed Sidati, senior Polisario diplomat in Europe.[70] The core of the new offering was unchanged – a referendum after a period of autonomy in which settlers could vote. Under the plan some 65 per cent of eligible voters would be Moroccan, according to Polisario calculations.[71] Where the original proposal gave the right to vote in the referendum to anyone who had been a resident of the territory for one year, the new version gave it to Sahrawis registered under the Settlement Plan process plus adults continuously resident in the Western Sahara since 30 December 1999. Morocco would not be able to flood the territory with new voters but the vast bulk of settlers would be able to cast a ballot. Again the Security Council extended the Minurso mandate for two months while the parties prepared their formal responses.

When Kofi Annan next reported to the UN Security Council[72] it was to deliver a bombshell. The reworked Framework Agreement should be endorsed by the Security Council, he recommended. Requests from either Morocco or Polisario to open negotiations to amend the plan should not be entertained, he said, arguing that nine previous meetings convened by Baker to further the Settlement Plan had achieved little. The parties should be pressed to show 'readiness to assume their own responsibilities and make the compromises necessary to reach a successful outcome to the conflict'. If the parties proved unwilling and the Security Council could not agree to pressure them, 'the Council may wish to consider whether it wishes to remain actively seized of this political process'. Morocco and Polisario were acting in their own narrow interests, not those of 'the population of the Western Sahara', he suggested.

Bluntly, the UN secretary-general called on the Security Council to force acceptance of the Baker proposal by Polisario and Morocco while denying the parties the opportunity to negotiate the terms of what remained a very loose proposal full of ambiguities. Behind this was the veiled threat of the UN washing its hands of the whole issue – a threat far more worrying to the Sahrawis than to Morocco.

Annan asserted that the plan 'provides a fair and balanced approach towards a political solution ... providing each side some, but perhaps not all, of what it wants' but did 'not require the consent of both parties at each and every step of its implementation'. Again his report referred to Morocco as the administrative power and again the basic concept of self-determination of a people whose territory had not been decolonised according to the process of international law was replaced, now by the notion of a future determined by 'bona fide residents'.

For the preceding months Rabat had been playing hard to get. Political parties had begun to express reservations about the Baker proposals. Driss Basri, former interior minister and strong man of Hassan II, dismissed by Mohamed VI, had even mischievously called for a straight integration or independence vote, saying autonomy would pave the way to Sahrawi statehood. In its response to the reworked proposals, Morocco first of all highlighted its core achievement, that Kofi Annan publicly agreed with Rabat's declaration that the referendum plan of 1991 was dead. The response[73] then sought to achieve two further objectives, final burial of the Settlement Plan and seizure of the inheritance.

The 'initial architecture' of the Baker proposals provided 'a viable alternative to the options set out in the Settlement Plan'. The 'third way' and the Settlement Plan should not be amalgamated but the former should replace the latter, the argument went. In other words, having achieved a transitional period of the Western Sahara under provisional Moroccan sovereignty, the kingdom's rulers wanted to remove independence as an option from the eventual referendum, however much the conditions were stacked in its favour. Annan's reaction was, in effect, to point out just how rich this was as a demand but nonetheless to suggest the ballot might include a third option of continuation of the division of authority envisaged in the Baker proposals. This in itself looked like a recognition that in the case of Morocco gaining a vote for integration, the autonomous powers enjoyed by the territory in the transition period might simply be rolled up overnight.

The reworked proposal, running to four pages, was somewhat more detailed than the original, which was little more than one side of paper. For example, it provided for a Supreme Court of Western Sahara and, no doubt to the chagrin of former and current political prisoners, asserted, 'In no event shall human rights in Western Sahara be protected to a lesser extent than is provided for in the constitution and laws of Morocco.' Rabat's second concern was to ensure the minimisation of the powers of the Western Sahara authority. So, it objected to what it considered an inversion of the logic of the original Framework Agreement, under which Morocco, with provisional sovereignty, agreed to delegate specified powers, so all powers not specifically delegated were assumed to be held by Rabat. The wording of the revised version opted for subsidiarity, the kingdom's response argued, so the local legislature would be responsible for all laws under powers not specifically attributed to Rabat. The kingdom also pointed out that the relationship between two supreme courts, one of Morocco and one of the Western Sahara, was problematic, not least when it came to the crucial issues of jointly held powers such as taxation, finance and security – precisely the issues that would determine who controlled the wealth of the territory in the interim period, if not beyond.

In his report, Kofi Annan said the 'ostensibly technical objections' raised (by both parties) suggested a lack of genuine will to achieve a political solution. This demonstrated a fundamental misunderstanding of Morocco's long-term strategy. With time it has strengthened its demographic and military hold over the Western Sahara, so progress towards a settlement through the UN is only desirable to the extent that it delivers more than the reality of occupation can achieve. The Framework Agreement offered that possibility, but the strategy remains one of extracting more and more from the international community while retaining the option of scuppering the Baker proposal if the benefits do not outweigh those offered by the passage of time in a context where there are no sanctions against occupation beyond (the not insignificant) one of lack of current foreign investment.

Polisario's response document[74] pointed to Morocco's success with this strategy, referring to 'instances the United Nations caved in without succeeding in stopping Morocco's manoeuvres'. The paper's preamble is angry, scarcely hiding the bitterness of the movement at the way the rights of the 'martyrs, exiles and Saharans faced with unspeakable suffering' it claimed as its constituency seemed to be erased. The Sahrawi people had the right to expect the right of self-determination to be safeguarded and not to be turned into 'a gathering to endorse, through its own participation, the integration of its country in the occupying power or, even less, a return of its repression, massacre and suffocation'.

The proposed referendum at the end of the interim period of autonomy would be 'both unfair and fatal to the Saharan people', unfair because settler voters would outnumber accredited Sahrawi voters by four or five to one (an increase on the previous estimate) and fatal because the returned refugees would 'be trapped there by the coloniser ... [which] would embark on as brutal a repression as it did in 1975'. Polisario then proposed a series of measures it claimed could resurrect the Settlement Plan.

Two years earlier, Polisario did not grace the Framework Agreement with a response; it simply reaffirmed its attachment to the Settlement Plan and suggested ways to expedite it. This time round circumstances forced it to respond, and respond it did in detail. Indeed, beyond the rhetoric and the restatement of firmly held principles, the Polisario response read like a negotiating position rather than a rejection – a hint at what was to come. It cited the experiences of East Timor and Rwanda as proof that the UN would have to protect the Sahrawis from Moroccan forces in the months before the autonomous government was formed. Where Morocco argued against subsidiarity to strengthen its provisional sovereignty at the expense of the autonomous government, Polisario denied the validity of Moroccan control over foreign relations and international agreements on the very grounds that this implied sovereignty. Furthermore, it called for the dismantling of the Moroccan administration in the territory as the logical accompaniment to the installation of an autonomous government. And then, just as Morocco's response demonstrated its concern over taxation, finance and security, the control of which areas would lead to control of the territory's wealth, so Polisario got down to the nitty gritty. Baker's proposal conferred competence over taxation and economic development to the autonomous power, it noted, adding that this implied but did not demand an end to the 'plunder' of phosphates and fisheries. Moroccan control of customs would seriously restrict the economic powers of the local administration, it asserted, and ceding Morocco the right to make international agreements binding on the Western Sahara or its resources was invalid according to UN legal counsel opinion regarding Morocco granting licences to oil companies off-shore the Western Sahara.

It is certainly possible to read the Polisario response as a request for clarification or negotiation over the Baker proposal. But Polisario denied this at the highest level. Abdelaziz said in June 2003 in an interview for this book that the Settlement Plan remained the only basis for agreement.[75] Brahim Mokhtar, another senior member of Polisario, said the detail of the document was intended to make it a '"No, because…" not a "No, but…" response', a demonstration that it was not viable.[76] Polisario officials had some idea what to expect from Baker and Annan but there was a real air of depression and confusion when they first read the Algerian response. Gone was the full rebuttal of Baker's ideas contained in the response of two years ago, a rebuttal so firm that it allowed Polisario simply to ignore the Framework Agreement in its own response. Now Algeria ignored the nub of the argument, the move to substitute a constituency of residents of the territory and returnees for the Sahrawi people. Where in 2001 Algiers had rejected the inclusion of settlers, in 2003 it simply called for the expeditious drawing up of the electoral roll.[77]

The core of Algeria's position had changed entirely, from rejection of the plan as contrary to UN principles to insistence on a series of safeguards. The proposal was transformed into 'a gamble for peace in the Maghreb', 'a historic compromise in favour of peace' on the part of 'the people of Western Sahara', who 'are entitled to live in guaranteed security and under effective United Nations protection'. The guarantees that Algeria called for included: a local UN presence big enough and empowered enough to ensure the proposal was implemented properly from beginning to end; agreement in advance by the Security Council to 'correct any deviation' in the implementation of the plan; assurance by the Security Council that the result of the referendum would be respected and enforced.

A previous Algerian call to introduce temporary UN sovereignty over the territory had been rejected by Annan and Baker, as the secretary-general said in his report. The same report reiterated the view that Polisario's call for an enforcement mechanism for the Settlement Plan would get nowhere in the Security Council because Morocco would not agree it. Annan was again reiterating Baker's assessment that the Western Sahara was not Kuwait and no armed international coalition would enforce Sahrawi rights. Minurso had, from the beginning, been under tough cost constraints. As the registration process dragged on, so had costs, and Annan again pointed out that half a billion dollars had been spent, way in excess of original estimates.

Tellingly, the Polisario newspaper carried a two-page commentary on diplomatic developments but devoted just a few uninformative lines to the Algerian position.[78] But within days the Polisario leadership was issuing a message of comfort, saying it was only the form and not the content of the Algerian position that had altered. 'The wrapping is soft but the core is hard – as a diplomat you have to judge by mood',[79] said Mohamed Khaddad, a key minister with responsibility for the UN process. In the context of the recent ending of the US–UK invasion of Iraq and the unsettling of relations on the Security Council, it was wiser for Algeria to be cooperative in tone, he and other Polisario officials explained. Abdelaziz maintained Algerian insistence on Sahrawi self-determination, and effective UN involvement could be found in the Algerian document and in subsequent remarks by President Bouteflika. Whether the change in Algerian tone and the relegation of core issues to the subtext and referential background was deft diplomacy or signalled a qualitative shift of position remains to be seen.

In fact, the combination of Polisario rejection and Moroccan reservations about Baker's new iteration looked likely to result in Annan's bluff being called. Ahead of the July meeting of the Security Council, Khaddad said the indications were that Russia and China would insist no solution could be imposed, France would back away from Baker because Morocco asked it to do so, and Spain would maintain its position of active neutrality. The US and UK supported Baker but would not go so far as to demand imposition.

For Polisario, killing off the Baker plan a second time would have been a victory but purely defensive. After twelve years of neither war nor peace, the social pressure to achieve some progress was building up in both the camps and the occupied territories. Indeed, the one thing the movement's diplomats liked about Annan's report was that it tried to inject a sense of urgency. However, their assessment was that the issue was not yet high enough up on the Security Council members' priority list for them to take decisive action. The task was to persuade them that their interests lay in dealing with the issue and doing so in a way that satisfied Sahrawi demands for self-determination.

At a meeting of the Polisario National Secretariat in June, it was decided to advise the congress scheduled for October that the time was not right to take up arms and that 'The situation is not yet mature maybe for seeking a solution.'[80] After the Iraq war and in the midst of the US Roadmap for Peace in the Middle East, the Sahrawis would again have to mark time. But meanwhile the message to be delivered at every opportunity, in an attempt to get the Western

Sahara moved up the priority list of the US in particular, would be that Polisario was and a Sahrawi state would be islands of calm in a turbulent Maghreb. Algeria had been at war with itself for a decade; Morocco had just suffered the Casablanca bombings and the growth of political Islam there was good for scaring Europe and the US; and there had just been a coup attempt in Mauritania. Within this context, Polisario would push for a return to the Settlement Plan, arguing that, now the movement had proposed a streamlined appeal process for voter registration, a referendum could be held in twelve months. Polisario secretary-general Mohamed Abdelaziz said:

> The only solution that has acceptance of the parties and the inter-national community is the Settlement Plan. We accept only that plan. We can make adjustments but it is the only basis. There is the need for the Sahrawi people to have a choice over the whole territory.

Then came a volte-face, proving there can be drama in the cor-ridors of power. Three weeks after Abdelaziz's firm insistence that the Settlement Plan was the only way forward, rumours emerged from Security Council member foreign ministries that Polisario would accept a US draft resolution endorsing Baker's proposals. On 10 July, Ahmed Boukhari, Polisario representative at the UN, confirmed it, saying the movement 'would be ready to contribute to the ef-fective exploration of Mr Baker's proposal to achieve the objective that cannot be renounced of the self-determination of the Sahrawi people'.[81] Tellingly, he spoke of 'the insistent wishes expressed by several countries ... including Algeria and Spain'. Polisario diplomats privately confirmed there had been pressure from 'friends'. The con-clusion is inescapable that Polisario had been leaned on. Indeed, one Algerian press report claimed that the prime minister, the minister for African affairs, and the ambassador to the UN had met with Abdelaziz on 28 June to persuade him to change position.[82]

The next days were spent qualifying the shift and explaining it. The movement now argued that the proposals had the virtue of moving things on after a long stagnation. They also reaffirmed the idea of self-determination and the need to remove Moroccan administration from the territory, it was said. By agreeing to go forward with the Baker plan, Polisario was agreeing to discuss the 'fatal' question of the electoral roll and the length of the transition period and the need for international guarantees, not to accept Baker's position. Mohamed Sidati, Polisario's leading diplomat in Europe, said the move was intended to 'to engage a new dynamic by trying to make concessions in form but not fundamentals'.[83] For Polisario, the Settlement Plan remained the preferred option, he said.

The shift in position badly wrong-footed Morocco. While Polisario too rejected Baker, Morocco could not be isolated. Now it was. Indeed, it looked as if the kingdom had fallen into a trap set by Algiers. Rather than look for ways to accept Baker's plan itself, the government in Rabat went into a spin, intensifying the volume of its rejection. Delegations of pro-integration Sahrawis visited foreign capitals with lurid warnings of tribal warfare in the territory and wider threats to the unity of Morocco if the proposals were ever implemented.

Within the Security Council, France quickly took Morocco's side, not only because of its long-established policy of uncritical support but probably also to further its competition with the US for influence over Morocco. A US draft resolution endorsing Baker and carrying the suggestion of implementation over the heads of the parties (although in no way suggesting forceful imposition) was opposed by Paris. While Paris did sterling work on Rabat's behalf, it was nonetheless discomfiting for the kingdom to see a rerun of the Iraq invasion line-up in the Security Council: the US, UK and Spain standing against France, which gained some backing from Russia and China. In the midst of trade talks, the Moroccan government was now standing against the US and being backed by a Security Council member with which the US had scores to settle.

Resolution 1495 was watered down with 'support strongly' replacing endorsement and the plan described as 'an optimum political solution on the basis of agreement between the two parties' (my emphasis). Thus, Morocco could say there was no element of compulsion, while Polisario could say the use of the indefinite article kept the Settlement Plan alive and the UN involved in the conflict. The open question was whether the US would maintain its new-found appetite for solving the Western Sahara dispute. Without that pressure on the parties, there was every chance that Baker's proposals would run into the same endless bickering that had stifled the Settlement Plan.

Even if Moroccan diplomats could claim the Security Council was not a total defeat, it was seen at home as a shock and a humiliation. Articles appeared in the mainstream press questioning the quality of the diplomatic strategy. Predictably enough, the establishment political parties rushed to reassert a national consensus over the Western Sahara issue, and the rhetoric against Algeria and Spain was ratcheted up again. But alongside these responses, ones that have almost a comfort factor, was a new one, a concern and an anger at the US. Morocco had been told forcefully that it was the junior partner in the relationship. *L'Économiste* was outraged:

> [Washington] forgets our 40 years of engagement in the Western camp, from the time of the Cold War and the first Gulf War, our efforts for peace in the Middle East, our democratic opening.... All this has cost Morocco, materially and morally. In recompense America cooks up a 'solution' for the Sahara that pleases Algeria, a country for 40 years pro-Soviet and base for all anti-American movements, today a great home of terrorism and an oppressive regime.[84]

While Morocco chewed over its relations with the US, Polisario for its part needed to consider whether it had now toppled on to a slippery slope that would lead to dilution of its most firmly held principles. It had achieved movement but had it achieved progress?

Notes

1. For detail on the diplomatic process of this period and the governmental structure of the territory under Spanish rule, see Robert Rezette, *The Western Sahara and the Frontiers of Morocco*, Nouvelles Éditions Latines, Paris, 1975; and Tony Hodges, *Western Sahara: The Roots of a Desert War*, Lawrence Hill, Westport CT, 1983.
2. Hodges, *Western Sahara*, p. 133.
3. 'Western Sahara – Advisory Opinion of 16 October 1975', International Court of Justice, The Hague.
4. George Joffe, 'International Court of Justice and the Western Sahara', in Richard Lawless and Laila Monahan, eds, *War and Refugees: the Western Sahara Conflict*, Pinter, London, 1987, p. 27.
5. 'Report of the United Nations Visiting Mission to Spanish Sahara, 1975', A/10023/Rev1, p. 66.
6. Ibid., p. 69.

7. Ibid., p. 85.
8. Ibid., p. 78.
9. Hodges, *Western Sahara*, p. 212.
10. Stephen O. Hughes, *Morocco under King Hassan*, Ithaca Press, Ithaca NY, 2001, p. 244.
11. Ibid., pp. 242–3.
12. Hodges, *Western Sahara*, p. 311.
13. Report by the Secretary General, S/22464.
14. UN Security Council resolution S/RES/690 (1991).
15. 'Fighting for Talks', *West Africa*, 25 December 1989–7 January 1990.
16. 'Truce Announced by Polisario', *West Africa*, 6–12 February 1989.
17. 'Halfway to Peace', *West Africa*, 20–26 February 1989.
18. 'Morocco Takes a Pounding', *West Africa*, 9–15 October 1989.
19. George Theodore and Thomas Llewellyn, 'Inside Western Sahara', *West Africa*, 20–26 November 1989.
20. Report of the Secretary General on the situation concerning Western Sahara, S/2001/613.
21. Report of the Secretary General on the situation concerning Western Sahara, S/2000/131.
22. S/Res/1301 (2000).
23. UN record of the meeting S/PV.4149.
24. Ibid.
25. Ibid.
26. Report of the Secretary General on the situation concerning Western Sahara, S/2001/613.
27. Marrack Goulding, *Peacemonger*, John Murray, London, 2002, pp. 199–214.
28. Reiterating the long-standing position, the newly appointed minister for human rights stated categorically in an interview with *Le Matin*, 8 January 2003, that 'no case of disappearance exists in Morocco'.
29. Report of the Secretary General on the situation concerning Western Sahara, S/2000/1029.
30. Hughes, *Morocco under King Hassan*, p. 269.
31. John Bolton, 'Resolving the Western Sahara Conflict', paper delivered to the Defense Forum Foundation 1988 Congressional Defense and Foreign Policy Forum, Washington DC, 27 March 1998. Bolton served as assistant secretary of state overseeing the formulation and implementation of US policy and diplomacy at the UN during the George Bush presidency and later worked in a *pro bono* capacity with James Baker after the latter was appointed as Special Representative of the UN secretary-general with regard to the Western Sahara.
32. Ibid.
33. Report of the Secretary General on the situation concerning Western Sahara, S/1995/779.
34. Bolton, 'Resolving the Western Sahara Conflict'.
35. Report of the Secretary General on the situation concerning Western Sahara, S/1995/779.

36. Frank Ruddy, 'The United Nations Mission for the Referendum in Western Sahara: Lofty Ideal and Gutter Realities', paper delivered at Georgetown University, Washington DC, 16 February 2000.

37. 'UN Officials "Worked against Polisario"', *Independent*, 15 November 1991.

38. Ibid.

39. Report of the Secretary General on the situation concerning Western Sahara, S/1996/343.

40. Report of the Secretary General on the situation concerning Western Sahara, S/1996/913.

41. Report of the Secretary General on the situation concerning Western Sahara, S/1996/674.

42. Report of the Secretary General on the situation concerning Western Sahara, S/1997/742.

43. Goulding, *Peacemonger*, p. 214.

44. Letter from Kofi Annan to James Baker, 5 March 1997, reproduced in the James Baker Virtual Museum, www.rice.edu/projects/baker/vrtours/jab30yr.baker37.html,

45. Report of the Secretary General on the situation concerning Western Sahara, S/1997/742.

46. Ibid., Annex I and II. Annex III comprises the Houston Agreement.

47. Minurso press release, 3 September 1998.

48. Report of the Secretary General on the situation concerning Western Sahara, S/1999/1098.

49. Report of the Secretary General on the situation concerning Western Sahara, S/2000/131.

50. Report of the Secretary General on the situation concerning Western Sahara, S/2000/461.

51. Ibid.

52. Report of the Secretary General on the situation concerning Western Sahara, S/2000/683.

53. Trip report on visit to Morocco, 28 April–2 May 1999, by the Subcommittee on NATO Enlargement and the New Democracies of NATO Parliamentary Assembly, May 1999.

54. Ruddy, 'The United Nations Mission for the Referendum in Western Sahara'.

55. Report of the Secretary General on the situation concerning Western Sahara, S/2000/131.

56. Report of the Secretary General on the situation concerning Western Sahara, S/2000/683.

57. Report of the Secretary General on the situation concerning Western Sahara, S/2000/1029.

58. Ibid.

59. Ibid.

60. Letter from Kofi Annan to James Baker, 5 March 1997.

61. Report of the Secretary General on the situation concerning Western Sahara, S/2001/613.

62. For the text of the draft, see Report of the Secretary General on the situation concerning Western Sahara, S/2001/613, Annex I.
63. Report of the Secretary General on the situation concerning Western Sahara, S/2001/613.
64. For the text of the draft, see Report of the Secretary General on the situation concerning Western Sahara, S/2001/613, Annex II.
65. 'Rapport d'information fait a la suite d'une mission effectuée au Maroc du septembre 30 au 3 octobre 1999', website of the French Senate.
66. Interview with the author.
67. Security Council Resolution 1429 (2002)
68. Text of television and radio speech of 6 November 2002, translated and distributed by Maghreb Arabe Presse.
69. Report of the Secretary General on the situation concerning Western Sahara, S/2003/59.
70. Toby Shelley, 'Polisario Dismisses UN Plan for Western Sahara', FT.com, 20 January 2003.
71. Sahrawi Press Service 18 January 2003.
72. Report of the Secretary General on the situation concerning Western Sahara, 23 May 2003, S/2003/565.
73. Ibid., Annex 3.
74. Ibid.
75. Interview with the author, 13 June 2003.
76. Interview with the author, 10 June 2003.
77. Report of the Secretary General on the situation concerning Western Sahara, S/2003/565.
78. 'Il Sahara il hurra', *Polisario Front* 386, June 2003.
79. Interview with the author, 12 June 2003.
80. Interview with Abdelaziz.
81. Efe news agency, 11 July 2003.
82. El *Watan*, 6 July 2003.
83. *Le Matin*, Algiers, 13 July 2003.
84. *L'Économiste*, 5 August 2003.

10

Polisario and the SADR:
Guerrillas, Refugees and
Their State-in-Waiting

Late at night in a tent in a Tindouf camp an elderly Sahrawi prepares glasses of tea for his wife, a friend and two visitors. The scent of gum arabic billows from the charcoal on the brazier and a bowl of camel milk passes from hand to hand. The old man speaks of 800 years during which the tribes of the Western Sahara have lived in the region. He describes tribal groups loosely confederated through a periodic assembly under the authority of the *Ait Arbiin*, a council of leaders that ensured trade relations, arbitrated disputes and organised Koranic education. The Sahrawi identity he describes was asserted in resistance to intrusion from north, south and east. The Sahrawis were never aggressors but aggressed against, a people who provided refuge for the persecuted he says. His wife adds to his reminiscence, ensuring the visitors realise that this identity was forged by women too – hadn't she been among the women who fought alongside their husbands at the battle of Liglayb?

Fifteen years later, across the berm and the minefields, under Moroccan rule, another veteran prepares tea, tossing occasional indulgent smiles at his baby as she wriggles on the lap of a visitor. When the ceasefire came in 1991 he was against it, convinced Polisario could turn things in three years more fighting. All his adult life he had been a guerrilla and now he had no role. He left the camps, handed himself over to Morocco, kicked his heels and raked over his memories in Rabat for a while, and now lives a hand-to-mouth existence with his wife and daughter. But he quietly continues to support the ends of a movement in which he sees no further role for himself. He is firm, even outspoken, in his defence of Polisario's leadership.

In a PR company office in the City a young, besuited Sahrawi, every inch the rising diplomat, does not drink the proffered filter coffee. Along with a more senior colleague to whom the air of the desert still clings, he sits with executives of Fusion Oil, briefing a financial journalist on an agreement between the Sahrawi Arab Democratic Republic and the company. Commanding several European languages, a shining smile and a smart haircut, he is the dapper if unaccredited ambassador of a state-in-waiting, a state with ministries and reshuffles, institutions and a constitution.

The evolution from the Sahrawi identity of Sidi Mustafa and his wife to the nationalisms of the retired fighter and the diplomat was hastened by the sedentarisation of the Sahrawis in the 1960s and particularly the 1970s. This brought them into contact with the infrastructure and organisation of statehood, Spanish statehood. As the mineral potential of the Western Sahara became evident, so Madrid began to invest in the colony. Laayoune, Smara and Dakhla (then Villa Cisneros) were built up. Spanish settlers arrived to work in the administration and the phosphate industry. Sahrawis too were recruited for the armed forces and for the mines and, albeit to a very limited extent, they began to go to school. As Hodges puts it: 'With its administrators and bureaucrats, soldiers and policemen, laws and regulations, schools and hospitals, Western Sahara started to look, to settled Sahrawis, like a country.'[1]

A Sahrawi commentator[2] suggests that Madrid's co-option and transformation of the institution of the assembly or *djemaa* in 1967 hastened the Sahrawis redefinition of themselves as a people rather than members of a tribal confederation. Despite the close control of the *djemaa* by the colonial authorities and the maintenance of a strong tribally based quotient in its membership, the fact that some one-third of its members were elected, and the very fact that the institution was presented as the voice of the Sahrawis, contributed to a new sense of supra-tribal identity. Indeed, former members of the *djemaa* interviewed in 2003 for this book were involved in a series of clandestine meetings between Sahrawi elders and young, educated Sahrawis in 1969 that led to the first nationalist political party.

Meanwhile, on the international stage the decolonisation process had been in full flood since the end of the Second World War. Hodges cites the telling UN statistic that, due to the influx of cheap sets from the Canaries, for every 1,000 inhabitants, 340 Sahrawis had transistor radios by 1972, compared to only 95 in Morocco and fewer still in Algeria.[3] So, increasingly, the Sahrawis' view of the outside world was one informed by concepts and news of decolonisation. Regionally, of course, Morocco gained independence in the late 1950s and then gained the Tarfaya Strip and regained the Ifni enclave and Tangiers. The Algerian war of independence raged until the early 1960s. As one Sahrawi elder, now living in Smara refugee camp outside Tindouf, said: 'The Sahrawis saw they were the only people in the Maghreb who had not got independence and when Spain offered a century of training and autonomy, the Sahrawis decided they had the same rights.'

And then the UN, without reference to the Sahrawis themselves, pronounced on the Western Sahara in 1964. Although at the diplomatic level the UN decolonisation process was a forum for Spain, Morocco and Mauritania to assert their claims, the Sahrawis nonetheless became aware that the territory on which they lived was being considered as unitary, as indeed they were. European colonialism and its successor were framing the Sahrawis' political perception of themselves as surely as they had framed the legal boundaries of the land.

The enervating influence of the Sahrawi community outside of the territory was another factor. Around 1967, young Sahrawis formed cells that coalesced in 1969 into the first identifiable, formal anticolonialist political organisation,[4] Harakat Tahrir. It was these cells that had held a dialogue with Sahrawi elders and together circulated a nationalist text around nomad and émigré communities.[5] The organisation was led by one Mohamed ould El Hadj Brahim ould Lebssir, known as Bassiri, a Sahrawi from Tan Tan. Among the cell members were later Polisario fighters and political leaders. Harakat Tahrir called for the achievement of Sahrawi independence in stages and by peaceful means. It emerged from a clandestine existence in June 1970 when it organised a demonstration in Laayoune. The demonstration was suppressed bloodily by Spanish forces. Bassiri was arrested and never seen again. In 1969, one El Ouali Mustapha

Sayed had already begun gathering together a group of nationalist-minded Sahrawi students in Morocco.[6] The suppression of Harakat Tahrir convinced the young Sahrawi militants that independence might require 'modern' political organisation, but it would also require altogether more traditional recourse to the gun. Harakat Tahrir advocated social reforms and abolition of the tribal structure, prefiguring Polisario's political agenda. In 1972, members of Harakat Tahrir combined with young Sahrawi activists studying in Morocco, Spain and Mauritania and formed an embryonic Sahrawi liberation organisation, a short-lived bridge between Harakat Tahrir and the Front for the Liberation of Saguia el Hamra and Rio de Oro – the Polisario Front – which was constituted on 20 May 1973.

Bassiri was born in Tan Tan but later lived inside the Western Sahara. Hodges[7] was told Bassiri was evacuated by Sahrawi fighters in 1957 to Morocco from Lemsid, a strange coastal spot south of Laayoune, site of a centuries-old Sahrawi cemetery and a sulphur spring. He studied in the Middle East before returning to Morocco and then to the Western Sahara as a Koranic teacher in Smara.

Bassiri's connection with the ethnic Sahrawi community in the Tarfaya Strip is echoed in the biographies of a number of Polisario figures. A document issued by the Moroccan government[8] cites, among others, the fathers of Polisario leaders Mohamed Abdelaziz, Mahfoud Ali Beiba, Bachir Mustafa Sayed, Mohamed Salem ould Salek and El Batal Sid Ahmed as Sahrawi fighters who settled in Morocco after the fighting of 1958. It was sons of this generation who won places at Moroccan universities where their political experiences determined them to establish what was to become Polisario. In 1975 the UN Mission recognised the politicisation of the Sahrawi community in the Tarfaya Strip, saying that in addition to visiting refugee camps at Tan Tan, Zag and Amakroud, it had met with representatives of several organisations.

The political connection between Sahrawis living in the Western Sahara and those in the Tarfaya Strip re-echoes in the political activism of Sahrawi students from towns like Assa, Goulmime and Tan Tan and in the figurehead role played in recent years by Assa-based nationalist, trade unionist, political prisoner and hunger striker Tamek.

The organisation formally inaugurated inside the Mauritanian border by El Ouali, charismatic first leader of the Polisario Front, and his companions, launched its first attack against Spanish forces on 20 May 1973, just days after its formation. A group of seven overran a small outpost at El Khanga.

By the time the UN Mission went to the territory in 1975, there was clear political competition within the Sahrawi community, and Polisario was evidently better organised:

> The Mission believes, in the light of what it witnessed in the Territory, especially the mass demonstrations, of support for one movement, the Frente Polisario, ... that its visit served as a catalyst to bring into the open political forces and pressures which had previously been largely submerged. It was all the more significant to the Mission that this came as a surprise to the Spanish authorities who, until then, had only been partly aware of the profound political awakening of the population.[9]

The Mission met with representatives of several political organisations claiming representation of the Sahrawis. In the Tarfaya Strip, it noted that every political figure presented to it asserted Moroccan nationality, attachment to the king and support for integration. Edouard Moha, head of the Mouvement de résistance pour la libération des territories sous domination espagnole (Morehob), told of his pilgrimage from capital city to capital city in search of sponsorship. A handful of fighters from a self-styled Front de libération et de l'unité denounced Polisario as a bunch of children. A representative of Istiqlal said the Moroccan nationalist party had many branches in the territory. But in the Western Sahara itself, 'the Mission did not encounter any groups supporting the territorial claims of neighbouring countries'.[10] The political contest was between two organisations.

Representatives of Partido de la Union Nacional Saharaui (PUNS), which advocated maintenance of strong ties with Spain after independence, denied being a creation of Madrid. Unfortunately the denial's weight was lessened by the remarks of one Khali Hena al Rachid, secretary-general of PUNS, who defected to Morocco during the Mission's visit and said that 'the Spanish authorities had chosen him to lead PUNS, with a promise he would become the head of government after independence, because he had been educated in Spain and had a Spanish wife'.[11] PUNS' programme for an independent Western Sahara was for economic modernisation, along with preservation and adaptation of 'religious and social traditions'.[12] It told the Mission it opposed radical social change. PUNS was the only organisation able to emulate in part Polisario's mobilisation of crowds during the Mission's visit. With Spain's withdrawal, PUNS evaporated, although some of its supporters rallied to Polisario.

The members of the Mission were met by Polisario demonstrations throughout the territory (although, interestingly, the leadership said it was less well organised in the south, perhaps because of the lower level of urbanisation). They found the front had 'considerable support among all sections of the population and especially among women who, together with the young people and workers, are among its most active adherents'.[13] As the Spanish found increasingly to their cost, Polisario was able to mine support from Sahrawis in the Spanish armed forces. During the Mission's stay, two units of the Tropas Nomadas mutinied, capturing their officers, and joined Polisario forces.

Political evolution within the movement

That women, the young and workers were most prominent among Polisario's supporters in 1975 hints at the political programme of the front. The first women's cell was set up in the first days of the organisation.[14] But while the programme, in common with those of other national liberation struggles of the era, used phraseology familiar to the European left, care was taken to root the movement in the Sahrawi traditions. The UN Mission had noted 'considerable conflict between the young people and the traditional social structure',[15] yet, as mentioned above, there had already been cross-generational political discussion for several years before Polisario was founded, a major achievement in a society where the custom is of deference of youth to age.

Just as the Moroccans convened a meeting of members of the djemaa to legitimate the Madrid Accords and Green March, so Polisario convened a meeting of djemaa members who had fled the advancing armies to reject the accords and demand independence. Earlier the Mission had noted that a number of older people, including sheikhs and notables, expressed sympathy for Polisario. Morocco and former Polisario members who have defected to Morocco frequently assert that Polisario's founders were either communist ideologues or students seduced by the romanticism of Guevarist politics of the 1970s. Certainly key founding members of Polisario had worked closely with Moroccan Marxists and to this day active support for Sahrawi student activities comes from the Moroccan far left. But to have attempted to indoctrinate a recently sedentarised population of a traditionally tribal society in an economy in the very first throes of development would have been futile. As one Polisario activist remarked, 'If they had told the Sahrawis they were communists, they would have killed them.' The suggestion that El Ouali and associates were closet Marxists who hid their schemes for social engineering and apostasy until they had lured Sahrawis to the Tindouf camps is similarly unappealing.

By the time of the Mission's visit, Polisario's programme called for immediate independence. But it is worth noting that this was not explicit in the very first days of the organisation. The founding constitution of the movement calls for lifting of the colonial yoke but the word 'independence' does not appear once. Omar Hadrami, a founding member who defected to Morocco in circumstances discussed below, maintained that El Ouali was originally more influenced by the pan-Arabism of Libya's Muammar Qaddafi, Polisario's original backer. In 1974 as Algeria adopted Polisario, so it promoted the notion of an independent Sahrawi state, said Hadrami.[16] In an interview with the author, an activist in the Western Sahara in the 1960s who joined Polisario but is now living under Moroccan rule said the objective of the front was always an independent state. A group of elders in Smara camp said it was when Spanish withdrawal loomed that they decided independence was their preferred option. It is known that El Ouali was for a while willing to entertain the idea of a Mauritanian–Sahrawi federation.

Polisario told the UN Mission that it wanted a republican government along socialist lines and with mass participation. Natural resources would be nationalised.[17] It denounced the *djemaa* and PUNS as agents of colonialism – though, as noted above, was willing to use a rump of *djemaa* members to support it once the Spanish link was broken. It said it opposed feudal elements of Sahrawi society. In its statutes, it also commits its militants to combating regionalism, nepotism and corruption.[18] It described the condition of women as deplorable and called for the improvement of social conditions. Islamic religious institutions were to be preserved.

In the context of a developed, well-established capitalist economy such a programme might be described as radical but scarcely a blueprint for a communist state. In the context of the Western Sahara in the mid-1970s it accorded quite well with the contemporary trends in the economy and society. Decolonisation would, in theory, remove Spanish control of natural resources, which would then be vested in the independent state. The only Sahrawis who might lose from this were a few notables who had hitched their star to the Spanish administration. Bar a few nominees to the administrative board of the phosphate company, the Sahrawis only gained from Bou Craa inasmuch as some were employed in the mine. Similarly, Sahrawis were not engaged in the fishing industry. Other natural resources had (and have) yet to be exploited. References to distribution of the benefits derived from natural resources to all sections of the population and to improving social conditions were vague enough not to be objectionable to anyone.

At the social level, Polisario was careful to respect religious sensibilities and, once it had declared the creation of the Sahrawi Arab Democratic Republic, it enshrined in the latter's constitution Islam as the religion of the state and the inspiration for its laws. At the same time, by opposing feudal or tribal elements in society and, indeed, by championing improvements in the lives of women, it could be argued that the front was pushing on a door already opened by sedentarisation and urbanisation. The reference to republican government, inasmuch as the Sahrawis had never had a royalty, can be read as a reaffirmation of independence from Morocco.

In the mid-1990s a new constitution was written for the SADR. With no mention of a socialist orientation, it maintained commitments to provision of a comprehensive system of social security and to public-sector development of natural resources. 'After independence, market economy and freedom of private initiative will be recognised',[19] the new constitution now said, nodding not only towards the global hegemony of market economics and ideology but also to social pressures in the refugee camps. The economy of the camps had been a non-monetary one but certainly by the late 1980s there were reports of cash circulating in small amounts, the proceeds of pensions from former Spanish employers, and of goods being brought in from Mauritania for sale.[20] Hadrami alleged there were inequalities in the camp, with functionaries able to ensure better provision for their families and members of the leadership procuring Land-Rovers and amassing camel herds.[21] So, after several years of ceasefire, the austere war-economy collectivism of the camps was relaxed and freer rein given to the trading traditions of the Sahrawis. By the late 1990s the principle of foreign investment in a future independent state was written into the constitution and a Polisario leader said 'the only way for us to survive as a country' was by becoming an economic and political reference point in the region. Fishery and mineral resources could be shared with Morocco and other Maghreb countries, he added.[22] Sahrawi enterprises would have priority but only as long as they proved themselves competitive, according to Fadel Ismail.[23]

In the camps the relaxation has brought the development of petty commerce and some artisanal work. Small shops selling basic groceries and household goods have sprouted, as have rudimentary repair sites for private vehicles, the number of which has increased enormously. Jewellery and leatherwork, much of it aimed at the solidarity and NGO market, is made and sold locally. There are some basic restaurants. Families own livestock. An estimated 4,000 young men have left the camps for migrant work in Spain. Their remittances, pensions from those employed by Spain before 1975 (and donations from Spanish families and organisations), allow many of the mud-brick houses that supplement or replace tents to have electricity generated by solar panels.

The palpable improvement in living standards for many families is clearly positive but it comes at the price of social change. For the migrant workers the economic liberalisation means one or two years of illegal work while awaiting residency rights. For professionals trained abroad and returning to work unpaid for their community it means the temptation to go elsewhere and market their skills or to forget their education and strive to set up a shop instead. For the whole community it means the growth of pilfering and petty theft, previously all but unknown.

The constitution of the SADR has been extended and revised on a number of occasions. There were three versions between the declaration of the state in 1976 and 1985. While the text of the constitution is clearly an important pointer to the aspirations of the Sahrawi independence movement, Bontems is absolutely right to caution against using it as a crude yardstick:

> Some writers have attempted to calculate, from the basis of these few written declarations, the extent of socialisation achieved by the Sahrawi regime. This method does not produce any convincing conclusions since it fails to reveal any of the SADR's originality, simply measuring the SADR's constitution against the ideal democratic model.[24]

It would be as naive to measure the degree of real personal freedom in the camps by the assurances in the constitution rather than by the reality imposed by the environmental and political circumstances in the Tindouf camps. Again, as Bontems remarks,[25] the constitutional text has often borrowed terms from a dominant Western political discourse and is, perhaps, in part for external consumption.

Polisario was and remains a front rather than a party. It has no formal membership. Rather, any Sahrawi who supports the objectives of Polisario is considered part of Polisario. Within the camps, in order to influence the policy of the front and of the SADR, one must be active in an organisation or institution and so have a vote in deciding its direction. As will be seen, the basic cell structure of the front (and of the state) reaches right down into the community. Subsidiary mass organisations for women, youth, workers are a further vehicle for mobilising the population.

Polisario is better compared to the Algerian FLN, which contained many shades of political opinion, including Islamist and Marxist, than to the PLO, which developed as an umbrella for organisations with particular loyalties or political programmes.[26] Necessarily, that structure ensures a high degree of generalisation in a political programme. But Fadel Ismail argued that within the entwined structures of Polisario and the SADR are the germs of a pluralistic polity expressed within a quasi-parliamentary institution: 'The currents of thought that exist are in essence just as much political (as in the

West) as social (regionalist and tribalist).'[27] He notes that the tribal basis of the UN identification process for the stalled referendum has reinvigorated tribalism and that this could have consequences at the political level. Indeed, he goes further and says that Polisario had been rigid and naive and had made mistakes in its campaign against tribalism. The movement should have recognised that it could not simply abolish in a few years a structure that had been a basis for social organisation for centuries.[28] At its ninth congress, Polisario said an independent Western Sahara would have a multiparty system after a transitional period. Like the FLN, Polisario might form its own political party after independence, said a Sahrawi diplomat, although he added that at present, with the range of views expressed, 'It's a hell of a job to run a meeting of Polisario.'[29]

Polisario and its base community in the camps have suffered from internal disagreements and defections over the years. Recently, Polisario officials have become more willing to acknowledge and discuss the issues involved and to concede mistakes. In part they have had to do this as Morocco has naturally taken every opportunity to publicise defections. But some, such as Fadel Ismail, have presented dissent as an opportunity to deepen the accountability of the leadership. Indeed, there may be times when it is in the interests of the leadership to publicise the pressures it is under. For example, with the Settlement Plan consigned to the waste bin by Morocco and the promotion of autonomy proposals, some Polisario officials were more and more willing to talk of anger among the ranks of the fighters and the difficulty faced by the leadership in defending continuation of the ceasefire. Arguably, presentation of a threat to the ceasefire could be used as leverage in the diplomatic game.

At the same time, the division of opinion may be a new expression of a political cleavage within the movement, one that might be another of Ismail's germs of political pluralism, a distinction between 'movementists' and 'statists'. As far back as the first half of the 1980s competition for pre-eminence between the ideological apparatus and the state apparatus was identified. Until 1984, Polisario institutions clearly dominated those of the SADR. As the SADR built its international stature, the emphasis shifted.[30] The ceasefire was contentious from the start, unpopular among some elements of the fighting force in particular. Well over a decade later and with little to show, the pressure to recommence combat could signal wider discussion of political direction.

A senior and early member of Polisario in a discussion with the author in early 2003 recognised not only a back-to-war tendency in the camps but also a minority constituency that might be tempted by material improvement. 'Some people are getting a normal life within an exceptional context', he noted, adding that for some exile was now normality and, by implication, could become acceptable in certain circumstances. Of course the quest for a 'normal' life or simply for lack of deprivation might also spur people to accept Moroccan calls to desert the camps and submit to Moroccan rule. Over the years a number of senior Polisario figures have defected. The Moroccan authorities produce defectors for visiting journalists and claim that many ordinary Sahrawis have handed themselves over. Certainly some rank-and-file Sahrawis have chosen to leave the camps and live under Moroccan rule, but there is little reliable evidence to support claims that the number is great. Indeed, there continue to be some Sahrawis who flee to the camps from the Moroccan-controlled zones each year.

Nonetheless, serious disagreement did emerge in 1988, a year when relations between the governments of Algeria and Morocco looked to be improving and some observers were forecasting Algerian abandonment of Polisario. It was also the year when the Settlement Plan with its attendant ceasefire was agreed. There are few sources of information on the events that took place. Ismail, a dedicated and very early member of Polisario (who died in 2002), who was also widely respected for his lack of dogmatism, talks of it as a period when cadres publicly opposed the arrogant and ad hoc actions of 'certain leaders'.

By his account,[31] cadres in the Political Bureau of Polisario protested at the actions of some members of the front's Executive Committee, accusing them of centralising power and developing a political oligarchy. The spark for the protests was the detention of political opponents of these leaders. In meetings organised by the Moroccan authorities, Sahrawis claiming to have been maltreated and detained for long periods in the Tindouf camps say that they were released because of popular demonstrations in the camps in 1988.

The Polisario leadership has admitted publicly that there were human rights abuses. They are explained as other national liberation movements have explained their own purges and detentions: as results of the tumultuous circumstances, with the assurance that 'the lesson has been learnt'. The events of 1988 created the climate for a 'Sahrawi perestroika', moves to ensure respect for human rights and freedom of expression. Polisario's structural solution was to replace the two organs with a single National Secretariat and improve the alignment of responsibilities with designated positions within the movement.

Ismail notes that the internal conflict coincided with a division of opinion over whether to go down the route of a ceasefire, but explicitly denies that the two issues were related.

A different version is given by Hadrami. He had been a member of the Executive Committee that Ismail said provoked criticism from cadres in the Political Bureau, although by 1988 was no longer a member. He was also head of military security from 1982 until his arrest in 1988. By his own admission he controlled much of the life of the camps and ordered arrests, although he asserts that the incidence of detentions fell under his supervision. Amnesty International's report on Morocco and the Western Sahara in 1996 does not mention names, but it does note that 'Some former Polisario figures who held positions of responsibility in the Polisario security apparatus, and who are alleged to have been responsible for human rights abuses in the refugee camps administered by the Polisario authorities in the south of Algeria, have since left the camps and are now in Morocco.'[32]

According to Hadrami's testimony,[33] there were large demonstrations and work stoppages in the summer of 1988. At the same time there was an organisational crisis within the SADR with a group of nominees for ministries refusing to take their posts. The protests, he insisted from his villa in Rabat, were supported by Sahrawis originally from the interior of the Western Sahara, whom he counterposes to a minority whose background was in the Algerian or Mauritanian Sahara. This latter minority, according to Hadrami, was sponsored by the Algerian government, while the majority, by 1988, wanted reconciliation with Morocco. The suggestion that Polisario itself operates on quasi-tribal lines is a theme of defectors. Abdellah Chikhatou Ali Salem asserted in April 1990 that there was an alliance of tribes at the base level and in the Sahrawi armed forces.[34] The assertion runs contrary to another theme, that until the early 1980s tribal identification in the camps was suppressed by such means as public self-criticism sessions. The charge of tribalism is levelled at dissidents. In August 1989, Polisario leader Mohamed Abdelaziz accused an unnamed group of officials, almost certainly including Hadrami, of tribalism.[35] Whether correctly or not, Hadrami's account clearly identifies individuals and views with particular tribes and origins.

Contrary to Ismail, Hadrami explicitly links the events of 1988 to the Algerian–Moroccan rapprochement, suggesting that there was a feeling that the Sahrawis should take the initiative in negotiations with Rabat. He said that the demonstrations were put down forcefully, with many arrests. Hadrami was arrested and held for several months until he was apparently rehabilitated and sent to Washington, whence he defected to Morocco.

A Polisario representative in Europe explains the events as a consequence of the evolution of Polisario from a tight-knit politico-military organisation to a movement of many thousands of people, sponsoring a state structure, engaged in international diplomacy and responsible for the lives of the community in the camps. The movement had not developed to cope with this evolution and that failure allowed room for individuals to claim powers and authority not allocated to them by any formal structure. Personal and policy disagreements became difficult to separate. Different individuals received support from different parts of the camp population and the demonstrations reflected this when tension mounted. But, according to the same person, the evident danger of tribal splits and the fact that almost all of the players maintained their attachment to the cause of independence were enough to bring the movement back from the brink. At the congress called in 1989, Polisario reformed its structures, a number of personalities involved in the 1988 dispute conceded mistakes and all reaffirmed commitment to the cause (as underlined by a series of military engagements shortly afterwards).

The structure of Polisario's state

The Sahrawi Arab Democratic Republic is Polisario's machinery of government. The institutions of the SADR and Polisario are intertwined, and the declaration and constitution of the state-in-exile are explicit about the relationship. In a riposte to the vote by *djemaa* members under Moroccan rule to approve the occupation of the territory, on 27 February 1976 Polisario proclaimed the SADR, with the approval of the other *djemaa* members. The proclamation at Bir Lehlou stated: 'In carrying out the will of our people the Polisario Front, with the unanimous agreement of the Provisional National Sahrawi Council, decided to constitute a government which will assume responsibilities for the continuation of the battle.'[36] The SADR was created by Polisario as a tool in the independence struggle. The preamble of the 1999 constitution of the SADR describes the Sahrawi people as being under the leadership of Polisario and declares the people's determination to achieve sovereignty of the SADR over the whole of its national territory.[37] Article 31 of the constitution states:

> Until the achievement of national sovereignty, the Polisario
> Front remains the political framework that groups and politically
> mobilises the Sahrawis, to express their aspirations and their
> legitimate right to self-determination and independence, and to
> defend their national unity and achieve the building of a sovereign
> Sahrawi state.

The secretary-general of Polisario is, constitutionally, the head of state of the SADR. He names the prime minister, whose cabinet is selected with reference to the head of state. The army, of which the head of state is commander, is an organ of the state under the constitution while remaining the armed wing of Polisario according to the front's statutes. A new head of state can only take office after the holding of a Polisario congress. The legislative Sahrawi National Council is formed after a Polisario congress according to rules laid down by the secretariat of Polisario.

The overlap between functionaries of movement and state is considerable. Among the September 1999 SADR figures who were also on Polisario's national secretariat were the head of state, the president of the National Council, the prime minister, the minister of the interior, the secretary to the presidency, the minister of health, and the minister of defence.

The state serves several functions for Polisario. It is an effective vehicle for the running of the exile community, organising health and education for example. It also is a means of mobilising the population. Externally, it provides a focus for the diplomatic struggle for recognition of the claim to self-determination. The number of states recognising the SADR fluctuates but is around 60 at present. It has been considerably higher in the past but Morocco and its allies have campaigned hard to reverse an embarrassing loss of diplomatic face. A major success for Morocco was India's retraction of recognition in 2000. On the other hand, in 2002, the newly independent East Timor recognised the SADR.

Sahrawi diplomats, some recognised as ambassadors, others merely tolerated as Polisario representatives, live on meagre resources. This is not a limousine lifestyle. Jeremy Harding describes the life of Lamine Baali, Polisario's man in London through the 1980s, turning round reports from the front, lobbying trade unions, trying to make sense of approaches by Trotskyist sects, 'making his way through the drizzle in a light grey suit to the Houses of Parliament'.[38] Lamine is now in Stockholm, his place currently taken by Lehbib Breica, operating out of a flat west of Paddington, his family split between the camps and Laayoune, battling for attention amid a decade-old ceasefire.

On the ground the structure of the SADR is formal and complex for a small population. The head of state, appointed (in practice reappointed) every three years, leads the executive. It is he who controls foreign policy and appointments as well as being head of the armed forces and nominating the prime minister. He also makes a number of important military, security and civil appointments, including regional governors or *walis*. He is not responsible to the legislature and can dissolve it. The government is described as the apparatus of the executive and is responsible to the head of state. The prime minister establishes an annual programme and budget for adoption by a council of ministers and approval by the legislature.

The Sahrawi National Council is the legislative organ of the SADR. Its fifty-one members are elected each eighteen months. The council meets in two annual sessions with commissions functioning between times. It considers the programme put forward by the government and if two-thirds of the members consistently oppose it, the head of state must choose between dissolving the council or picking a new cabinet. The council can censure the government. Along with the prime minister, deputies of the National Council can propose legislation.

There is a judiciary that is declared independent, starting from tribunals of first instance and culminating in a supreme court.

The organisation of the state reaches right down into the populace with a mesh of committees, congresses and councils. The camp community administered by the SADR is divided into four *wilayat* (provinces), each with six or seven *dawair* (communes), in turn divided into *baladiyat* (districts). Then there are administrative bodies dealing with production, education, health, social issues and so on. Each *daira* is administered by a local council, composed of committee heads and a popularly elected leader.

At the *wilaya* level there is a regional council comprising the leaders of the *daira* councils, directors of government departments in the *wilaya*, and a representative of the Red Crescent. The council is headed by a *wali* who is appointed by the head of state and who, as a member of the national secretariat of Polisario, has a political as well as administrative function. Indeed the political organisation and mobilisation of the *wilaya* feeds upwards to the *wali*, again intertwining Polisario and the SADR. Within each *daira* are cells of five to eleven members. These each elect a leader who represents the cell at the section level. The sections elect representatives to a *wilaya* level body headed by the *wali*. The congresses held at each administrative level are a channel for the elaboration and explanation of policy decisions originating from the Polisario congresses that, in principle, take place every three years. For Bontems,

> The originality of the SADR lies in the positive use that is made of the Sahrawis' deficiency in number. Every inhabitant of the Tindouf region has political, economic and ideological roles – the state and ideological machinery completely intertwine. Political and economic activities are not separated under this democratic system, and election to a position of technical responsibility (economic or administrative) often leads to one of political responsibility. The reverse is equally true.[39]

Firebrace contrasted the mobilisation of the Sahrawi refugee community with experiences elsewhere:

> This total participation of refugees in the smooth running of camp life is unique. The running of the camp in other refugee situations is the task of only a few. In the difficult context of enforced exile, frustration, alienation and boredom are usually common factors. But in these camps, the Sahrawi administrative structure ensures the involvement of all.[40]

He was writing in the 1980s, before the ceasefire. Since then, frustration, alienation and boredom have grown, prompted not only by the passage of so much time in so unforgiving an environment but also by the ceasefire itself. People have busied themselves building houses but time hangs heavy and, with neither a war to fight nor a vote to cast, there is no horizon. The return of the men from the front meant the same tasks needed to be shared among a much larger number of adults. That men have edged women out of some jobs such as security work or heavy lifting has brought little complaint but there is unhappiness among some women that they have been squeezed out of less onerous functions. The lower levels of the political and administrative hierarchy, previously the preserve of women, are being encroached upon. The National Council has thirteen women members but at the ministerial and National Secretariat level they are barely represented.

Then the social change caused by economic liberalisation has, as mentioned above, altered the social pressures on people. Some have access to private income and this has enabled restitution of the practice of giving dowries, only given symbolically during the first years of exile; it has also added a new concern to young people's lives. The liberalisation has recognised and sanctioned a degree of social inequality as well. While some are able to afford small luxuries, for many eating enough is a challenge. In August 2002, the UN High Commission for Refugees and the World Food Programme made a joint appeal for more food aid and funds for the camps, saying their populations otherwise faced malnutrition.

Traditions such as the Sahrawi tea-drinking ceremony remain firmly in place, if only to fill some of the long, hot, empty summer hours, but other aspects of Sahrawi tradition risk being lost.

The oral history of the people is not being systematically preserved. Without this knowledge, the younger Sahrawis often have only the haziest idea of what their homeland was and is like, how their great-grandfathers fought the French, how their grandfathers coped with Spanish rule and their parents escaped Morocco. As the television replaces family conversation, the glue that ties generations of resistance is weakening, although an apparent rise in the incidence of praying suggests another aspect of traditional life may transmogrify to cope with new political realities.

Notes

1. Tony Hodges, 'Origins of Saharawi Nationalism', in Richard Lawless and Laila Monahan, eds, *War and Refugees*, Pinter, London, 1987, p. 38.
2. Mohamed-Fadel ould Ismail ould Es-Sweyih, *La République Sahraouie*, L'Harmattan, Paris, 2001, p. 37.
3. Hodges, 'Origins of Saharawi Nationalism', p. 48.
4. There were instances of armed activity by groups of Sahrawis during the early 1960s despite the crushing joint French and Spanish military action of 1958 that drove Sahrawi fighters into the Tarfaya Strip where their organisation was further crushed by Rabat when the strip was ceded to the kingdom. See Ismail Sayeh, *Les Sahraouis*, L'Harmattan, Paris, 1998, pp. 40–43.
5. Interview with Sahrawi elders, Smara camp, June 2003.
6. 'Les révélations d'Omar Hadrami', *Jeune Afrique*, 23 October 1989 p. 25.
7. Hodges, 'Origins of Saharawi Nationalism', p. 49.
8. 'Different Periods of Population Exodus from the Sahara to the North of Morocco', available on www.mincom.gov.ma.
9. Report of the United Nations Visiting Mission to Spanish Sahara, A/10023/rev1, p. 59.
10. Ibid., p. 64.
11. Ibid., p. 86.
12. Ibid., p. 61.
13. Ibid., p. 64.
14. Interview with member of first women's cell, Smara camp, June 2003.
15. Report of the United Nations Visiting Mission to Spanish Sahara, A/10023/rev1, p. 39.
16. 'Les revelations d'Omar Hadrami', p. 26.
17. Report of the United Nations Visiting Mission to Spanish Sahara, p. 63.
18. Mohamed-Fadel, *La République Sahraouie*, p. 91.
19. Reproduced in Sayeh, *Les Sahraouis*, p. 176.

20. Claude Bontems, 'The Government of the SADR', in 'The Politics of Exile', Third World Quarterly, vol. 9, no. 1, January 1987, p. 184.
21. 'Les révélations d'Omar Hadrami', p. 31.
22. Interview with the author, 1999.
23. Sayeh, Les Sahraouis, p. 110.
24. Bontems, 'The Government of the SADR', p. 173.
25. Ibid.
26. That said, there are perhaps more obvious parallels between Polisario and the main constituent group of the PLO, Fateh.
27. Mohamed-Fadel, La République Sahraouie, p. 103.
28. Sayeh, Les Sahraouis, pp. 90–91.
29. Interview with the author, April 2003.
30. Bontems, 'The Government of the SADR', p. 175.
31. Sayeh, Les Sahraouis, pp. 102–6.
32. Amnesty International, Morocco/Western Sahara, 18 April 1996, p. 14.
33. 'Les révélations d'Omar Hadrami', pp. 22–34.
34. Agence France Press report, 20 April 1990.
35. Agence France Press report, 10 August 1989.
36. Proclamation of the first government of the Sahrawi Arab Democratic Republic, available on www.arso.org.
37. 1999 constitution of the SADR, reproduced in full in Mohamed-Fadel, La République Sahraouie.
38. Jeremy Harding, Small Wars, Small Mercies: Journeys in Africa's Disputed Nations, Viking, London, 1993, pp. 113–62.
39. Bontems, 'The Government of the SADR', p. 181.
40. James Firebrace, 'Lesson and Prospects', in Lawless and Monahan, eds, War and Refugees, p. 169.

11

War:

The Unbroken Chain

The peoples of the Sahara were tenacious defenders of their independence in the face of European incursion. France pitted men like the soldier Laperrine and the latter-day warrior monk de Foucauld in a crusade against the Tuareg and later against the Sahrawis. The drive to establish control and lines of communication from the Mediterranean, across the Sahara and into the French-controlled Sahel was marked by ill-fated expeditions. In 1880 one Colonel Paul Flatters was sent to survey a route for a trans-Saharan railway, a French obsession of the colonial era. The reduction of his column by raiders to 'two clutches of human debris'[1] assumed mythical status. The brutality with which resistance was met is reminiscent of Conrad's Kurtz in its terminology.

In the first years of the twentieth century France consolidated its grip on the Maghreb, establishing a protectorate over the Moroccan sultanate and moving against the resistance of Saharan tribes in the Adrar region of what became Mauritania, as well as in the Algerian Sahara. Pressed from the north, south and east, those fighting against France found refuge in the Western Sahara where Spanish rule was entirely notional, limited to an embattled outpost on the Dakhla peninsula. In 1916 Cap Juby – now known as Tarfaya and within southern Morocco – was occupied, only to become another beleaguered encampment from which it was unsafe to venture. As Lindqvist relates, in the 1920s Cap Juby took on a new significance as a French airline needed it as a stopover for flights from Toulouse to Dakar. Between Cap Juby and Dakar, one in six flights ended in a crash or emergency landing. Altogether, 121 pilots were lost, for: 'when the pilot in his thick leather overalls, "heavy and cumbersome as a diver", clambered out of his cockpit – then, if the rescuers did not get to him in time, what awaited him was captivity or death at the hands of hostile nomads'.[2]

From the 1880s Sahrawi resistance to European rule was increasingly centred around the charismatic *marabout* Ma el-Ainin. This legendary figure, who originated from the Niger river not from the Western Sahara, established the town of Smara as a religious and trading centre between 1898 and 1902. He organised assistance to those fighting France in the surrounding regions and received weapons from the sultan of Morocco. By 1909, France had been goaded enough to commence raids into the Western Sahara. In June 1910, Ma el-Ainin's forces were routed by French troops as he made a bid for the sultanate, angered by its increasing capitulation to French demands. He died weeks later, leaving his son, el-Hiba, to continue the struggle. Sahrawi tribes continued to resist in Mauritania. After one particularly successful attack on a French garrison, Lieutenant Colonel Mouret retaliated with a strike against Smara in 1913. They found the town deserted but destroyed much anyway, blasting Ma el-Ainin's council chamber. The damage remains to be seen today.

The fighting continued throughout the 1920s and early 1930s but the French noose tightened as control was established over Tindouf, allowing forces in Mauritania and Algeria to link up, and then over southern Morocco. Spain began to take a grip of its nominal colony while France bolstered its military presence around the Western Sahara and demanded joint action against the Sahrawi raiders. The Spanish advance inland met no resistance, according to Hodges,[3] who says the Sahrawis had decided that they preferred the relatively peaceable Spanish to the troublesome French. Sahrawi elders say they reached agreement with the Spanish that the latter would be permitted to stay in the Western Sahara on certain conditions, one of which was that the Sahrawis kept their weapons.[4] Spain established a base at Smara with outposts further south and agreed with France the administration of the tribes that straddled the borders. The clusters of small, domed houses around the market at Smara date from this era, one of the minor architectural curiosities imported by the Spanish administration.

Active resistance petered out and the Sahrawis continued their lives largely untroubled by Spanish colonialism until Franco began to realise that the territory had economic potential. As France granted independence to Morocco under a sultan deemed more compliant than the rebel forces that had emerged in the Rif and the Atlas, and as the Algerian war of independence intensified, the Sahrawis took up weapons again. Sahrawi units allied themselves with autonomous Moroccan guerrilla forces in the south of the kingdom. Again, French positions in the Tindouf region were raided by Sahrawi fighters. Fighting flared in northern Mauritania. French forces recommenced hot pursuit strikes into the Western Sahara. The ghost of Ma el-Ainin had returned to haunt the colonial administrations.

The Sahrawi fighters attacked Spanish positions in Boujdour, Layoune and Argoub in 1957 and 1958. Madrid and Paris decided on joint action and in February 1958 French troops from Bir Moghrein, Nouadhibou and Zouerate in Mauritania and from Tindouf in Algeria crossed into the Western Sahara while Spanish columns pushed out of Layoune, Dakhla and Tarfaya and paratroopers landed in Smara. Sahrawi accounts say the colonial forces embarked on a campaign of deliberate destruction of the nomads' means of subsistence, with some 85 per cent of livestock destroyed.[5]

The uprising was crushed, with thousands of Sahrawis displaced into the Tarfaya Strip and the Tindouf region. As the UN Mission found out in 1975, assessments of the numbers who fled north and east were subject to considerable variance, not least because of their significance in any referendum. In 1958 Spain handed the strip over to the Moroccan king's army on the understanding that it would not serve as a base for further insurgency. Sahrawi accounts say it took the royalist forces three months to subdue the Sahrawi fighters in Tarfaya.

The chain of Sahrawi resistance has worn thin at times but never been broken. The exploits of Ma el-Ainin's warriors link with the memories of Sahrawi elders still alive in the late 1980s who fought in the 1920s and 1930s. Their sons took up arms in the 1950s. And some of their sons, in turn, formed the first fighting units of Polisario as it adopted the age-old tactic of the *ghazzia*, or raid, from 1973.

After its first engagement at El Khanga, Polisario staged a series of minor raids throughout the territory, launching its first sabotage attack against the Bou Craa conveyor belt in October 1974. By early 1975, Sahrawis recruited into the Spanish police and military had begun to defect to Polisario. The embarrassment of the Polisario military operations combined with the growing political support for the movement, which became so obvious when the UN Mission reached the territory. But it was political embarrassment rather than a military threat to Spain that Polisario posed at this point. The Mission's report passes over guerrilla activity in the territory prior to its visit in a few lines in its report, referring in the same breath to bomb attacks in Layoune attributed to Moroccan sympathisers. It cites a number of unattributed attacks, often near the Moroccan border, and an attempt, apparently by either Moroccan troops or Moroccan sympathisers, to capture a border post. But during the Mission's stay in the region, Polisario pulled off a publicity coup, taking fourteen Spanish troops prisoners as two Tropas Nomadas patrols defected, and then taking the Mission members to meet the captives.[6]

When Moroccan forces swept into the Western Sahara to the east of the Green March coup de théâtre, Polisario fighters harried them as best they could before turning to the task of evacuating refugees eastwards. That task became more urgent as Morocco turned in February 1976 to a campaign of bombardment of refugee columns, which many older Sahrawis recall with horror. The work of the fighters was complemented by non-combatants who crossed back into the territory to guide refugees and to recapture their livestock.

The second half of the 1970s and the early 1980s were the years when Polisario was at its most daunting as a military force. Mauritanian forces were entirely inadequate to defend their territory against incursion, let alone hold the swathe of desert bequeathed them by Madrid. Attacks on the iron ore mines at Zouerate and on Nouakchott by Polisario columns of hundreds of fighters in fast-moving vehicles ensured Mauritania's exit from the struggle. But this was not before France had used its air power to attack Polisario forces and not before Morocco had established what a Mauritanian diplomat called an occupation in all but name of areas south of the Western Saharan–Mauritanian border. With an initial 40,000 troops in the Western Sahara, Morocco's army was a more formidable adversary, but guerrilla attacks as far west as Layoune took place. Morocco lost its first aircraft, a US-supplied Northrop F-5, in January 1976. After Mauritania's withdrawal, Morocco doubled the size of its army in the territory but found itself more stretched than ever.

With Mauritania out of contention, Polisario was able to redeploy fighters further north and launch its Houari Boumedienne Offensive.[7] It concentrated its attacks on isolated outposts, from August 1979 assaulting Lebouirate, Mahbes, Farsia, Jediria, Haouza, and Guelta Zemmour, points that Morocco was forced to abandon.[8] In the same year, guerrilla fighters struck in Tan Tan and other parts of southern Morocco.

The extent of Moroccan territorial control was shrinking. By 1981, Rabat's forces controlled no more than 10 per cent of the Western Sahara, according to Polisario. Casualty figures for engagements vary to the point of bearing no relation. Polisario regularly detailed numbers of Moroccan troops killed or wounded or captured, sometimes running into hundreds or even thousands. Names of some prisoners or purported enemy casualties were given, along with lists of equipment said to have been destroyed or taken. Equally regularly Morocco denied the claims.

The remnants of defensive ditches and walls along the line of the Bou Craa conveyor belt and the prevalence of minefields across the territory bear testimony to the pervasive threat of attack from raiders. From the end of 1979, the Moroccan army began to implement a new strategy on US advice. Large, semi-autonomous units with air support were to push out of southern Morocco and prevent further incursions there. Among the tasks would be the relief of the strongpoint at Zak, which Polisario claimed to have isolated. A series of engagements were fought in the Ouarkeziz hills. Later, expensive search-and-destroy columns were sent lumbering across the plains of the territory, following the US model. The Polisario fighters simply disappeared into the desert. According to Hughes, it was at this point, when Hassan II himself was describing the war as reaching the threshold of the intolerable, that the CIA was predicting the monarch's day were numbered.[9]

But in 1981 Morocco commenced a new strategy born, by some accounts, of success in limiting the effectiveness of Polisario raids within the so-called 'Useful Triangle' of the territory with the ditches and walls and minefields mentioned above. Over a period of six years, bulldozers piled rock and sand into a 10-foot-high barrier stretching a staggering 1,500 miles, running parallel to the Algerian and the Mauritanian borders. Military outposts were located at small intervals along its length at observation points and in larger forts. Ditches, minefields and razor wire added to the defences, while artillery and air support could be called in, and rapid reaction units were located a couple of miles inside the wall. High-tech monitoring equipment scanned the desert. To man the defences Morocco doubled its military presence in the territory again, to 160,000 men. The Moroccan army now intended it to be Polisario that was confined to just 10 per cent of the territory. Incidentally, the wall would also severely limit Polisario's ability to disrupt maritime activity – over the years, numerous attacks had been launched against fishing and leisure craft offshore the Western Sahara. As the defences were built, attacks continued inside the Western Sahara, including around Boujdour, Lemsid, Dakhla, Bou Craa and Smara.[10]

Polisario attempted to prevent the walls or berm from being built but was unable to do so. Using its limited and ageing artillery capability exposed its forces to air attack, and hit-and-run raids were no more than an irritant. It claimed some victories, including a major one in October 1984 at Zmoul Niran near Zag. But now Morocco claimed to be inflicting severe casualties as the guerrillas attempted to storm their way through the unfamiliar new defences.

The guerrilla movement tried to put a positive spin on the wall strategy of Rabat, asserting it was a sign that Hassan II needed to lower the intensity of the conflict and was acting from a position of weakness. But it had to concede that the berm was a problem. Brahim Ghali, SADR minister of defence, said, 'During the years 1982–1984, we recognise we experienced some difficulties, entirely naturally, in respect of the new mode of combat imposed on us'.[11] A major period of adaptation had been required, he said. The wall would become a tomb for Moroccan troops, he promised.

Moroccan prisoners of war held by Polisario describe a miserable existence manning the wall, told they faced Cuban and Vietnamese mercenaries. The climate is insufferable to those not used to it. Provisions for the conscripts are minimal and some say they received neither training nor weapons. Indeed, a few even defected. Guerillas soon found they could penetrate the wall in small numbers, and, to make the point, numerous journalists were taken on probing expeditions. Larger battles were reported along the wall, for example at Adheim Oum Ejloud in August 1987, when nearly 200 Moroccan troops were said by Polisario to have been killed, and at Tichla the previous month.[12]

Ironically, it was after the ceasefire had been agreed in principle that the Sahrawi fighters believed they had mastered the wall and that within two or three years they could turn matters to their advantage and win concessions from Morocco at the negotiating table. So, against a background of duplicity and incompetence at the UN and in a bid to push Hassan II into further talks, Polisario forces went on the offensive in late 1988. A series of major confrontations took place. At Um Dreiga, up to 2,500 fighters assaulted a 10-mile section of the berm, and Morocco, in a rare admission, acknowledged heavy losses, including the death of a senior field commander.[13] The confidence gained in these battles was to underpin a suspicion of the ceasefire on the part of Sahrawi fighters that has remained throughout the years of stalling and vacillation over the Settlement Plan. Frequently, Polisario officials have warned that a return to fighting was possible. In reality, the ceasefire has held and the warnings are little heeded, believed to be a case of the boy crying wolf too often.

The wall was and is expensive in terms of the hardware and manpower needed to maintain it, and Sahrawi fighters can penetrate it. It has already been remarked that Baker once quipped to a Moroccan general that Texas had a similar length border with Mexico but could not afford a berm and defences such as Morocco had built. But it succeeded in doing what no other military strategy had done, keeping the war outside of the vast bulk of the territory. It was the perfect military complement to Rabat's policy of prevarication at the diplomatic level and later during the course of the voter registration exercise, giving as it did the space and the time Morocco needed to deepen its colonisation and integration of the Western Sahara.

With the sedentarisation of the Sahrawis, the early Polisario fighters were drawn largely from the towns within the territory or in the surrounding areas. Hodges says they were mostly young, skilled workers in their early twenties, often employed by Fosbucraa.[14] By the beginning of 1975 they probably numbered no more than a couple of hundred and were poorly armed. In theory, Libya supplied weapons as well as radio broadcasting facilities. In reality, although some fighters were trained by Libya, Algeria was not at this point willing to let weapons get through from Tripoli.

The exile of 1975 provided Polisario with a willing population from which to recruit and, numerically, the contest would have been relatively even had Mauritania been the adversary. Polisario fielded forces of several hundred fighters in its raids deep into Mauritania with its army of just a few thousand. But, as been noted already, the Moroccan army was quite another proposition, putting an initial 40,000 men into the territory and ending up with four times that number. Most of the troops were conscripts but the army was large and well armed and able to count on air support. The extent and provenance of Rabat's armoury is revealed in Polisario's military museum, where South African equipment of the apartheid era sits alongside US and French weaponry. After a decade of ceasefire and despite the rhetoric of an 'ethical foreign policy', the UK government was upgrading howitzers deployed in the Western Sahara. Sahrawis in Layoune report the presence of at least one British weapons trainer for a period of several months in late 2002.

Polisario's manpower has been estimated by Cordesman at between 3,000 and 6,000 fighters in 1999.[15] The same assessment attributes to them up to 100 old Russian-designed tanks, 60 armoured personnel carriers and around 100 artillery pieces, including mortars. More important and unquantified by Cordesman are the lighter vehicles, Sagger anti-tank guided missiles and the Sam surface-to-air missiles that cost Morocco at least a dozen aircraft during the years of fighting. Morocco, just to give a sense of the imbalance, had 524 main battle tanks, 785 armoured personnel carriers, reconnaissance and scouting vehicles, and over 2,000 pieces of artillery, mortars and missile launchers, excluding anti-aircraft weapons.

However, while it may be true that Polisario's mobilised forces through the ceasefire amount to a few thousand fighters, there is no doubt that the number of fighters available is vastly greater. Prior to the ceasefire, women predominated in all economic and social activity in the refugee camps precisely because men of fighting age were under arms. As one observer noted, Polisario could mobilise a high proportion of the above-16 male population of the camps inside twenty-four hours.[16] That would give a total potential fighting force of tens of thousands.

The ability of the Sahrawi forces to wage war against a vastly bigger army for over a decade and a half has frequently (and correctly) been attributed to traditional guerrilla strengths – knowledge of the environment, employment of hit-and-run tactics – but Bhatia notes another, the ability to retain experienced fighters. In a random sample, he found a mix of veterans with seven or eight years' experience and more recent inductees with one to three years under arms. Certainly up to the implementation of the ceasefire in 1991, there were frontline fighters who had fought in 1975.

The issue of prisoners of war is one that Morocco now highlights internationally as well as domestically. There is some irony here, as for many years the kingdom refused to recognise their existence publicly. Indeed, Polisario alleges Morocco obstructed the repatriation of some POWs. Since the late 1990s Rabat has improved the international perception of human rights in the kingdom and that has given it the opportunity to launch an offensive against Polisario, which at the time of writing still held some 900 Moroccan POWs, some captured in the first months of the war, making them the longest-held prisoners of war anywhere in the world.

From the moral high ground it now claims, Morocco says that POWs have been treated with brutality, interrogated and forced to work, in contravention of the Geneva Conventions.[17] It also maintains that the POWs should have been released after the ceasefire came into effect and that for its part the handing over of 66 Polisario prisoners in October 1996 was the final meeting of its obligations.

For Polisario the Moroccan prisoners are pawns who serve several purposes. For years, like the display of captured weaponry, they were proof for visiting politicians and journalists of military successes. Now their existence is acknowledged inside Morocco, to some extent they keep the issue of the conflict in the public eye. Then, periodic release of batches of prisoners in response to interventions from governments and agencies may be a useful diplomatic tool although, arguably, each release simply puts the spotlight back on an issue that serves Moroccan propaganda purposes. Since 1987, around 1,000 POWs have been repatriated in groups.

Polisario disputes Moroccan claims to have liberated all the POWs it held (let alone accounted for the civilians who have disappeared in the occupied territories). In November 2001, the International Committee of the Red Cross said the fate of 150 former Polisario fighters remained unknown. The men Polisario holds, it holds in part in the hope that an exchange is possible although it would likely be an exchange of Moroccan prisoners for confirmation of Sahrawi deaths. Finally, there is the argument that prisoner release, like the cessation of hostilities, was intended to be part of a process leading to an act of self-determination. While that process is stalled, its individual elements are contingent.

Pressure to release the POWs has grown, and some nationalist Sahrawi human rights activists living under Moroccan rule say privately that they would welcome a release. Legal and moral arguments apart, Morocco is flinging back accusations of human rights abuse in order to draw the spotlight away from its own activities, they say.

The October 2003 congress of Polisario was scheduled in large part to air the question of whether to return to fighting given the stalemate in the diplomatic process. The intention would have been twofold: to re-energise the population of the camps and assuage their frustration after twelve years of neither war nor peace, and to prompt movement on the political stage. There was no illusion that Polisario would win a military victory but rather that Europe and the US would be alerted to a further step in the destabilisation of Morocco with the consequences that would have in terms of migration, national security and economic interests. However, by June 2003 it appeared that the leadership had decided to caution against a return to armed struggle, saying the dust needed to settle in the international arena after the invasion of Iraq before a clear path forward could be determined.

Notes

1. Fergus Fleming, *The Sword and the Cross*, Granta, London, 2003, p. 40. Fleming provides an excellent account of French colonialism in the Sahara through the lives of Laperrine and de Foucauld.
2. Sven Lindqvist, *Desert Divers*, Granta, London, 2000, p. 16.

3. Tony Hodges, *Western Sahara:The Roots of a Desert War*, Lawrence Hill, Westport CT, 1983, p. 64.

4. Interview with the author, Tindouf camps, 1988.

5. SADR Ministry of Information, *La Republica Arabe Saharaui Democratica: pasado y presente*, 1985, p. 37.

6. 'Report of the UN Visiting Mission to Spanish Sahara, 1975', A/10023/Rev1, p74.

7. Polisario Front, *Sahara News*, 31 July 1987.

8. Stephen Hughes, *Morocco under King Hassan*, Ithaca Press, Ithaca NY, 2001, pp. 251–61.

9. Ibid.

10. Polisario Front, *Sahara News*, 31 July 1987.

11. Interview with Algerian daily newspaper *El Moujahid*, n.d., c. 1987.

12. Polisario Front, *Sahara News*, 31 August 1987.

13. *Middle East International*, 23 September 1988 and 7 October 1988.

14. Hodges, *Western Sahara*, p. 162.

15. Anthony Cordesman, *Military Balance in the Middle East: III, North Africa Country Analysis*, Centre for Strategic and International Studies, Washington DC, 1998, p. 9.

16. Michael Bhatia, 'Western Sahara under Polisario Control', *Review of African Political Economy* 88, June 2001.

17. Briefing document issued by the Moroccan embassy in London to journalists in April 2002.

12

Endgame

What is sure is that we will not stay here. I have spent twenty-nine
years in the desert. I have three daughters and they will not grow
up in the desert. We are not condemned for the rest of our lives to
be refugees, especially when we can make a change. And we can
make a change.[1]

The determination of Sahrawi nationalists is matched by their recognition that the issue of the Western Sahara can only be satisfactorily
resolved if it moves up the priority list of the UN Security Council.
This is a necessary but not sufficient condition for resolution.
Moments before uttering the above heartfelt declaration of Sahrawi
intent to be agents in their own future, the speaker said there would
be no solution without US commitment. Mohamed Khaddad, senior
Polisario diplomat, made the same point, saying in mid-2003 that
the Western Sahara was not yet enough of a priority for the Security
Council, and the potential presence of commercially exploitable
quantities of oil there was not yet an issue for the powers.

For both Polisario and Morocco, there is the perennial question
whether to play a waiting game or adopt an activist strategy in the
dispute, to the extent that they are able to influence the arena in
which the dispute takes place.

In the 1970s and 1980s the Western Sahara became part of the
collateral damage of the Cold War. In a dispute between the obliging
and pro-West Moroccan monarchy and a Third Worldist, Non-Aligned
Movement activist, and Opec price hawk, like Algeria, it was clear

which way the US would veer. For France, too, preservation and protection of the Moroccan regime was and is important in terms of maintaining French economic, political, military and cultural influence in North, West and Central Africa. Again, given the choice between siding with Rabat or with a movement supported by Algeria – with all the baggage of Franco-Algerian relations – the choice was obvious. The Sahrawi preference for Spanish as a second language threatens to drive a wedge into the *francophonie*.

Ironically, while Polisario received diplomatic support from some governments with close ties to Moscow through the 1970s and 1980s, it equally achieved recognition from many that did not. And while Cuba provided education and training, the tales of Cuban and Vietnamese fighters in the Western Sahara were as much a Cold War myth as were later Moroccan claims that Polisario was training Islamic militants was a myth generated to exploit Western concerns after the Iranian revolution. Moscow itself was more interested in securing major trade deals with Morocco than supporting Polisario. So, the Western Sahara issue was an innocent victim of a global competition in which it did not participate.

The end of the Cold War and the Settlement Plan coincided, and the Western Sahara could, for some years, be put in the (Nearly) Closed file. The twin trends of economic globalisation and growing US military and political interventionism have generated a new interest in Washington in Maghreb affairs. The US and the EU agree on the need for stability in the subregion and they both want the Algerian and Moroccan markets to be open for business. For the US the need for stability is of strategic importance. For the EU it is of immediate and very direct importance, determining as it does the flow of natural gas, migrants and drugs. Within the overall agreement, there is competition. Europe and the US are rivals for North African markets, for instance, while France and Spain may compete for economic and political influence. However, for the Western Sahara, it could even be that increased US and French activity in the Maghreb delays a settlement, for both countries have increased their interaction with Algeria. Given the state of Algerian–Moroccan relations, this necessitates a careful balancing act that is likely to be expressed in caution over initiatives involving the Western Sahara. France opted to side with Morocco in its rejection of the second version of Baker's plan while the US used its muscle to push a diluted resolution through. But the very fact that the resolution was diluted suggests that Washington will seek to cajole Morocco and Algeria into an agreement over time. After all, if the aim is to create a stable single market safe for US investors, alienating one or other of the key partners is not the path to follow. That said, where some had feared the Western Sahara would slip from the agenda after the occupation of Iraq, it has actually risen as the US seeks to diversify its sourcing of oil imports away from the Gulf and secure stability in strategically important regions.

What can safely be said is that for the US and France and, indeed, the other Security Council members the fate of a quarter of a million Sahrawis is a matter of supreme indifference except to the extent that it impinges on their economic and political ambitions.

Polisario leader Mohamed Abdelaziz, in an interview for this book, expressed the way the Western Sahara has been buffeted by external events in another way. He remarked that the last thirty years of Sahrawi history have been influenced in a major way by three deaths. The first was the death of Franco, which saw Madrid change course from offering self-determination to partitioning the territory between Morocco and Mauritania. The second death was that of President Boumedienne of Algeria. According to Abdelaziz, Boumedienne's foreign minister and the Moroccan foreign minister of the day held talks in Bamako after Mauritania withdrew from the conflict. There were indications that Rabat was disposed to offer much more than the slice of territory Mauritania was evacuating, he suggested. Then Boumedienne died and Hassan II decided the pressure would ease. Malian invitations to further talks were turned down. The third death was that of Hassan II in 1999. Abdelaziz believes that Hassan II had the flexibility and authority to deliver a satisfactory solution, particularly as new international pressures came into play in the Maghreb. Since his death, Morocco has reverted to slogans not heard since the late 1970s, Abdelaziz said.

Morocco as the de facto power in the territory has benefited from the contingent nature of the Western Sahara issue for the international players. Like Israel in the West Bank and Gaza, Morocco in the Western Sahara has used time and indifference to its advantage to create facts on the ground, calculating that if push ever comes to shove, the realities of settlement and demography will outweigh international law. So, an academic like Thobhani finds it possible to write in his notably Moroccan-influenced book: 'The reality is that the bulk of Western Sahara has, to all intents and purposes, become Moroccan, and to harbour any thought of independence is only a delusion.'[2]

For Rabat, recourse to the UN route has been used only when its benefits seemed likely to outweigh those offered by the passage of time. Thus, agreement to a referendum came only when the military pressure on Moroccan forces was becoming unbearable. The registration of voters under the Settlement Plan has always been hostage to Moroccan attempts to enlarge the electoral roll. The first iteration of the Baker plan was accepted, but the clarifications seen in the second iteration tipped the balance just enough to prompt rejection and a return to the passage-of-time track.

The prolongation of the 1991 ceasefire has presented Morocco with additional advantages. While, with a conventional standing army inside its own territory and a large population from which to conscript, Morocco is able to maintain and strengthen its military capability, the same is not true of Polisario. It is likely that the movement's military capability will have been eroded by loss of experienced fighters due to age and deterioration of hardware. At the same time, the situation of neither war nor peace has put new strains on the population of the refugee camps, whose lives are no longer defined by struggle but by demoralising waiting. Morocco exploits this by highlighting defections and claiming that large numbers of ordinary Sahrawis have left the camps. Then there are the effects of liberalisation of life in the camps. The standard of living has risen, but with it have come new social pressures, a less collectivist spirit, migrant labour, allegations of the growth of crime. For some there may even be a normalisation of exile that saps the will to continue with the struggle.

This said, the passage-of-time track does have disadvantages for Morocco. One is that the unresolved status of the dispute means that foreign investment in the Western Sahara has been virtually non-existent. Indeed, investment from the Moroccan private sector has been negligible too. Should oil be found in commercial quantities offshore the Western Sahara, Morocco does not have the capability to develop fields and would require foreign partners. It is an open question whether US and French (or indeed other) oil companies would go so far as to pump oil from the waters of a non-self-governing territory without legal clearance from the UN. The legal process itself would push the Western Sahara up the international political agenda as it did, briefly, in 2001 when Morocco issued reconnaissance licences to Kerr–McGee and Total. Morocco's ability to continue to absorb the costs of occupation is privately questioned by at least one historically supportive permanent member of the Security Council.

Also, like its adversary, Morocco is buffeted by forces beyond its control or foresight. Spain's period on the Security Council was always a concern because it would introduce an alternative European view of the Western Sahara, but that months into Spanish membership Washington and London would wage war on Iraq and Madrid would support them against France was unforeseeable. Equally unforeseeable was the election of a socialist party government in Madrid in the spring of 2004, a backlash against the Aznar administration's handling of bombings in the Spanish capital. The election result prompted energetic Moroccan and Polisario lobbying, the former looking for a return to the Gonzalez era and the latter counting on the new government's dependence on pro-Polisario regional parties.

The dust has yet to settle in the Security Council, due in part to continued French scepticism about US plans for Iraq, which leaves Morocco in the uncomfortable position of drawing support from Paris against Washington while negotiating a trade agreement with the latter.

At the tactical level, Polisario recognises there are times when it must simply wait. Despite all of the talk of pressure to return to the armed struggle, the National Secretariat decided even before accepting the Baker Plan to go into the October 2003 congress saying the circumstances were not right. The diplomatic victory over Morocco that summer meant the leadership could go to the congress showing there had been movement of a sort.

At the strategic level, Polisario recognises that the US and European need for stability in the Maghreb provide it with its only leverage. It must demonstrate that a Sahrawi state would increase rather than decrease stability and, by extension, that continuation of the dispute would have deleterious consequences for the big powers. The question that then presents itself is whether to adopt an active role, whether to exacerbate tensions. Leaving aside scale, logistical feasibility, implications for the people in the occupied territories and whether Algeria would permit it, the aim of a return to the armed struggle would not be achievement of military victory but to give Europe a war on its doorstep to underline the fragility of the Maghreb and remind it of the consequences of a crisis in Morocco. However, the danger of breaking a ceasefire would be a deeper and broader international attachment to the French school of thought that Moroccan stability is best guaranteed by support for the regime.

The referendum and independence of East Timor were triggered by political and economic crisis in Indonesia. Crisis in Morocco would raise similar strategic concerns for the US and more immediate ones for Europe. Is there cause to believe Morocco is on the road to chaos? The economy is weak. Its agriculture is vulnerable to drought, its fisheries to depletion of stocks, its industry to energy costs, its tourism to international tension, its phosphate exports to world markets, and its migrant remittances are not providing the support that was hoped for. Unemployment and poverty are abiding, and a growing legal and illegal Islamist wave is garnering committed support that the established political parties have not had for decades. US trade representative Robert Zoellick praised Morocco at the 2003 World Economic Forum meeting in Jordan as a model of a successful start to economic reform.[3] But it is questionable whether the urban poor see much gain from, say, the privatisation of the state tobacco company. Millions of rural Moroccans will be affected by extension of trade agreements with Europe or the US into the agricultural sector. Political reform inside the country has shown little conviction and, after the Casablanca bombings by a radical Islamist faction, may not be continued. The government has proclaimed greater commitment to the alleviation of poverty. Democracy and decentralisation continue to be watchwords of the administration. But the disjuncture between rhetoric and reality is growing.

Morocco is fragile. So, is it in the interests of the Sahrawi national movement to weaken it further in the hope of an East Timor scenario or to strengthen reformist elements in the hope of changing

Moroccan policy? Perhaps the two options converge in an autocratic state where pressing for reform can provoke repression and chaos.

In either case, the Sahrawis who are positioned to be agents for change are those living under Moroccan rule. Since 1999, it is they who have asserted Sahrawi rights. There have been explicitly political manifestations – the rallies to greet Daddach on his release from prison, Tamek's explicit sympathy with Polisario, the portraits of El Ouali and Che Guevara at student events in Agadir, the masked youths attacking police posts. More often protest has taken on the form of a civil rights movement, the project pursued by human rights activists to break down what they call the wall of fear and build a civil society. But it is clear the civil society they are building is a Sahrawi civil society on Sahrawi land. The prisoners they often were themselves and the prisoners they campaign for are political prisoners in their eyes. It does not lessen in the least the value and sincerity of their work as activists for the unemployed, students, families of the disappeared, prisoners, pensioners, to say their activity is informed by a strong attachment to a Sahrawi right to self-determination.

The protests that started in Laayoune in 1999 and were echoed in Smara two years later have been portrayed by some as purely economic in nature, and indeed the demands made were economic and no one who was then involved in talks with the authorities was so foolhardy as to raise illegal political demands. But it is absolutely clear that the protesters' economic demands were within a well-understood political context of job discrimination against Sahrawis, dispersal of students to Moroccan universities, rewriting of contracts and pensions for Sahrawi miners, let alone the context of the referendum process that at that very moment was on the cusp of implementation or abandonment.

The linkage between the economic and the political for the Sahrawis was recognised and highlighted by Khalli Henna ould Rachid. A wealthy Sahrawi deputy mayor of Laayoune and a former minister in the Moroccan government, he ardently espouses integration. Talking of the Laayoune events of 1999,[4] he described the economic and social situation as 'catastrophic, explosive even', adding that 'There is today a cocktail of social and economic crisis but also of political questioning.' He said the economic situation, with abnormally high dependence on the state and the lack of agriculture, industry and tourism, was specific to the Western Sahara but that 'the measures to take are of an essentially political nature'. He continued, saying Morocco must not forget that there is 'an external enemy, an enemy that works, that feeds the difficulties of the actual situation'.

Some Polisario officials downplay the politicisation of the protest movement inside the territory, saying that the absence of an explicit political agenda means it is not ready or able to lead the nationalist movement. Nonetheless, there is growing realisation that, as one SADR minister put it, the occupied territories are currently 'the only door we can push on'. Of course, acknowledging the occupied territories to be the fulcrum might entail risks for Polisario. The Palestinian struggle from the time of the first intifada till now has been marked by power struggles between a PLO structure formed in exile and a popular and autonomous movement inside the occupied territories. The decision of the PLO leadership to negotiate the Oslo agreement was, in part, a move to reassert its control over the national movement.

Inside the Western Sahara, in the Tarfaya Strip and in the Moroccan universities, Sahrawi activists are determined to be agents of change. Their immediate demands are often social and economic but are always in the broader context of the demand for self-determination. There is growing evidence that their activities are winning the interest and even sympathy of some Moroccans as the Sahrawis engage with Moroccan trade unionists, students and human rights activists. As the rise of political Islam and the eclipse of the popular base of traditional Moroccan political parties hints, there may be an appetite for new, less territorially defined concepts of Moroccan nationhood. There is simply no telling how strong or weak is popular Moroccan commitment to the 'southern provinces', although the need to maintain double salaries and subsidies for settlers suggests their attachment is economic rather than emotional.

If Baker's plan is pushed forward it will require more clarification, more definition of the powers of the transitional authority. The length of the transition period will be fought over; so will the terms and implications of any third option beyond independence or integration. The reliability of UN guarantees will be tested to ensure there is no repetition of the murderous rampages that sullied East Timor's referendum. That is all in addition to the primary battle over the composition of the electoral roll, the battle that surely will determine the future of the Western Sahara.

In 1975 the Sahrawis, then under Spanish occupation, convinced the UN mission through their demonstrations and delegations of their desire for self-determination. Under another occupation they now face the challenge of persuading the international community that any process towards a solution must have their consent and input. Supporters of independence will, of course, face repression and organisations devoted to integration will be created just as they were by Spain. But, as 1999 proved again, popular protests inside the territory do reach the attention of the Security Council. Despite the tremendous obstacles, the people inside the occupied territories are unconstrained by the geographical isolation of the Tindouf camps or by pressure from a powerful ally increasingly confronted by new domestic and international imperatives.

If the Baker proposals are stalled, whether by obstructive negotiation or by a US decision that the time is not right to push them further, the movement Polisario's leadership needed to show to its constituency at its October 2003 congress will prove to have been a mirage. The camps will remain isolated and their inhabitants deprived of the means to affect their future. In these circumstances, if Sahrawi nationalism is not to stagnate, it will be incumbent on the activists inside the Western Sahara and inside Morocco to push forward with their project to build a civil society and, perhaps, at the points of contact to 'infect' Moroccan society with the germ of rebellion.

The task of building a Sahrawi civil society has an importance beyond carrying forward the struggle for Sahrawi rights now and in the immediate future. It is also a duty of stewardship of an uncertain more distant future. When, one day, the refugees return it may be as part of a negotiated process and under international protection. More darkly, there is a scenario whereby their return might be forced by withdrawal of support. In that latter case, it would be for the movement in the occupied territories, with its long years of acquaintance with Morocco, to recast the Sahrawi struggle in new circumstances, perhaps as 'the Basques of the Maghreb', a role they have so far rejected. In the case of a negotiated return as part of a peace process that led to independence, those who worked for civil rights under occupation would have to ensure their values were nurtured in a Sahrawi state.

Notes

1. Brahim Mokhtar, minister of SADR government, interview with the author, June 2003.
2. Akbarali Thobhani, *Western Sahara since 1975 under Moroccan Administration: Social, Economic and Political Transformation*, Edwin Mellen Press, Lewiston NY, 2002, p. 266.
3. *Financial Times*, 24 June 2003.
4. *Maroc-Hebdo International*, 9–15 March 2001.

Index